# Also available at all good book stores

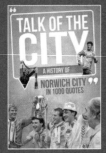

9781785310355

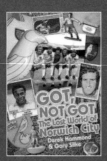

9781909626577

9781908051462

9781905411702

9781905411528

9781785315442

9781785314476

9781785315312

9781785314995

9781785314384

9781785315411

9781785314902

In His Own Words

# LIFE

on the Inside

In His Own Words

# LIFE
## on the Inside

PETER MENDHAM

With Edward Couzens-Lake

First published by Pitch Publishing, 2019

Pitch Publishing
A2 Yeoman Gate
Yeoman Way
Worthing
Sussex
BN13 3QZ
www.pitchpublishing.co.uk
info@pitchpublishing.co.uk

ISBN 978 1 78531 489 6

Typesetting and origination by Pitch Publishing

Printed and bound by TJ International Ltd, UK

# Contents

## DEDICATION

For Ross and Jamie. I brought you life.
You brought me joy. x

# Preface

MOST OF the original notes I made that ended up being used by Ed and I as the foundation of this book were written as I sat in my locked cell at both HMP Norwich and HMP Highpoint. I then expanded on those initial thoughts and recollections whilst taking a four-week sabbatical from work in the winter of 2015/16.

Continuing to do so, to recall and record so many memories from my life, then and now, and either with just my pen and some paper in an empty room or in the company of Ed has been an emotional struggle and something that has been increasingly difficult for me to do, and I would think you would have already guessed why, for many clear and obvious reasons.

From the very beginning, I wanted my book to be honest and to tell the story of my life and career in an honest and straightforward way. No glossing over of events, no hiding place and no excuses. It's presented here as it happened, my life before, during and after football, during which, in each of those instances, I went through some incredibly dark and difficult times and still, in truth, continue to do so to this day. That will never change.

On the positive side, there have also been some incredibly happy memories that I have enjoyed looking back on and sharing with you here.

I know that many people have already judged me and have decided that I am a bad person. More still will object to my writing a book about my life and will say that I should not be able to profit or gain publicity from the crime that I committed back in October 2006.

I understand and respect their opinions and would do or say nothing to try and persuade them otherwise.

A day rarely goes by, even now, when I don't read, see, or hear of yet another person's opinion of me. What sort of person I am, the things I've done, the things I haven't done. Either that or how good, bad, or, in some cases, utterly hopeless I am as a person or was as a professional footballer.

But all they are, and can ever be, are opinions. The only person who can tell the whole story and be relied upon to tell the truth, good and bad, is me.

Everyone else seems to have had their say.

Now it's time for me to have mine.

Peter Mendham

# Foreword

*by Ken Brown*

PETER MENDHAM, ultimately may not have had the most straightforward of lives but as a footballer, for me, he was exceptional. His is the classic story of 'local boy made good'. At his peak, he was so good that sometimes the only person who didn't realise quite how good he was, was Peter himself.

I remember when he first came into the team at Norwich, playing alongside Martin Peters. 'Mendy' was in awe. He was just the same when he lined up alongside Martin O'Neill and all the other top players we had at Carrow Road over the years.

Yet Peter deserves to be remembered in his own right for the important part he played in those teams and should be reminded just how highly his team-mates rated his contribution. His work rate, for example, was phenomenal; his engine powered the team through on so many occasions and, in addition to that, he weighed in with some important goals too.

Peter was the genuine article, a local lad who loved his football, who loved his team and gave everything he had, even when he was battling through a serious injury. He was also always eager to learn and never stopped listening to whatever I, my coaches or any of the senior players might have had to say on his or aspects of the game in general.

He was an important part of the team that won the League Cup at Wembley in 1985, although he maybe let the joy of the occasion get to him a little too much by wearing that dodgy headgear afterwards!

He also supported the football team and the city off as well as on the pitch, getting involved with various groups and organisations that served the local community. I often used to say of Peter, 'If you cut him open, he would bleed yellow and green' – I think that is as true of him today as it was then.

I am both delighted and honoured to have been asked to write this foreword for Peter's book. His life may not have turned out as any of us would have expected but on the pitch and in the dressing room he was a manager's dream and, over the years, has become a good friend.

I wish him well.

Ken Brown
Manager Norwich City FC 1980–87

# Introduction

A MEAGRE gathering of 8,369 souls scattered themselves about the wind-blown terraces and stands at Selhurst Park on Saturday, 25 January 1986.

At least two of those in attendance weren't fans of either Crystal Palace or Norwich City. I know that because Allan and Helen were friends of mine, friends who I'd convinced to make the trip over to South London with me in order to watch the game.

Allan, who remains a good friend to this day, supports Liverpool. I'd long forgiven him the error of his ways as he'd often admitted he enjoyed watching Norwich and, on that particular afternoon, Ken Brown's team did little to convince him otherwise. Norwich won 2-1 to establish a club record of ten away games without defeat.

Towards the end of the game he leaned over and said to me, 'Who's your player in the number-ten shirt?' It was, of course, Peter Mendham who'd opened the scoring on the day with a well-taken volley and had, as was the way of things at the time, bossed the opposition, a team that featured such footballing luminaries as Jim Cannon, Ian Wright and Andy Gray with his usual consummate ease.

I have to admit, my first thought was that Allan, who sported a head of fierce ginger hair at the time, was showing a little solidarity with a fellow redhead.

But it was about more than that.

'He's a good player,' said Allan. 'Very decent. He'll play for England one day.'

A bit of an outlandish claim at the time. But, as it turns out, one that wasn't that far from becoming a reality.

Peter Mendham was, as Allan had worked out, a very good player indeed. One who was full of energy, covering every inch of the pitch. I'd love the stats wizards to let us know how many kilometres he ran in a match. I know that, at the time of writing, anyone who covers between 11 and 12 kilometres over the course of a game is considered to have set a very high standard and it is, indeed, an admirable sign of energy and commitment to their team's cause. But I'll tell you this now, Peter Mendham would have covered that distance in every game he played in as standard.

Pete played the game as he has lived his life. He puts 100 per cent into absolutely everything he does. Whether that was a man-of-the-match performance at Carrow Road, a day's fishing at Barford Lakes or helping one of his many loyal customers with a house removal, he'll have done so with a smile on his face and a commitment to excellence from beginning to end. And again, as standard.

He was living and enjoying the good life when, completely and utterly against character, he committed the horrific crime against his then girlfriend on that never-to-be-forgotten October evening in 2006 that changed both their lives forever, an act of madness that he will always have to live with and one that is now an easy frame of reference for anyone who mentions his name in conversation.

It's just as likely he'll be remembered as Peter Mendham who went to prison for stabbing and nearly killing his girlfriend as it is Peter Mendham the gifted midfielder who was a shining light in the Norwich City team throughout the mid to late 1980s. Peter will be the first to admit he did a terrible thing on that day. It was a brutal crime and one that, rightly, subjected him to not only the full force of the law but the contempt and, in some cases, hatred of many of the people who used to idolise him as a footballer.

Peter knows that, no matter what else he does in his life, the events of that night and his incarceration which followed will never be forgotten, nor will he, by many, ever be forgiven.

He will never ask for sympathy or forgiveness from anyone.

But he has decided that in a world of whispers, gossip and all the stories that have appeared about him in the intervening years, it is time he was given the opportunity to tell the story of his life and career as a professional footballer as well as the events that led up to his time in prison and what followed afterwards.

It's all too easily forgotten that Peter played football in one of the great Norwich City sides and was able to learn his craft alongside such well-known names and larger-than-life football figures like John Bond, Kevin Keelan, Martin Peters, Martin O'Neill, Justin Fashanu and Mike Channon, which is, in itself, a tale worth telling. The local lad made good who wasn't, at one point, even earning ten per cent of what the club's highest-paid player was being paid per week.

This is a revelatory tale about top-flight football in the 1980s: the players, the matches, the managers and the incidents. It's also a story about what happened to him when his career was ended by injury, and the hand that he was dealt by life which led, eventually, to those dark and desperate days spent at Her Majesty's pleasure. And his attempts to rebuild his life, career and reputation in the years that followed. Not all of it will make for easy reading, and it certainly didn't make for easy living as far as Peter is concerned.

He still has his bad days. But he has a lot more good ones now. But we both know you're more interested in the bad ones. Well rest assured, they're all in here.

Peter doesn't hold back. He never has and he never will.

Edward Couzens-Lake
July 2019

# Prologue

I WAS in utter despair.

How could I have done such a terrible thing?

I've always tried to live the life of a good and decent man, one who had, as a young boy, been sent to Sunday school to learn about and absorb those timeless virtues of love, honour and compassion. I hadn't, I'll admit, been all that keen on going to Sunday school in the first place but, despite that, I couldn't help but agree with the lessons I learnt there and had vowed, from that early age, to try as best I could to treat others as I would expect to be treated myself, but this good and decent man had just seriously injured the woman he loved more than anything or anyone else. More, perhaps, than life itself.

Life had been good to me. I was fit and healthy, as blissfully happy as I had ever been. Through a mix of hard work and good fortune I'd enjoyed a decent career as a professional footballer before, having left the shelter of the game altogether, securing a job that I thoroughly enjoyed, not something a lot of ex-pros I knew were able to admit to. I had money in the bank and lived in a beautiful cottage on the banks of the River Wensum in Norwich with a brand new sponsored Seat car parked in the driveway. I looked forward to getting up every morning, especially those that I could spend with the woman I loved and cherished so much – the woman who was now lying in my hallway covered in blood after I'd stabbed her in the back with a kitchen knife.

### *Charlotte*

I'd met Charlotte at my local gym where I'd previously seen her coming and going a few times before we were introduced to one another by the instructor who took the spin classes I was doing. Charlotte had really stood out from the crowd at the gym because, unlike most of us who'd be clad in sweatshirts and jogging bottoms as we arrived and departed, she was always very smartly dressed. Now that we'd been introduced I felt confident enough to follow that up by passing the time of day with her whenever we saw one another, a quick 'hello, how are you?' that eventually developed into us really starting to get to know one another at the gym's Christmas Party that year, which was held at the Holiday Inn at Norwich Airport.

It was simple enough stuff really. We sat together at the party and for its entire duration just talked about anything and everything really; it felt as if, for those few hours, there was no one else in the room at all, let alone that there was a typically raucous festive party going on in the background. Christmas duly came and went, and as the new year approached we found ourselves keeping in touch more and more by just texting one another, until early that January we finally arranged to meet again properly over a coffee, the first 'proper' date that we had as a couple.

More dates followed. Nothing too outlandish or extravagant, just the two of us meeting somewhere in or around Norwich and having a chat, revelling in, as anyone in the same situation does, that special feeling that comes with getting to know someone that you like more and more. We continued meeting on this basis until, now resolved to wanting to take the relationship further, I took the plunge and asked Charlotte if she'd like to come out to dinner with me.

Oh joy. She said yes.

We had, by now, learnt a great deal about one another. I knew, for example, that she was still living with her ex-partner and her daughter, not the sort of situation you'd expect your date for the evening to still be in, but as Charlotte had explained she felt she could not, at that time, leave the home they were still sharing as it was being completely renovated.

Despite that, however, she very much regarded herself as a single woman who had been more than happy to spend time with me, including, as things had progressed, a lovely and intimate meal together. It was a memorable evening that we both thoroughly enjoyed, the beginnings of a proper and committed relationship with one another.

The highlight of my week was always on the Saturday and Charlotte swiftly became a big part of that day. In the mornings I'd coach upwards of 120 boys and girls at Eaton Park in Norwich alongside my very good friend Malcolm 'Macca' Sparrow. We'd finish there at around midday, which is when, if Norwich City were playing a home match at Carrow Road, I'd make my way there to commence my day's work as part of the club's hospitality team. This would usually involve me greeting either the match ball or programme sponsors as they arrived for the game, starting with me introducing myself to them at the directors' entrance and being with them for the rest of the day, before and after the match as well as sitting with them during the game.

Life was good. I thoroughly enjoyed my work as well as, on those days I was 'on duty', the responsibilities I had as a representative of Norwich City Football Club. I was fortunate enough to be a lifelong fan of the club who had also had the privilege of playing for them, and I'd enjoyed every second of my time at Carrow Road. Yes, there had been more than one opportunity to move to another club during my time there – Leeds United, for example, were very interested in signing me at one time. But I never really wanted to leave and was not at all frustrated that I spent all of my career with the Canaries. I'd been a player, now I could be a fan again and I looked forward to meeting those fellow fans who came along to the games, many of whom were really interesting people who were nearly always excellent company. It all made my job very easy, that's if you can even call it a job because for me at that time it was a privilege to do it. I'd happily go the extra mile with 'my' guests and would often arrange for them to meet one of their footballing heroes, be it a Norwich player or, as was sometimes the case, a member of the opposing team on the day, a player who might, of course, have been someone I once lined up alongside or played against myself.

It was always an enjoyable afternoon for me and I hope it was for all of the people I hosted. Yet, fun as it was, by the time the last of our guests for the day were leaving the ground, my thoughts would turn to the evening that was to come and what Charlotte and I would be doing together, the perfect ending, at this time in my life, to what had already been a wonderful day.

So yes, life was good. Very good in fact.

CHAPTER ONE

# The Linnet

*I knew that I was, like all of my mates, meant to be
going along to Alderman Catleugh school when I was
11 but was told by my dad, who I'm sure had gone
in to have a quiet word with the school's headmaster,
that, regardless of the fact we weren't in his school's
catchment area, we were a Gaywood family and I'd
therefore be going to a Gaywood school.*

YOU'VE PROBABLY heard of King's Lynn but I'm not so sure
that you will have heard of Gaywood. Whenever I read something
about myself, it usually refers to the fact that I was born in King's
Lynn, the Norfolk market town that sits on the River Ouse, that
grey and silt-rich river that acts as the gateway to The Wash.

That bit is true enough. My first home was on Regent Street,
which is in the centre of King's Lynn. But, for various reasons, not
least the fact I went to school in Gaywood, it remains the part of
the town I am most closely connected with.

Fittingly, my day of birth was a Saturday, the day of the
week which I looked forward to more than any other, especially
during my playing career. There's an old rhyme that claims that
'Saturday's child works hard for a living'. That might have been
written by Mel Machin, my old coach at Norwich (and more on

Mel later on) except that he'd have rewritten the whole thing so that working hard for a living applied to all the other days of the week as well, Sunday included.

Gaywood was, at least before it was swallowed up by Lynn, quite a substantial village in its own right. And a prosperous one at that. Gaywood Hall, seat of the ancient Bagge family, was built on the site of a medieval palace that was the home of John de Gray, who didn't do so bad as he ended up being appointed as Bishop of Norwich.

He'd have had no problem declaring himself to have been a proud man of Gaywood. Nothing much has changed since then to be honest. If you ask a Gaywood man or woman if they're from Lynn, they'll look at you in a funny way and say, 'No, I'm from Gaywood.'

I was the second of four children born to Bill and Molly Mendham. They lived in Regent Street in Gaywood, which isn't far, if you're familiar with the area, from the Majestic Cinema. Bill worked in the town docks driving cranes and forklift trucks. He was a hard man who didn't suffer fools gladly, especially as far as his children were concerned. That especially applied to Paul, my older brother, who would, as you do when you're growing up, look to see how far he could push Dad before he responded. In all honesty, Paul should have learned early on where Dad's boundaries, at least as far as the behaviour of his children was concerned, were drawn in the sand and made sure he didn't cross them. Because if he did, that's when Dad's leather belt would come off and my brother would know all about it. Dad would be going at it with Paul whilst I'd be hiding under the kitchen table, pleading with my dad not to hit him, but usually to no avail because Dad had made it a point of honour that no one, not even his own children, would get away with showing him any sort of disrespect. That's the kind of man he was and I guess it reflected his own upbringing, and, just as importantly, how things were at the docks, the sort of working environment that didn't take kindly to any sort of man other than those who grafted hard and knew how to put in a proper shift, but were also good with their fists.

I've made Dad sound like a bully but that's not my intention. He was a product of that time and would have been no different to any other man in any other working family then, no matter where they lived. If we did as we were told, worked hard and, in doing so, kept on the right side of Dad and Mum, then they'd do whatever they could for us to ensure that we were happy.

Both Dad and my Uncle Les saw active service during World War Two. They were identical twins which meant they had hoped to end up serving in the same battalion, but any dreams they had of doing so were thwarted at King's Lynn railway station on the day that Dad reported for duty, along with my Uncle Les, only to be told by the sergeant at the station that he was being posted to a regiment up in Scotland.

'I can't go that far,' protested Dad, adding, 'I'm a Norfolk man, I want to be with my own kin – and that includes my brother here.'

Dad was referring to the Royal Norfolk Regiment, but no such luck. Off he went to Scotland so he could start his training with the Royal Army Medical Corps, whilst Uncle Les ended up being sent down to somewhere on the south coast of England, so about as far away from my dad as you could possibly get! The Army, of course, would not have considered this an issue at all. Everyone had to do as they were told and go wherever they had been ordered to go, but, for all that, it was still a bitter blow for my dad to be separated from his brother as the notion of family togetherness and strength through being together, including through adversity, was very important to him.

Take Christmas, for example: there was never much money to go around as Dad's was the only income (he truly thought a woman's place was in the home and would never have considered letting Mum go out to work) so it had to be spread around our little terraced house as carefully as possible. They certainly excelled at this at Christmas, which was always special, a time when all the family would get together at our home and enjoy themselves, Dad included. But, with family being so important to him, he'd ensure that all of my assorted aunts and uncles would dutifully call round for a glass of beer (sherry for the ladies) with plenty of fizzy pop on the go for Paul and myself as well as Steve, my younger brother, and Lynne, who had the unenviable role of being the youngest out of all of us and sister to the three Mendham boys; that couldn't have been an easy task for her at times, but I have to say she coped with the three of us quite magnificently!

I think there must have been quite a few Mendhams around at that time. If you look at the old census forms from 1891, you can see that there were 105 Mendham families living in Norfolk alone, which was nearly a quarter of all the Mendhams living in the UK at that time. It did feel at times, as I grew up, that most of them seemed to all congregate at my parents' house every Christmas for a jolly before all going their separate ways, never to be seen or heard of again until 12 months down the line.

I started school quite early, indeed. I would have been four when I was taken along to the St James' Infants School for the first time. Mum didn't want me under her feet at home for any longer than was necessary. Not that I minded. I was an energetic and inquisitive child who needed the stimulation that school would bring and I made the most of it from the very beginning. St James' put a heavy emphasis on sport, especially the St James' Junior School for Boys, which was where you 'went up' to at the age of seven. It was part of everyone's daily life at the school and I soon found myself enjoying running as well as trying out for, and getting into, the school football team, where the Formula One driver and present-day commentator Martin Brundle, who was a year older than me, was a regular team-mate.

We were very lucky at St James' in having good sports teachers. Someone can have all the talent in the world at their chosen sport at the age of seven or eight, which can be enough, albeit if a lot of other things fall into place, for them to end up as a world-class performer and household name when they get older. Take, for example, Tiger Woods – when he was only three, he shot a score of 48 over a nine-hole golf course before going on, at six, to win a pitch-and-putt competition that saw him up against boys three or four years older than him. Even more remarkably, he first shot a score of under 80 when he was only eight, a phenomenal achievement. Luckily for Tiger, and this is such a crucial factor for anyone in any sport, he had a mentor and guide alongside him all the time, that person being Earl, his father.

Because even at a very young age, youngsters who enjoy their sport and are showing signs of excelling at it all need someone to nurture that talent, to encourage them and make training fun, something they look forward to and want to do, because if they don't then the easiest decision a seven- or eight-year-old will ever make is not to bother with sports practice again. He or she just wants to have fun. Look at, for example, Lionel Messi, one of the greatest footballers there has ever been. When he was just nine years old, the directors of the club he trained with, Newell's Old Boys in Argentina, would ask him to practice keepy-ups on their pitch. If he did 100 he knew he'd get an ice cream. That was incentive enough for the young Messi, who once did 1,100 keepy-ups just so he could have another ten ice creams! The coaches he was working with knew exactly what they were doing. By making training fun and putting in these little incentives, Messi wanted to succeed and improve from an early age. Had they not been quite so committed to him and just left him in a group of another eight to ten boys, he might have lost interest and never turned into the player that he ultimately became.

The teacher in charge of games and PE at St James' School was Alan Fry. He had that exact same approach with his teaching that Earl Woods or Messi's coach would had done; he wanted everyone, no matter what their standard was, to enjoy playing games and to look forward to their weekly sessions. That was an approach which meant that anyone with a genuine natural talent for what they were doing would soon shine. It baffles me to this day how some children will do just about anything they can to get out of PE at school. It should be the highlight of their week, a chance to get outside into the fresh air and run around with a ball or whatever and just have fun.

Maybe some are put off because they don't think they are any good or will ever be in the school team or the first to be picked. That's such a shame. You don't have to excel at any sport, just enjoy it. That is what a good teacher or coach should be focussing on with young children, making sure the sessions are fun and leave everyone with a smile on their face – which is what Alan Fry did. He was very dedicated and gave everything he could to ensure that his young and lively charges had fun, regardless of what the sport was. He had a big influence on me with all the enthusiasm and commitment he demonstrated to everyone back then. It was infectious. I wanted to improve because of Alan and become a better player. He was always there for me, encouraging me to do just that, to better myself in the game in every way he could think of. Yet he'd have given just as much time and effort to those children who could barely kick the ball straight, never mind do anything else with it. It didn't matter to Alan, he just wanted us to have fun and, you know what, every single one of us did. The man was an absolute diamond.

The other subject I enjoyed at St James' School was geography. However, it wasn't so much for my longing to immerse myself in the fascinating world of ox-bow lakes (come on, how many of you still remember how they are formed?), weathering, erosion, myriad Mercator maps and the capital cities of the world. None of that mattered much to me in the slightest. What did matter was my geography teacher. Her name was Miss Tate, and to the young Peter Mendham she was someone who had been sent down to earth by the gods. I thought she was gorgeous and, in the way that many a ten-year-old will, I fell totally and utterly in love with her. I paid the price for my infatuation, mind you, as one day I wrote 'I LOVE MISS TATE' on a piece of scrap paper and passed it over to one of my friends. What do you think happened? Yes, she saw what I was doing and intercepted that piece of paper, opening it in front of me and the rest of the class. She went a little bit red as she did so, but not half as red as I must have gone! Luckily, she didn't share my message with my classmates but she did send me to see the headmaster so I could show him what I'd written. I dare say I wasn't the first or last young man he'd encountered in his office who'd fallen for that particular member of his teaching staff.

I was at St James' School until I was 11. Football was, by then, already playing a very big part in my life, but I didn't neglect my other subjects too much and certainly didn't get into serious trouble. I'd have my moments of mischief, just as we all do at that age, but would always have, lurking at the back of my mind, the thought of what Dad might do if he got home from the docks one day to find out I'd really misbehaved at school. He'd chuckle or tut-tut a bit in response to some of my less-serious escapades, but that leather belt of his was always conveniently nearby if needed and I knew that he wouldn't hesitate to give me a wallop if he thought I'd overstepped the mark.

By the time I was 11, we had moved from Regent Street into a nice new house on the Grange Estate in a small village called South Wootton, which is about two miles north-east of King's Lynn. It's a pleasant enough little suburb where nothing much really happened, though if it did you could be sure someone would be keenly watching from behind their immaculate net curtains. It was a great place to live if you were growing up as the roads were much quieter, with the added bonus that there was a lot more green space for all of us kids to run wild in, including a sports field within a few minutes' walk of our cul-de-sac. All of the local children used to gather on the playing field on a daily basis until there was enough of us to have a decent game of football, we'd all then head off to the sports field every evening and, in the best childhood traditions, continue playing until it was nearly dark and the streets were echoing to the multiple calls of parents wanting their children to come home. I'd be enjoying our games as much as anyone, but if I heard my Dad's voice shouting out my name I'd stop whatever I was doing and head straight home without waiting for a second invitation.

Our new house was in the catchment area of a local secondary modern school known as Alderman Catleugh, but, unlike all of my mates on my road, I didn't go there and wouldn't have done even if I'd wanted to. No, my fate was to go to the notorious Gaywood Park school, locally renowned for being just about the toughest school with the hardest, meanest and most streetwise intake you could think of. And that was just the teachers. No, seriously, Gaywood Park did have a reputation at the time for being the school where all the local hard nuts went, or at least the school where they were meant to be if they weren't bunking off and hanging out in the town centre. I knew that I was, like all of my mates, meant to be going along to Alderman Catleugh school when I was 11 but was told by my dad, who I'm sure had gone in to have a quiet word with the school's headmaster, that, regardless of the fact we weren't in his school's catchment area, we were a Gaywood family and I'd therefore be going to a Gaywood school. It might also, of course, have had something to do with the fact that Dad thought I needed toughening up a bit, and if he was thinking that I would, like him, end up working at King's Lynn docks, then it wasn't so much an academic education that I needed as one that would leave me streetwise and able to look after myself.

Alderman was considered to be an all-round better school, and no wonder. It didn't, for example, include the massive Fairstead Estate in its catchment area. Fairstead, or 'the Stead' as it was known locally, was one of the biggest council estates in the whole of East Anglia and one which, unfortunately, housed a few undesirables, many of whom were reputedly sent there by assorted London councils keen to get them off their hands and make them someone else's problem. Given the choice, then, most local families would have sent their children to Alderman. But not my dad, it was Gaywood Park for me and that was the end of it.

My first day at senior school rolled around, and whilst all of my mates headed off in one direction I went in the other, and I ended up going to the school I should never have gone to for five years. Not that this particularly bothered me. For all of Gaywood Park's problems, I'd heard some very good things about the teacher there who was head of PE and games called Steve King.

Steve worked alongside another teacher, Barry Chandler, who had played a fairly decent level of football in his time but was now more interested in passing on his knowledge and experience in the game to others. Another teacher who had a great influence on me at this time was Tony Gayton. They all ended up having a huge influence on my life and fledgling career in the game, something which I will always be grateful to them for.

Barry soon had me playing in the Year One (11 to 12 year olds) team but quickly realised that I was already too good for this level so he promoted me into the Year Two (12 to 13 year olds) team where, despite being a bit smaller and younger than everyone else, I more than fitted in, as did two other lads, Robert Linford and David Goose, whom Barry had also 'promoted' from the first-year team.

Because of our age (we were two years younger than some of the lads we played against, a big difference when you're 11 and they're 13), Barry knew we'd need to work on our stamina and fitness as well as build up our physical strength, which meant lots of cross-country running, especially in the large park in the middle of King's Lynn, which is known as The Walks, although, funnily enough, I can never remember 'just' walking in there, all I did was run! I actually got quite good at cross country and ended up representing Norfolk at two English Schools Cross-Country Championships which were held in Derby and Portsmouth, and I was proud to be representing my county.

I'd spend a lot of time running there on my own, usually at weekends but sometimes after school and into the evenings. Most of the other kids my age would be out mucking about on their bikes or just messing around with whatever the latest craze was, but not me. I was, even then, becoming more and more dedicated to doing whatever I could to be as good a footballer as I could possibly be. I don't suppose it would happen today;

not only are there a lot more distractions out there for children of that age but, given how the world has changed in the years since I was going out for my solo runs, most parents are very reluctant to let their children out of their sight. That's especially true in the evenings, and, for all the negatives there are about the current younger generation spending all of their free time in their bedrooms playing computer games, at least their mums and dads know where they are. I would, at least, have someone to run with on occasion as I'd kept in touch with one of the lads I went to St James' School with, so on more than one occasion it would be me and my mate Tony Hunt pounding the lanes and footpaths in and around The Walks, taking in all the local landmarks like the tennis courts and the Red Mount Chapel.

I mentioned earlier on how I tended, for the most part, to behave myself. That's true enough and I'm not going to contradict myself here too much. But I did have my moments and it would have been at around about the time I was really getting into my running that I found myself distracted enough one afternoon to engage in that great teenage occupation of a spot of light scrumping.

Scrumping, for those of you who are either not old enough or simply too cool to have heard of it, is the act of pilfering fruit from an allotment or someone's garden, usually with the intention of eating it straight away. This was certainly my intention at the time as I was feeling rather hungry, something that people who know me well will agree is not particularly unusual. The object of my desires was an orchard that was set in the grounds of a large house that was situated in the Gaywood Road, not too far away from where the old Lynn Tech, now the College of West Anglia, is. There was a great abundance of ripe apples hanging from the branches of the trees in this orchard and I couldn't help myself, I had to have some of them. Unfortunately I was so intent on filling both my stomach and my pockets with lovely ripe fruit that I didn't notice the owner of the property running up to me until it was too late.

## *Busted!*

I could hardly plead innocence as, let's face it, the evidence was overwhelmingly against me. There I was in her orchard, half-eaten apple cores at my feet with more fruit stashed about my person. There was little point in me claiming that it was an accident or I'd taken a wrong turn whilst I was out on my run. The aggrieved lady wouldn't let me go until the police had arrived, which I felt was a little mean-spirited of her. Mind you, I didn't run off either so maybe, deep down, I'd accepted that I was in the wrong and was ready for whatever fate might have in store for me. With my dad, that might have involved his old leather belt, but for whatever reason (maybe he'd done a spot of scrumping in his day) he wasn't too mad at me and the scrumping episode was soon forgotten.

I guess if I did have a taste for apples then I could have quenched my thirst in one of the many pubs that are dotted around King's Lynn and the surrounding area. I was never particularly interested in going out for a drink though, as right from my early teens I'd had my heart set on becoming a professional footballer and knew, even at that age, that pubs and alcohol were not something that would help me achieve that lofty goal. So I got into a few other things, notably fishing, something that I still love to do to this day whenever I have the chance. My favourite fishing haunts at the time were the Babingley River as well as the long ponds on Loke Road in King's Lynn, the latter a location that many a committed fisherman or woman who grew up in the town will be more than familiar with. It's a place where, rod and line wise, you learnt the angling trade along with all of your mates, who were just getting into it and, just like you, all making the same mistakes such as getting your line all tangled up, losing hooks and, more often than not, managing to prick yourself in the finger whilst you tried to get a worm on to the hook.

If I wasn't out fishing then there is a fair chance that if I wasn't training you'd have found me at one of two cinemas in King's Lynn at that time. The two options we had were either the rather grandiose Majestic or the more humble Pilot which, sadly, has now long gone. The Majestic was a must for me and all of my mates every Saturday morning when they used to put on a series of films for the local children – quite an ordeal I would think for all the hard-working staff there at the time who were rather more used to small and relatively genteel audiences every evening. I'd also go along to the King's Lynn Sea Cadets meetings on occasion – the closest, I guess, I ever got to following my dad and having a career on or in the water, but it wasn't for me and I often wonder if my dad had ever thought he'd end up accompanying one of his sons, probably me, to work every morning down at the town's docks and being disappointed when that never happened.

Mind you, I think he was more pleased with me when I started to show an interest in girls. Maybe he was looking forward to meeting them whenever I brought one home. The first girl I was really interested in (if you disregard my schoolboy infatuation with Miss Tate) was Margaret Benefer. I did have more than a little crush on her. She lived near King's Lynn Library, which wasn't too far away from Gaywood Park school, so I would never have been able to use the excuse that she lived too far away from me. Even somewhere like Castle Rising, which is only a few miles away from Lynn, might as well have been on the other side of the universe at that time, so it would have been pointless if I found myself fancying someone who came from there or even further afield, the glamorous surrounds of seaside town Hunstanton, for example. But no, Margaret was local and, as far as I knew, she wasn't going out with anyone, so there was no reason for me not to ask her out on a date with the possibility of sitting in the back row at the Majestic foremost in my mind. It should, I guess, have been the beginning of a wonderful friendship, my first girlfriend and all the memories that go with it, of holding hands, stolen kisses and letters that have SWALK written on the back of the envelope, but no, it never happened. As much as I wanted to ask Margaret out, I could never quite summon up the courage to do so, and in the end, despite all of my romantic hopes and dreams, I was just too shy to even talk to her.

I had my first genuine sexual experience with a local girl when I was 17. She was a little bit older than me and was probably expecting big things in every sense of the word from the young, fit and athletic Peter Mendham. Sadly for both of us that didn't end up being the case at all; in fact, the whole thing was something of a complete and utter disaster for me.

I don't suppose that's particularly unusual in young men, even today. I was, like so many of my friends, very good at all the talk and acting as if I knew exactly what I was doing, but that was anything but the case. Sadly, though, that wasn't my first sexual encounter as my childhood innocence had been taken away from me at a much earlier age. I had, when I was a lot younger, been dispatched up the A149 coast road to Heacham in order to enjoy the occasional night under canvas and just enjoy being away from the town for a few days. These ended up being trips I never used to look forward to as the man who was charged with looking after me on these trips was someone Dad knew, and someone who, over a period of around four years, would regularly make his way into my tent and sexually abuse me whenever I was there.

This man was regarded as a family friend, someone who would always receive a warm welcome and a cup of tea whenever he knocked on the door. He and Dad got on really well, with Dad especially liking the fact that he seemed to enjoy spending time with us all. It meant, as far as he was concerned, there was someone he could rely on to take us off his and Mum's hands on occasion and spend time with us. Dad trusted this man with his kids, never knowing, for one second, that his trust had been betrayed in the worst possible way.

He would put on a great show of being a family friend when Dad was around. But once he was on his own with me he didn't care what pain and suffering he inflicted as long as his sexual needs were sated. He'd also tried to abuse my brother Paul, but fortunately Paul was, by the time he was on the prowl, streetwise enough to know that he had to avoid him and his company at all costs. That didn't particularly bother him. He still had access to me and the nights I was forced to spend in his company at that campsite in Heacham still provoke memories that keep me awake at night and return me to that state of complete and utter hopelessness that I knew then. Had Dad known he was doing this, of course, he would have taken the law into his own hands but he never did as my attacker was able to manipulate me in such a way that I became convinced it was a secret that could never be known or shared by anyone other than the two of us. I knew it was wrong and the whole scenario, as it played out, used to make me feel as uncomfortable as hell, but I felt as powerless in terms of doing something about it as I did in stopping him from doing so in the first place. It certainly never occurred to me to say anything to my dad about it.

Later on in my life and just as I had started my professional career, Dad got in touch with me to say that the man in question, who was still one of his best friends, was seriously ill and not expected to live for very much longer. Would Peter, he'd asked my dad, care to go over and see him one last time? I didn't want to of course, the memories of all the things that had taken place in that tent all those years ago were suddenly very vivid ones again, but at the same time I couldn't think of a reason not to go that would have satisfied Dad, other than telling him the truth about what had happened at that campsite in Heacham. So I went along to see him in order to please my father, realising, as so many thoughts raced through my mind during that brief visit, that the man who was lying there in front of me, slowly dying, had been the reason I had, on the day that I thought I was going to lose my virginity, completely frozen, unable to move or even talk, much to the distress of the young lady I was with who must have ended up being a little bit scarred by the whole experience herself.

I was too young to know what he was doing to me was abuse. Over time it just became part of what we did when we were at the campsite, and although I didn't like what he was doing I also knew that a lot of things grown-ups asked or expected you to do weren't particularly nice, but you just had to put up with it. Even as I got older and began to realise that what was happening wasn't right I became very frightened at the prospect of heading out to the campsite, but I must have hidden it well as no one in the family ever picked up on my sudden reluctance to head out to Heacham for a long weekend. I eventually plucked up the courage to speak to him about what he was doing but was told that I wasn't, under any circumstances, to say anything to anyone about him or the two of us, so, not wanting to upset anyone or make my dad cross, I did as I was told and kept quiet. Eventually, many years later, I brought up the subject with my older brother Paul and told him what had happened. Paul listened and then told me that he'd tried to abuse him as well but, being a little bit bigger and older at the time, he'd pushed him away and he'd never bothered him again after that one attempt.

Despite everything that went on there, I do still have, thankfully, some good memories of the campsite, which was perfect for getting away for a few days, even if it meant having my immediate family around me for the duration. It therefore became, between April and September every year, a second home for the Mendhams and we'd be there, complete with a few essential belongings, on the first weekend it opened every spring, no matter what the weather was like. The tents we made our home were fairly large, around 16ft square and made of a solid-wood frame with a heavy duty canvas over them.

No nonsense then, and far superior to the flimsy things you see being sold in shops and garden centres today. So, for every dark and dreadful memory I had of the place, I could, at least, try to blank it out with some of the good ones, treasured memories spent with Mum and Dad, my brothers and sister, them and other members of the camping fraternity whom we got to know at the time and considered to be our friends. It sounds, admittedly, not much of a big deal.

Most people had caught the foreign travel bug by then and were jetting off to sun themselves on the beaches of Spain and Portugal, but not the Mendhams. We were happy enough to drive 15 miles or so out of town and, come rain or shine, spend our precious free time under canvas in Heacham. And what a great place to be it was. We had a beach on one side of the campsite with woodland and a river on the other. It was a well-kept secret, a place known only to the privileged few, picturesque beyond belief and with an abundance of wildlife to watch, particularly rabbits. I remember us heading over to the nearby town of Hunstanton ('Hun'stun' as its referred to locally) and to its fairground for a bit of fun and a laugh on the ghost train and dodgems. It was pitch black by the time we returned to the campsite and I was enraptured by the sight of what seemed to be thousands of pairs of rabbits' eyes glowing in the reflection of my dad's headlights. That memory prompts another one, the story my grandad told me about how to catch a rabbit. It's easy really, all you need to do is get a big stone and put some pepper on it, then when the rabbit comes along and sniffs the stone it promptly sneezes and in the process knocks itself out on the stone.

No wonder that campsite is the source of some of the best and worst memories of my younger life. I prefer to focus on the good ones. Like finishing at school in July and looking forward to spending six long and glorious weeks in Heacham. We cycled all the way there from King's Lynn at the start of one holiday and I spent the entire summer in a tent, my days full of what would now be considered rather old-fashioned pursuits for a boy to take part in, lots of swimming and fishing as well as playing tennis, rounders and, of course, football. We had everything we needed there. The tent had a gas cooker and fridge, a set of bunk beds, a single bed plus a large sofa bed, which is where Mum and Dad slept. It was 'glamping' way before it became fashionable, just us and the great outdoors. No television and, of course, no mobiles or other devices to suck away your time and gaze. A wonderful and innocent time that we all so thoroughly enjoyed.

Much later on in my life, and shortly before my father passed away, I shared my story about what happened at the campsite with him. Poor Dad, it came as a great shock to him but he was glad that I told him, difficult as it was for me to do.

By the time I was 12, I was really getting into my football in a big way. Steve King and Barry Chandler, my teachers at Gaywood Park, were continuing to encourage me to practise as much as I could and I'd taken that advice seriously, so much so that even when I was walking to and from school I'd have a tennis ball or, if one wasn't readily available, a pair of rolled-up socks at my feet. I grew so committed that you'd rarely, if ever, not see me walking along and controlling a ball of some kind (or the socks) as I walked to and from school. As far as I was concerned, the two most important items I took to school with me every day were my packed lunch and something to kick on the way there and back as well as all points in between. Pens, pencils, textbooks and homework, they soon all became afterthoughts to me on my 'school run'; as long as I had something to eat and a ball at my feet, I was content because I was now living and breathing football in every waking moment, as well as dreaming about it when I was asleep. Football was all that I ever wanted to do in my life and I made sure that every opportunity I had to practise, train and play the game was one that I seized upon with relish.

One thing I'd come to realise was that I wasn't as strong with my left foot as I was with my right. I knew, there and then, that I could never expect to make it in the game as a professional if I could only kick and control the ball with one foot. It amazes me today that commentators and media pundits refer to Premier League players as having a 'weaker foot'. They're earning in excess of £100,000 a week and can't kick with one of their feet? Why on earth have they never practised being stronger on that side of their body? They'd be far better players as a result of that extra effort.

I wasn't going to be like that. I didn't want there to be a weakness in my game. So I established a personal training routine that would put the emphasis on improving my kicking with my left foot. That involved me wearing one of my carpet slippers on my right foot whilst on my left I'd wear a football boot. The footballs we had to play with back then were heavy old leather things, especially if it had been raining, which meant if I kicked with my right foot it would hurt as I only had a slipper on. This was incentive, therefore, to use my left foot as much as I could, and that is exactly what I did. More often than not I'd be practising on my own anyway as my friends didn't always want to play, not as much as I wanted to anyway. So I'd spend a lot of time perfecting my skills and making sure I could control, kick and pass the ball equally as well with both feet, an asset which served me well throughout my career as it meant that the managers I played under could consider me as an option on the left side of the pitch as well as through the middle and on the right. These little training sessions were occasionally interrupted by my giving some other sports a go. I was, for example, quite handy at both the long and triple jumps at school whilst I also took time out to have a few games of cricket, but that didn't last very long as it was far too slow a game for my liking and I found it very hard to get excited about a sport that revolves around nothing happening for much of the time.

It was around about this time that my grandparents took me along to my first 'proper' match as a spectator. Tim and Elsie Mendham were my dad's parents and they'd clearly noticed how keen I was on the game and decided, as big fans of the local team, King's Lynn FC, that they'd take me along to watch one of their matches. I knew where the club played as I'd run past their stadium many times on my training runs in The Walks; indeed, that's the name of the ground that the Linnets, as they are known, play at. I'd never been to watch them though so was, understandably, very excited about seeing them in action. I can't, sadly, remember who they were playing or even if they won the match, but I do recall finding it all great fun and wanting to go again. Grandad Tim was wonderful company, someone who you would unhesitatingly call a 'proper' grandad, a man who had a garden shed full of wonderful tools that he would use, as grandfathers do, to make just about anything you could care to ask. Both he and my Nan Mendham encouraged me in my football and would always ask me, without fail, how I was getting on with my training or how my school matches were going. It saddens me to this day to think that they both passed away before they got the chance to watch me play in the First Division for Norwich City as it would have been a wonderful way for me to have repaid them for all the faith and support they showed me when I was younger.

I can remember the first Norwich City match that I attended as if it was only a few days ago. It was the second leg of a League Cup semi-final tie against Manchester United in January 1975 (so I would have been 14) that Norwich, who'd drawn the first leg at Old Trafford 2-2, won by a goal to nil in order to reach the final, where they'd play Aston Villa. There were nearly 32,000 people packed into Carrow Road that night who, along with a very excited Peter Mendham, enjoyed an absolutely thrilling match, one that saw the legendary Canaries goalkeeper Kevin Keelan make two absolutely extraordinary saves, one from Alex Forsyth and another from Sammy McIlroy. It was a game and occasion that fuelled my desire to become a professional footballer myself and take part in nights and games such as that one and in front of such a boisterous and demanding crowd. Norwich fans have never been slow to let their team know when they weren't happy with the way they were playing and, back then, would very publicly display any dissatisfaction by lobbing the blue cushions that used to be placed on every seat in the main stand on to the pitch. But I didn't want to be throwing the cushions, I wanted to be out on the pitch and playing so well that no one would ever dream of lobbing one my way. The first opportunity I had to do so that summer wasn't with Norwich but with Peterborough United, who invited me down for a trial match. They were seen as quite a progressive club at the time and had, in Noel Cantwell, a manager who'd taken Coventry City into European club competition as well as, three years earlier, won the Fourth Division title with Peterborough.

They would have been a good club for me to join then but, despite my playing well in the trial match at London Road, nothing came of it. At around about the same time, I was invited up to

Nottingham Forest for a trial with them, an even more exciting prospect really because at that time they'd just been taken over by Brian Clough. Unfortunately, the chance to impress Cloughie never came about as on the day of the trial I managed to miss the bus I was due to catch at the start of my journey north and wasn't invited again. Looking back now, I do wonder if, deep down, I didn't really want to go all the way up there at all and maybe didn't make as much effort to get that bus as I might have done. Maybe deep down I was still waiting for the opportunity to have a trial for Norwich to come along and had realised that if I ended up signing for another club, even as an apprentice, my chances of playing for the Canaries might have disappeared altogether.

I didn't see being rejected by Peterborough as a disappointment but came to regard it as a vital lesson that I was determined to make the most of. I knew I was a good player, even at that early age, and came to accept that Peterborough hadn't turned down the opportunity to sign me because I wasn't capable of making the grade. What I had begun to realise is that I needed to address other aspects of both my game and my character on the pitch because, as decent a player as I was, I was also rather quiet and withdrawn, someone who, perhaps, wasn't as visible or vocal as he could have been, especially when things weren't going well. What I needed to do, I realised, with the same sort of commitment I had to improving my ball control, sprinting and gym work, was to work on my confidence, to express myself more both on the field of play and in the dressing room or at training, to come across, in other words, as someone who had the self-belief and positive attitude to match his game.

CHAPTER TWO

# Fledgling Canary

*It was a tough week. Early starts, late nights and lots
of hard work in between, with little mercy shown to
those who weren't up to it, even at that stage. There is
a lot of churn amongst schoolboy footballers, it was the
case with me back then and remains that way today.*


WHEN PEOPLE ask me now what a young player, say someone
who is doing well with their school team or at schoolboy level, can
do to give themselves as good a chance as possible of progressing
into the professional game, I always tell them that absolute
dedication to the game and practice is essential. It might now
be considered a bit old-fashioned to say 'practice makes perfect'
but for football it's especially true and as important today as it
was when I was starting to push on in the game myself when
I was 13. Youngsters today have so many more distractions in
their lives than my generation ever did, yet if they're serious about
becoming a professional footballer then he or she needs to put all
those distractions aside and focus on nothing but their football
training, coaching and playing. Even when they're not doing any
of those three things, they need to be thinking and planning about
when they will next be doing so. It's also important to practise
when they're on their own. Don't let anyone else being around

be an excuse for them not to practise. They can, just as I did, put together little drills they can do on their own. If there's a convenient wall close to you, for example, and preferably one where constantly kicking a ball against it isn't going to annoy the person who lives in that house, make a target on it and aim to hit that target with the ball every time from various distances, making sure they are able to do so with both their right and left foot so they become what is now referred to as a naturally two-footed player, of which, in the modern game, there still aren't that many.

It's about dedication – I was told that, and thanks to people like Alan Fry at St James' School, I never forgot how important it was to show that in order to make a career in the game. It helped, of course, as far as I was concerned, that I also received plenty of encouragement, especially from my grandparents. They'd come and watch all of my games and were always very supportive of me. I hope that the current generation of 11-, 12- and 13-year-olds trying to progress with their football have the sort of support and encouragement that I did, but whenever you hear or see some of the so-called 'competitive parents' today yelling and screaming at their children from the touchline when they are playing, you do wonder if it isn't enough to put them off wanting to play the game for life and that would be a real shame.

By the time I was 14 I was so into my football there seemed little time for anything or anyone else in my life. I was playing for fun and making the most of every match I played. Looking back at that time now, I can't say for certain that I was playing with the set intention of becoming a professional footballer. I hadn't, for example, done what so many young lads of the time did and written to clubs to ask for a trial. That was something my good friend and former team-mate Jeremy Goss did, something which saw him get trials with Aston Villa and Southampton before he ended up with me at Norwich. I just wanted to play. So by accident rather than design my own big breakthrough came about almost without me realising it was happening! I was in the fourth year (14- to 15-year-olds) at Gaywood Park school but had been selected to play for the fifth year in a game against our deadly rivals from just across the road, King Edward School, or KES as it has always been known. It was a local derby of sorts with a bit of needle attached to it because KES was a grammar school at the time, so, not surprisingly, we regarded them as the posh kids that needed to be taken down a peg or two, whilst the KES lads saw us as the local yobbos who were also in need of the same thing. It wasn't a game for shrinking violets and I was, along with everyone else at Gaywood Park, looking forward to a good game and, of course, a win.

Unbeknownst to me, two Norwich City scouts were at the game. They were Fred Davies, who'd been a goalkeeper for Wolves, Cardiff and Bournemouth before moving to Norwich at around the same time as John Bond was appointed Norwich City manager, and Basil Hayward, who'd spent most of his playing career at Port Vale in the 40s and 50s before going into coaching. He'd been manager of Gillingham and non-league Telford United before being appointed as Norwich City chief scout in 1974. Fred and Basil weren't there to run the rule over me, however. Their interest was in my mates Robert Linford and David Goose who I mentioned earlier and who had, only a short time before then, caught that bus at that start of the journey to Brian Clough and Nottingham Forest that I had missed. Rob and David continued to be in demand, and they had, like me, played their way into all of their school sides and it was now pretty much agreed that of all the boys playing football in the King's Lynn and West Norfolk area they were just about the most promising. Rob and David had already been watched by scouts from quite a few other clubs and, determined not to miss out on two local lads as they'd done in the past (Norfolk-born Trevor Whymark slipped through the Canary net, signed for Ipswich instead and ended up playing for England!), Fred and Basil were stood on the touchline, notepads in hand, ready to get Rob and David up to Carrow Road for a trial with the Canaries.

It was a good game and I played well, more than holding my own in a midfield that was made up of lads who were a lot bigger and more physically developed than me, so much so in fact that at the end of the match Fred and Basil came up to me, introduced themselves and asked me if I'd be interested in coming up to Norwich for a week's trial during the half-term holiday, which wasn't far away. I was as surprised as I was delighted and had no hesitation whatsoever in saying yes, doing so, of course, without thinking of the not inconsiderable problem of how I was going to get from King's Lynn to Norwich and back every day for a week. The actual distance isn't that great – it's about 40 miles by road but that's no good for a 14-year-old who's going to need to use public transport – and forget the train because if you want to get to Norwich from Lynn that way, you've got to go via Ely which is in Cambridgeshire!

Luckily for me, Dad was more than happy to take me up to Norwich, although in the days I was playing for the youth team we'd be leaving at five in the morning so he could get me there in time. We had to play all of our games away from home at the time, so the earlier we had to leave Norwich on the team bus to get to a game, the earlier Dad and I had to be up, ready and away in the mornings. He and a lot of other people gave so much of their time and petrol to get me to places at that time and I'll always be very grateful to all of them.

Fred and Basil had seen enough in me to know that I had the potential to make it in the game. There are never any guarantees if you're a good schoolboy footballer; being one of the very best there is at 14, 15 years old doesn't mean you're going to make it into the full-time game. Every club in the land will have stories of schoolboy prodigies who were strongly tipped to be the next big thing, only for them to slip into obscurity and never be heard of again. Take my friends Rob and David, for example; they were considered to be two of the very best schoolboy footballers in East Anglia at that time, yet Rob never made it past that level in the game, whilst, although David went on to play at a fairly decent standard, he never attained the heights in the game that many thought him capable of. Having the potential to go all the way –

and this counts in all sports – is one thing, but having the desire, the commitment and sheer bloody-mindedness to turn it into something more tangible is something else. I was nowhere near being a professional footballer myself at that time either. Fred and Basil had seen the raw material was there but had no idea if I'd be able to push on from there. And there were weaknesses in my game that I'd have to work on and improve if I was to have any chance of pushing on. I was a little quiet during games so would need to be a little more verbal and talk more during matches, something that comes with self-confidence and, to an extent, a willingness to take on some responsibility. I also needed to work on my physique and bulk out a little, something that came through going to a local gym and learning how to use weights, something I soon enjoyed doing, so much so, in fact, that I still do so to this day.

So I was building myself up both in terms of my confidence as well as my build. As for the football itself, well, ability wise, I was above average but no more than that. A fast and tenacious right-winger who was good on the ball and had a bit of pace about him. All well and good of course and a promising foundation to build on. But there was, as I soon learnt, much more for me to do and learn. It was a tough week. Early starts, late nights and lots of hard work in between, with little mercy shown to those who weren't up to it, even at that stage. Clubs like Norwich would arrange for upwards of ten or 15 boys to come in for a trial, yet if at any time during that week someone looked like they wouldn't be able to reach the standard required, someone would have a quiet word in their ear and they'd be gone, never to return. Remember I mentioned Jeremy Goss earlier, the Gossy who seized the footballing imagination of the country with his goals and performances in Norwich's UEFA Cup run in 1993? He went along for that trial at Aston Villa that he got through writing to the club but had barely been on the pitch there before he was taken to one side by one of the club's coaching staff who sent him on his way with the words, '... you will never be a professional footballer as long as you live. Get yourself off, get changed and off to the station, get yourself home and get yourself a real job.' [1]

Brutal. But that's how it was. I'd tasted this for myself after my experience with Peterborough United. It still is, maybe more so now. Gossy had the determination and drive to prove that Aston Villa coach wrong. But for every young player who digs in and does just that, another 99 will take that sort of message to heart and drift away from the game before they've even started. I was lucky, I made it through that week's trial and on the Friday met up with Basil Hayward who told me that the club liked what they'd seen and wanted me to sign on what was then known as associated schoolboy terms for two years. That would take me up to the age of 16, which is when the club would have another decision to make, that of deciding whether or not to offer me an apprentice professional contract, which would be for another two years and, if all went well, the prelude to being offered your first full-time professional deal when you turned 18. That was now my obvious goal and I wanted nothing more than to do just that.

My week's trial with the club was hard work. Football clubs didn't make allowances for your age or the fact you were in a new and unfamiliar place with a lot of pressure now heaped upon your shoulders. It was sink or swim and even though I was still just short of my 15th birthday I already knew I had to perform or I'd be out. Maybe that knowledge, of already being aware of what was expected of you through the experience I'd already had at Peterborough, had toughened me up a little and given me just that little bit of an advantage over Robert, David and the rest of the lads who were up at Trowse that week.

We played two games during that week, the first against a team of schoolboys from Watford. We beat them 5-2 and I played well, scoring a couple of goals into the bargain, so my confidence was up by the time the second game of the week came around, which was down at Cheshunt against one of Tottenham's

---

1  *Gossy*, Edward Couzens-Lake (Amberley Publishing), 2014.

schoolboy sides. That game ended in a 0-0 draw and was a lot tougher. The Tottenham lads had a lot of quality about them, even at that age, and I often wonder how many of them who played in that match made it in the game.

When we weren't playing games we were training. And we trained hard. I knew that if I didn't work hard enough to impress those shadowy figures that were standing on the sidelines then I'd be told, again, that I wasn't good enough, then I might have wanted to pack it all in. Being turned down by Peterborough was one thing but that had been a 'dry run' in my eyes for the real deal, this trial, the one with my local club and whose fortunes I'd long followed. Mind you, for all that, I had never been solely a fan of the Canaries as I'd been growing up. That's because the first football team that really caught my eye was Leeds United, the team that Don Revie had led to near total domination of English football for just under a decade from the mid-1960s onwards.

They had that touch of arrogance about them that I liked, a swagger that came with the confidence that they were the best players and best team around, and if you wanted to beat them then you had to play at your absolute best and hope against hope that at the same time they had a bit of an off day. What most attracted me to them though was something a lot more simple. It was their all-white kit! The sight of that on players like Billy Bremner, Johnny Giles and Eddie Gray was enough for me to want to join the Leeds United fan club, and for a while my bedroom walls were covered with team pictures as well as a load of individual players including Gary Sprake, Paul Madeley, Paul Reaney and Jack Charlton. I also loved the famous club badge which was known as 'smiley', but most of all I liked, and wanted, a pair of the tags their players wore at the top of their socks which showed their shirt numbers. It was a gimmick of course but one that was way ahead of its time, designed and introduced, I am convinced, to lead to thousands of football-loving boys and girls across the country, Leeds fans or not, to demand that their parents bought them some!

The colours adorning my bedroom walls were now very definitely yellow and green. My trial went well and I was duly signed by the club on schoolboy terms, a big thrill for me of course and for my dad, even though he knew it would mean him putting many more miles on the clock of his car as he drove me up to Norwich in order for me to meet my commitments at the club as well as taking me anywhere and everywhere else that my football 'duties' necessitated. The Canaries were, at that time, a club that was on the up and up, thanks mainly to the efforts and vision of John Bond, who'd been appointed as first-team manager in December 1973. Bond had previously been manager of Bournemouth and had, upon joining Norwich, made sure he was joined at the club by both players and coaching personnel he was familiar with and trusted. One of them was his old West Ham team-mate and his former assistant at Bournemouth Ken Brown, who ended up having more of an influence on my career and life than anyone else in the game. They'd joined a club that had only just escaped relegation at the end of their first season in the top flight and had found things even more difficult the second time around, so much so that Ron Saunders, the man who led the Canaries to their first-ever promotion to the elite level, had walked out of the club following a home defeat to Everton. John and Ken did everything they could to arrest Norwich's slide during that 1973/74 season, but the Canaries were, by now, a side in desperate need of both new players and ideas, and it showed in their on-field performances as they ended the campaign in bottom place.

Bond's arrival at Carrow Road not only saw them promoted back to the old First Division at the end of the 1974/75 season, but also saw a swift and decisive era of change sweep over the club both on and off the pitch as he made it a priority to bring the Canaries business model up to speed. One of the best things he did was arrange for the club's reserve and youth teams to be granted full membership of what was then called the South East Counties League.

The Canaries up until then had to play all of their games at that level away from home due to their opponents claiming that Norwich was too far away for them to travel to. Ludicrous I know, but true. Bond regarded this, rightly, as totally unacceptable and eventually persuaded the Football League to permit Norwich to play as full members of the South East Counties League and on a traditional home and away basis rather than having to travel for every single game as we had been doing. This arrangement particularly suited the younger players at the club such as myself because the Canaries schoolboy and youth teams had also been arranging and playing occasional friendly matches against local teams such as Great Yarmouth, Lowestoft and, of course, King's Lynn.

You'd be forgiven for thinking that the players at these, and other, local teams would look forward to having the opportunity to test themselves against the best young players from Norwich. Which they did. But not always for the right reasons. There would always be a clutch of embittered veterans in the non-league ranks, players that had either never come close to making it as a professional or those who had been taken on but ultimately rejected by a league club and who were now finding their level in the non-league game.

There's nothing wrong with that of course, but nonetheless there would always be a few of them who thought they deserved more than playing at Eastern Counties League level and who would, as a consequence, enjoy taking their frustrations out on the young lads who were wearing a Norwich City shirt they, fancifully or not, thought they should be wearing. The tackles in those games would be high and not so handsome and it came as a great relief to all concerned when the club's youngest players were able to compete against their peers on a weekly basis rather than risking life and limb when playing against a defender who might have been twice their age and size as well as still suffering from the ill effects of the six or seven pints of Norwich Bitter he'd put away the previous evening.

It certainly wouldn't have done me a lot of good. I dread to think of what might have happened had I, an aspiring young right-winger, come up against any of those old-school full-backs in some of those matches. They'd have caught sight of me, this slight kid with a big smile and mop of red hair, and have wanted to break me in half simply because I was playing for Norwich City and they weren't. Mind you, as my physique wasn't as good as it could have been at the time, I would probably have struggled to make an impression anyway and the general consensus of the coaches at the club when I first arrived was the same as that of Fred and Basil in that I had more than a good chance of having a career in the game but it would more likely be as a traditional midfielder. I had bags of energy and thanks to all of that practice I'd done on strengthening my left foot I could hit a decent pass with either, an invaluable asset for any midfielder and for his manager as it means you can slot into any position in the middle four or five with relative ease.

The big personalities at the club when I joined as an associated schoolboy, aside from John Bond himself, were Kevin Keelan, Ted MacDougall and, most of all, club captain Duncan Forbes. Duncan was a massive character, a giant of a man in every way. He wasn't particularly tall; indeed, he stood at a little under six foot. Yet he seemed and most certainly sounded a lot taller than that! He had a loud and very commanding voice, one that a football reporter once famously asked him to keep down to a mere 'roar'. What a man, a true leader and someone who would instantly have the attention of everyone around him when he started to talk. Then there were the players that Bond brought in from his former club, most notably of all the striking partnership of Ted MacDougall and Phil Boyer. They were both players I'd watch in training whenever I got the chance, with Phil's work rate even in a training match standing out. People say he did all of Ted's running for him and they were right. But what a finisher Ted was. He was alright as long as he was left alone to do his own thing, whether that was in and around the club or on the pitch during a game.

For both the schoolboys and apprentices at the club back then, actual contact with any member of the first team squad was pretty minimal. It's not like that today of course; indeed, the footballing philosophy at Norwich City now aims to encourage mixing between all the age groups as much as possible. We'd watch them training when we could, although it was best not to get too close to them in case one of the senior pros or members of the coaching staff decided there were a few little jobs that needed doing around the place. The logic behind that thinking was that if, as a young player, you started to get ideas above your station or began to think, maybe, that all the hard work had been done and that you'd made it as a player, then a little bit of humility didn't do you any harm at all, especially if it brought you back down to earth and kept your otherwise out-of-control spirits in check. We didn't, as was the case with most clubs, have a specific professional in the squad who we solely reported to, it was more of a case of us helping out whoever needed someone at that time so you had to have your wits about you if the shout went out for someone's boots to be cleaned, although when I look back at some of the tasks we were asked to do, cleaning someone's boots was probably one of the more pleasant ones!

The training ground at Trowse was nothing like the state-of-the-art facility the club has at Colney now. In fact, it was in pretty poor condition all round, with most of the training areas we used set back well away from the main pitch which was used by the first team. But even that wasn't really fit for purpose, as flints would often work their way up through to the surface of that pitch, sharp enough, as you might guess, to cause quite a nasty cut if you came into contact with them. The club's way of dealing with this problem was to get all of the apprentices together on one side of the pitch before one of the ground staff would order us to 'form a line'. We'd then all proceed, in this line, to walk across the pitch, making sure we picked up any flints that were showing. We must, in truth, have looked like a load of policemen looking for evidence at a crime scene!

We trained on our own for much of the time. Indeed, picking up and disposing of those rather nasty looking pieces of flint was just about the only time we were allowed anywhere near the first-team pitch. So, for most of the time we were stuck out at the back somewhere other than on Thursdays, when we'd all join up in one big group in order to work our way through a session that John Bond was very fond of called 'Threes'. This involved having three players starting out positioned on the halfway line with the middle of the three having possession of the ball. He'd pass the ball to one of the other players that made up that little trio, with the third following the pass before overlapping, before both the first and third players split off to make a little run, either to the near or far post, with the player in position making a pass to one of those who was making the run.

It was a very repetitive routine that we would practise time and time again for most of a morning. So we'd moan about it and not hold back from doing so. Professional footballers get bored very easily and tales you may have heard about them falling out with a manager or coach because of their perceived poor opinion of how training sessions were put together may well, in a lot of cases, be true. It happens. Yet, because we did it regularly, it started to work for us in games, so much so that in some instances I found myself in the right place at the right time to score without even having to think about what I was doing or where I was running, it was just an automatic reaction to the situation we were in during a game.

One of the best coaches I ever played under was Mel Machin, a former player at the club who worked as Ken Brown's assistant. Mel, and I won't have been the first person to have revealed this, played 'bad cop' to Ken's 'good cop' and little got past his watchful eye. He had very high standards, especially as regards fitness, but I found that motivational; the more Mel implored, cajoled and drove us to raise our own standards of fitness, the more I wanted to improve. Rarely a day would go by without Mel getting himself wound up over something or what someone had done, whereas

John Bond, for example, would rarely get too rattled, although I do remember him getting frustrated with Kevin Keelan who would, in matches as well as in training, come out and catch the ball in one hand; they'd have many an argument about Kevin's habit of doing that.

Between working hard on the training pitch and ensuring that whoever's boots I was told to clean came back to them looking brand new, things went well at Trowse and in the summer of 1976 I was duly offered a new two-year deal at the club as an apprentice professional. This was the culmination and reward for all the hard work and dedication I had put in but not just during those previous two years on schoolboy terms but before then when I'd gone out training every night, setting myself all those little routines and exercises aimed at making me a better player. It was all done with this in mind, of a football club recognising that work and the potential that you clearly have and giving you the opportunity to push on from there. Mind you, back then, as now, there would always have been a few lads who might have thought they'd arrived once they got taken on as apprentices, but if you did that then you wouldn't last very long and I knew that if I thought I'd had to work hard in order to get this far then now, at 16, the hard work really began.

One of the aspects of my football apprenticeship that I found most difficult was being away from my mum and dad. Yes, I now had a very real chance to play for Norwich City as a professional footballer but there was a price to pay for that opportunity and that was the homesickness that I suffered because I was now expected to live in digs near to Trowse rather than come in every day from home. But it wasn't just my parents I was missing, it was also, and maybe even more so, my grandparents, especially those on my father's side. They'd been the ones, if you recall, who'd taken me along on many an occasion to watch King's Lynn play at The Walks where I'd stand, resplendent in my blue-and-gold bobble hat and scarf combo as well as the matching rattle. Nan and Grandad Mendham were football mad and were so excited when I signed on as an apprentice for Norwich. But not as excited as me, mind you. All I could think of now was how proud I'd be when they both came along to watch me play for the youth team for the first time. But not only that, I also wanted to tell them about everything I'd been doing at Trowse, and on one particular weekend when we didn't have a game I arrived home to tell my dad that I was going straight over to Nan and Grandad's to share all my news with them, only for Dad to tell me I couldn't go and see them.

Why not? I'd been looking forward to doing so from the moment I'd left my digs but now Dad was telling me that I wasn't able to do so. He then broke the news to me that my grandmother had passed away, but, not only that, they'd already had the funeral. In other words, I'd been in Norwich completely oblivious to the news as my parents had chosen not to tell me she had died. I was so upset and angry with my dad and told him that they should have let me know so that I could at least have come home for Nanny Mendham's funeral, but I guess that they were, in their own way, trying to protect me and had decided it was best I was left to get on with my apprenticeship without the upset or interruption the news would have brought to my tightly organised routine. Now I was at home they felt able to tell me, knowing that in a day or so I'd be off again and would be able to focus on my football and, as my dad told me, 'do it for Nanna'.

The summer of 1976 was one of the hottest and driest on record, conditions which not only made training in the extreme heat uncomfortable but also had an effect on the pitches we played on. In one of the early games of that pre-season, it might even have been the first one that we played, the pitch that the game was being played on was rock hard without even the tiniest bit of give in it. Honestly, it was like running around on concrete. At half-time I came in and sat down ready to take in some liquids and to hear what our coach thought about our efforts so far. Noting that my feet were particularly sweaty, I bent down to take off my football socks hoping, as I did, that there'd be a nice clean and dry pair I could wear at the bottom of the skip all the kit came in. It wasn't sweat that my feet were soaking in, however, it was blood, and lots of it; indeed, both of my feet were a not so healthy shade of claret. All the running I'd done in new football boots and on that unforgiving pitch had quickly given me blisters. Except they were no longer blisters. They'd not only burst but, worse than that, all the skin around them and on the soles of both my feet had all but completely worn away.

With the adrenaline I'd been running on throughout the first half now ebbing away as I sat in the dressing room contemplating my feet and the small pools of blood that were gathering on the floor near them, I realised that they were now beginning to hurt! John Bond, who'd come down to watch the game and see how some of his younger squad members were developing, walked over to where I was sat and commented that he couldn't believe how I'd got to half-time with my feet in such a state. Nor, to be fair, did I. That was it for me, I came off and after having my feet cleaned up and covered with a variety of dressings and sticking plasters proceeded to watch the second half of that game from the bench. My dad, who'd come along to watch me and the team, was probably wondering where I was by now and why I hadn't come out with the rest for the second half. Bearing in mind that he was a bit of a hard man, he probably thought a lot of fuss was being made about nothing and that I could easily have got through the second half!

The club didn't want to see any of its young players unnecessarily injure themselves, so at the beginning of the following week I found myself in receipt of a credit note that entitled me to go to Tom Stevenson Sports in Norwich to get some better quality football boots, which I duly got, four pairs in total, which comprised of two pairs of moulded and two pairs of screw-in studs for matchdays and training. I was very pleased that the club had helped me to do this, not least because in my first year (1976/77) as an apprentice I was being paid just £16 per week, with £12 of that due to be spent on my lodgings.

I've already mentioned how homesick I was at that time and how much I'd missed being at home and with my family, especially my dear grandparents. It may sound a bit strange being homesick when you are 'only' staying somewhere that's a few miles away from your home as I was in Norwich at that time. After all, it's a little less than 50 miles between King's Lynn and Norwich, hardly a great distance at all and miniscule when you consider Norwich would have had young lads from all over the country, including from Northern Ireland, coming over on trial as well. I could, at least, get home for the occasional weekend if we didn't have a game and even if that meant me leaving late on the Friday afternoon and having to come back again on the Sunday afternoon, I seized any and all chances to do so.

The lads that had come over from Ireland weren't so lucky in that regard. But then if you are away from home for the first time – and especially if you're young and used to being with your family – then it doesn't really matter if you're one mile away from home or 1,000. If it's not your house, your bed and your family there with you, then it's always going to take a bit of getting used to. There were, inevitably, some right horror stories doing the rounds amongst some of the apprentice professionals about how dreadful their lodgings were but I was lucky to have really good ones with Bob and Muriel Gell, who were a lovely couple who lived on Sumpter Road in Norwich. They did their absolute best to make me feel part of things and a member of their family which made things a lot easier for me. If I had, I think, been at some of the digs that I heard about at that time, I would probably have gone home and forgotten all about being a footballer!

One thing that always helped me forget my homesickness was training and playing in games at the Trowse training centre. I also had, as I've already said, lots of additional jobs to do whilst I was there in the day. There was cleaning the first-team players' boots of course, as well as giving the changing rooms a good wash and scrub on a regular basis. We also had to get the brooms out after matches and sweep clean the Carrow Road terraces. It was hard work and not at all glamorous (I wonder what the young lads at Chelsea or Manchester City would say if they were told they had to sweep up at the stadium after a match today?) but I loved it, even getting down amongst the muck and grime as it meant I was doing something that I always wanted to do and this was part of it.

The routine of the apprentice footballer at Norwich didn't change much from day to day or even week to week. We could pretty much work out what we'd be doing at the beginning of May by the time we were a couple of weeks or so into pre-season training with things planned out for us as follows:

| | |
|---|---|
| 9am | Report to training ground at Trowse. Prepare boots and kit for first and reserve-team players (who have the luxury of arriving for work at 10am!) |
| 10:15am | Training starts – all teams/age groups. |
| 12:00 noon | Training finishes. First and reserve-team players head home, or to the golf course! |
| 12:30pm | Apprentice professionals clean and hang up first and reserve-team players' kits, clean boots and have a quick lunch. |
| 2:00pm | Apprentice professionals' afternoon training sessions – mostly agility work and weights. |
| 3:00pm | Apprentice professionals finish training for the day, but then have to do additional work scrubbing and mopping the dressing rooms as well as the general areas at the training ground. |
| 5:00pm | End of day. |

It was hard work. Regardless of the fact that we were seen as future members of the first team at Norwich City, we weren't expected to slacken off in our duties at all. If you did or were seen as not putting a shift in then you'd not only hear all about it from the management but also from your fellow apprentices. Yes we were professional footballers in the making, and yes, and this is a fact that holds as true today as it did back then, the club would have been hoping that one or two of us might, one day, have made them a lot of money on the transfer market, but when it came to scrubbing boots, cleaning out the dressing rooms and sweeping the terraces we were general dogsbodies and were subject to no privileges at all and there were certainly no baby Bentleys to be seen anywhere!

We all made sure that we kept in the good books of Betty Filby at Trowse; she was the lady in charge of the laundry rooms there and we'd all spend time with her either getting some worldly advice on all manner of things or just having a bit of banter – and she could more than hold her own with a group of excitable teenage lads, I promise you that.

John Bond had made sure that he had some excellent coaching staff around him at the club and I found them all inspirational figures who I enjoyed working with and learnt a tremendous amount from. One of them was John Sainty who, along with George Lee, did a lot of work with the associated schoolboys and apprentice professionals. George was quite a character. He'd originally signed for York City in 1936 at the stroke of midnight on his 17th birthday, becoming, in the process, the youngest professional footballer in the history of the game at that time. World War Two interrupted George's career, but he soon settled back into his familiar rhythm and made ten appearances for England as well as playing for Nottingham Forest and West Bromwich Albion, who he lined up for in the 1954 FA Cup Final. He joined Norwich as a coach in 1963 and remained at the club until 1987. He was a man who'd pretty much seen and done it all in the game, and from an early age, as well as having fought in a war, a man who won my instant respect for all he achieved both in the game and in life itself.

John Sainty had worked his way through the youth ranks at Tottenham Hotspur, representing England schoolboys during his time at the club. Sadly for John, however, he was forced to leave Tottenham in order to pursue his footballing dream. He went on to play for Reading, Mansfield Town and Aldershot as well as

Bournemouth, where he struck up a long-lasting friendship with John Bond.

Little wonder, therefore, that Bond opted to take Sainty with him from Bournemouth to Norwich, where he excelled in his work with the club's younger players and was, like George, someone I had a lot of time and respect for. John has been in the game a long time now, but he still knows a good young player when he sees one, for it was John who, when he was working in a similar role at Southampton, spotted and signed Adam Lallana from the Bournemouth Centre of Excellence for just £3,000.

To be able to see in someone who is just 12 years old the sort of talent and potential to go as far in the game as Lallana has (Southampton made a profit of just under £25 million when they sold him to Liverpool in 2014) is a tribute to John's deep knowledge of the game and skills as a coach, something which we were benefitting from on a daily basis as he worked with us at Norwich.

Then there was Mr Brooks. Ronnie Brooks. He was an absolute gem of a man, a supportive father figure for us all. Mind you, Ronnie had a loud voice and was getting the hairdryer out a long time before Alex Ferguson ever did. You knew all about it when Ronnie had a pop at you, make no mistake about that. But, for all that, he cared passionately for us and would go to great lengths to protect us or get a lad out of a spot of bother if, for whatever reason, he found himself in trouble of one kind or another. He was certainly looking out for us when, after we'd won a youth-team tournament in Germany and celebrated rather too hard as a result, more fool us as we had rather underestimated the strength of the local refreshments that were available and there were soon some sore heads and upset stomachs about the place.

Ronnie was ready for it though and busied himself the morning after the night before by making sure we were all up, dressed and ready for our flights home. I've little doubt that most of the lads would have been left behind had it not been for Ronnie.

At the start of the second year of my apprenticeship I was voted the head apprentice (HA) at Norwich City, which was a nice gesture from the rest of the lads and for me a bit of an honour and a role I was more than happy to carry out. It also gave me a bit of a boost at exactly the right time as with it I'd been given, in effect, a 'vote of confidence'. I was a player who needed to be told he was doing well and praised whenever he had a good game or performed particularly well in training so, yes, my confidence at the time was, perhaps, a little bit lacking.

I certainly didn't have the self-confidence that my good friend Mark Barham had. He had that certain swagger about him that told you he knew he was a good player, which he most certainly was, good enough for England and, I am sure, a career that would have included a lot more England caps as well as a move to a top club and plenty of winners' medals to go with that, had Mark's career not been so cruelly and abruptly brought to a halt by injury.

Maybe they'd all realised how enthusiastically I'd go about the job and had picked me for that reason! That or no one else fancied the responsibilities that the HA had, which included the upkeep of the manager and his coaching team's dressing room as well as laying out their kit and cleaning their boots. Hard work, yes, but it had a bit of an advantage in that it helped me to slowly build a bit of a rapport with John Bond and his staff; so much so, in fact, that whenever the first team or reserves needed an extra player to make up the numbers in their end-of-session training matches, I'd usually get the nod and have to trot over to their pitches in order to take part. I knew that this was as good an opportunity as I'd ever get to impress and worked really hard whenever I got to take part in one of these sessions, something which, I am convinced, persuaded John Bond to give me a chance in the first team when I was still only 18 and, as I'd have been the first to admit, still learning so much about the game.

I suppose that deep down I knew that my time had come. That second year of my apprenticeship had been a very productive one for me which was, of course, exactly what the club was looking for in all of us. My performances in both training and matches were becoming a lot more consistent and my body was changing as a result of all the work I was doing in the gym. I'd gone from having a very lean frame to a much more solid-looking one and was developing muscles in places I didn't think it was possible to get them. I was, with that, also gaining in physical strength, something which, at that time, was an absolutely vital asset for any midfielder to have in the English game.

You only have to think about some of the top-class professionals who played in my position in the late 1970s and early 1980s, players like Jimmy Case and Graeme Souness at Liverpool; Brian Flynn at Leeds United and Steve Williams at Southampton, not necessarily the biggest of players, but they were all extremely compact and strong units who you couldn't easily knock off the ball. I had to be as strong as players like that were if I was to stand any chance of competing against battle-hardened pros like them.

John Bond and Ken Brown's background and football experience spoke for itself. They had been, and remained, big names in the game, two men who had enjoyed excellent playing careers that had seen them achieve things at the highest levels of the game. Take John Bond, for example. He played in nearly 450 first-team matches for West Ham and won an FA Cup winners' medal with them whilst he was there as part of the side that played in the European Cup Winners' Cup competition the following season.

Yet, if anything, Ken Brown's playing career surpassed John's for he, unlike Bondy, not only won an FA Cup winners' medal but was part of the West Ham team that won the Cup Winners' Cup in 1965, wearing the number-five shirt in a starting XI that also featured Johnny Sissons, Martin Peters (both of whom went on to join Norwich as players under John and Ken) as well as Geoff Hurst and Bobby Moore. Ken even went on to play for England, his one appearance coming in a 2-1 win over Northern Ireland at Wembley in 1959.

Yet, for all that John and Ken brought to the club, one of the greatest assets at Carrow Road at the time was the equally high calibre of all those other coaches I have just mentioned. Admittedly, neither George Lee or John Sainty had enjoyed playing careers that echoed those of John and Ken, but they were excellent coaches whose philosophies on how the game should be played echoed those of Norwich's more well-known managerial team. Terry Medwin, on the other hand, had also enjoyed a good career as a player; he was part of the Tottenham squad that won the league and cup double in the 1960/61 season. Prior to that, he'd represented Wales in the 1958 World Cup, the highlight of which for him would have been scoring the winning goal in Wales's 2-1 win over Hungary (the same Hungary that had beaten England 6-3 and 7-1 a few years earlier) in the play-off match that saw them reach the quarter-finals of that year's tournament.

How could you not learn when one of your coaches as a young player was a man who had played and scored in the World Cup? More to the point, how could you not want to learn from the likes of Terry as well as George and John? There were some, of course, who didn't want to, they had already been beguiled by the bright lights of Norwich and the twin temptations of women and alcohol, tempting to us all, myself included. Yet, as much as I enjoyed a glass of beer or the company of a nice young lady, I was more driven and committed to making it as a footballer and that continued to be my prime focus even if the 'muck and grime' aspect of it was about as far removed from the perceived glamour of living and working as a professional footballer as it was possible to get.

But for every pair of boots I scrubbed and every row on the Carrow Road terraces that I swept clean, there was, as a sort of payback, plenty of football to play and I was now getting a run of games in the South East Counties League, many of which were against our peers at some of the top clubs in the country at the time such as Arsenal, Chelsea and Tottenham. Norwich also entered the FA Youth Cup in the 1974/75 season but we didn't get very far in the competition that year, losing 2-0 at Fulham in the first round. Ipswich won the South East Counties League at the end of my first season at Norwich (then went on to win it the following two seasons as well) with Tottenham finishing as runners-up.

It would have been great, of course, had we been in contention to win it ourselves but the Canaries were still rebuilding their youth and schoolboy ranks after the arrival of John Bond so it was going to take time for us to establish ourselves, even at that level. The important thing was that we were playing regularly against the cream of the crop from some of the biggest clubs in the country, the sort of invaluable experience of playing a whole season's competitive fixtures that young players haven't been able to benefit from so much in recent years.

Most of our games were played on Saturday mornings with an 11am kick-off. This was usually because sides wanted their young players to be available for first-team duties later on that day, 'duties' in this case including sweeping the terraces after the game and cleaning out the communal bath as well as seeing to the players' boots.

I didn't mind. It was usually a bit of a mad rush to get back to Carrow Road in time for the game but, on some occasions, we'd do so and I'd find myself a place in the tunnel so I could watch the first team in action. I remember being there for one of the biggest games of the 1976/77 season against Manchester United, who were then on a 12-game unbeaten run and would, in addition to that, end that campaign by beating Liverpool in the FA Cup Final.

They had a great side at the time, one that included Stevie Coppell, Lou Macari and Gordon Hill, but we pretty much outplayed them on the day, winning 2-1 thanks to goals from Colin Suggett and Kevin Reeves. It should, therefore, have been a great day for everyone at the football club, but it's now more remembered for the rather large hooligan element of Manchester United fans at that time who took their team's defeat very badly and ended up, on the final whistle, trashing the Barclay Stand and throwing missiles at anyone who dared to come near them, including the members of the Norfolk Constabulary who were on duty that day.

That game was played a week before my 17th birthday on 9 April. I had, by then, pushed on a bit and was looking to start some games for the reserves in what was then called the Football Combination. Two of my best mates at the time were Phil Lythgoe and Mark Halsey, two exceptionally talented young footballers of whom big things were expected, particularly Phil who'd been voted as the best young player at a youth-team tournament in Holland that we played in that year. Mark, meanwhile, was someone who I already knew as I had run against him in an 800 metres race at a school in Thetford when I was representing Norfolk, whilst he wore the colours of his native Essex. Mark was another good young player, a midfielder who was tough in the tackle but, hard as he was, he could also play a bit and, like Phil, he was very much seen as someone who'd been a first-team player at Norwich. Unfortunately for Mark, he got sent off on his debut against Newcastle at the end of that month and never really recovered from that and ended up playing only two more games for Norwich before dropping into non-league football with Yarmouth Town and Wroxham. Phil, on the other hand, fared a little better. He made his first-team debut for Norwich a little over a month after his 18th birthday in a 3-1 home defeat by Manchester City and didn't look at all out of place in a Norwich side that included big-name players like Kevin Keelan, Colin Suggett, Kevin Reeves and Martin Peters.

Mark and Phil's elevation into the first team made me even more determined to do so myself. John Bond certainly had no hesitation in giving his young players a go if he thought they were good enough. In addition to Mark and Phil making their bows in that 1977/78 season, there were also first-team debuts for goalkeeper Clive Baker (who was 19), Mark Nightingale (20) and Greg Downs (19), all of whom had been team-mates of mine in the South East Counties and Football Combination sides. I was delighted for all of them of course, and as I was still only (and only just) 18 by the time the 1977/78 season ended I reckoned I still had a little bit of time on my side – but not much because, as

I saw it, those lads were all now ahead of me and in the first-team picture, something that I was determined would also apply to me by the end of the following season.

Regardless of the fact that I hadn't yet been given the opportunity to make my first team debut yet, I knew that I couldn't be very far off. I was, by early 1978, training a lot more with the reserves as well as making up the numbers when needed in the first team, where I'd started to take note of another player who had, in a similar vein to myself, come through the ranks at Carrow Road and was now starting to get a few games at that level. His name was Doug Evans. Doug was, like me, a very competitive midfielder who'd joined the club as an apprentice in 1972 and was a similar sort of player to me, the sort of man who I'd be looking to rival for a place in the team by the end of the season.

I'd figured that by the time of the last league games the following April I'd be 18, the age at which a lot of young players at the club were first given their chance, one that you had to make the most of if you were going to impress the manager – and, as quickly as John Bond would give you the opportunity if he thought you were good enough, he also wouldn't hesitate to drop you from his plans completely if he didn't then think you were up to it.

It was, as far as I was concerned, going to be something of a 'make-or-break' couple of years for me to win a contract and get ever closer to running out on to the Carrow Road pitch as a first-team player or, and this wasn't a very nice thought, putting my few belongings into my old duffel bag after our last match and leave both Trowse and Carrow Road for the last time at the end of my apprenticeship with only the stresses and strains of looking for a new club to think about – or, worse than that, thinking about getting a 'proper' job.

One reason for my optimism was, perversely, the club's worsening financial situation. Norwich were reported to be around £250,000 in debt at the start of the 1977/78 season, something that meant there wasn't going to be a great deal of money available for John Bond to spend on new players. This gave me and all the other second-year apprentices much to reflect upon. Surely we would be far more to the fore in both Bond and his coaching team's thoughts now? Having said that, one of the remedies that the club had to resort to in order to clear some of the debt wasn't one which was greeted with much enthusiasm by any Norwich fan, myself included, as it saw the departure, for a fee of around £135,000, of Phil Boyer to Southampton.

Phil would be missed, something which became brutally obvious almost straight away. The club had been in the middle of a pre-season tour to the West Country when the deal taking him to Southampton went through, meaning that the club was short of strikers, a fact that became very clear when in the three friendlies we played down there we scraped a 1-1 draw to Torquay United and lost to Exeter City (5-0) and Plymouth Argyle (3-0).

Three games played, nine goals conceded and only one scored in return. It was very clear where John Bond needed to strengthen the team. Unfortunately for me, it wasn't a problem that he would find an answer to by turning to a 17-year-old midfielder by the name of Mendham!

# CHAPTER THREE

# First Team

*As for me? Well, I had just about the best seat in
the house and was loving it!*

I'D SET myself the target of making my first-team debut by
the end of the 1977/78 season and went into it determined to be
noticed by the manager – and for all the right reasons. But I also
knew that, for all the effort I was making, I wouldn't be anywhere
near the first team that August because John Bond, as willing as
he was to give young players their start in the game, wasn't likely
to give the nod to a 17-year-old apprentice in the opening game,
even if the team's pre-season had been a disappointing one.

Doug Evans got a start in that game, however; an impressive
3-1 win over West Ham at their old Upton Park ground which gave
everyone a buzz that carried over into training in the week that
followed. Middlesbrough were our opponents for our first home
game, and everyone knew that with another home match to follow
three days later, this time against QPR, there was every reason we
could start with three wins on the bounce and top the table. Bond
named an unchanged side for the Middlesbrough game, one which
was instantly forgettable for they were a dour outfit, one that was
heavy on the ball and in the tackle and we struggled to break them
down. They even took the lead when their impressive number four,

who I later learnt was an ex-Tottenham apprentice by the name of Graeme Souness (I wonder what became of him?) scored via a deflection off our wall from a free kick. Souness was playing in front of an uncompromising defence that included the likes of Stuart Boam and Willie Maddren, two players who weren't shy to put themselves about a bit; however, their defence also contained, at left-back, Terry Cooper, who'd been one of the Leeds United players whose poster I'd have pinned to my bedroom wall back in Gaywood. So, tough as it was to watch Souness and co make their mark on both the game and the legs of my team-mates, I also enjoyed watching Cooper, who always seemed to have time and space on the ball and who was, if I'm honest, a level or three above most of his team-mates in what he was able to do with it.

The game ended in a 1-1 draw with Roger Gibbins scoring for us, as did that follow-up fixture against QPR. On that occasion, Roger opened the scoring shortly before the half-hour mark then Dave Needham, who went to two consecutive European Cup Finals with Nottingham Forest, equalised shortly before the final whistle.

Three days after that game, John Bond put Viv Busby on the transfer list. I didn't really get to know Viv very well, as he was the very personification of the senior professional; he was 28 and had played in over 250 league games as well as, two years previously, in the FA Cup Final for Fulham. I did know that he could be a bit feisty and that he and John Bond didn't always see eye to eye, but Bond knew that he was a goalscorer who could come in and hit the ground running, which was exactly what he'd done the previous season when he'd been brought in as a like-for-like replacement for Ted MacDougall. Now, with Ted long gone and Phil Boyer having followed him to Southampton in the summer, we were likely to lose our third striker in a year, a considerable blow for any club to have to take, let alone Norwich, for whom, with the financial side of things a little precarious, getting a replacement with a similar playing pedigree and experience to them was going to be a challenge for even a manager of John Bond's talents.

Viv moved to Stoke in November but played his last game for us in a 1-0 win over Bristol City on 10 September. That had, as it turned out, been a vital win as a week earlier we'd headed north to play Manchester City and had been well and truly turned over to the tune of 4-0, with Mike Channon and Asa Hartford, both of whom would end up being future team-mates of mine, amongst the goals.

That defeat hadn't gone down at all well with the Norwich fans, something that was reflected in the attendance for that Bristol City game which was just under 14,000 with a section of them giving Bond no little stick during the match. Viv started but was replaced by Roger Gibbins who got our goal, his third in four games.

Roger had turned out to be something of a bargain signing for us. He'd started at Tottenham but hadn't made the grade there so had ended up at Oxford United, for whom he'd only played 19 games before Bond signed him in the summer of 1976. He was certainly proving to be popular with the crowd and I remember him being cheered when he came on during that game, the cheers for him also, I suspect, a sign of our fans' discontent with Viv Busby, the man he was replacing.

With Roger and Kevin Reeves now the club's two first-choice strikers, it was clear that an experienced head or two was needed in the side to not only steady nerves a bit but to give the other young players that were finding their way into first-team contention a bit of on (and off) field guidance. Roger was still only 22 and Kevin was still in his teens, whilst another Kevin, the manager's son, was 20. Another youngster, Mark Nightingale, who made his debut in early October was also 20. Another striker, Phil Lythgoe, was just 18 when he made his first team bow in the return fixture against Manchester City in January 1978, a game that Norwich lost 3-1.

I was, by now, desperate to be given a chance myself, and when Greg Downs, at just 19, made his debut on 27 March 1978 in a 4-0 defeat at Ipswich (one to forget) it was all I could do to stop myself from knocking on the manager's door and asking him why he seemed to be giving just about everyone a chance to play in the first team apart from me?

My big break finally came in the spring when, just nine days after my 18th birthday, I was offered my first professional contract. I hadn't exactly given up at that stage but on turning 18 was beginning to realise that, as far as the schoolboy and apprentice ranks at the club were concerned, my time had come and it was time to shape up or get shifted out. So many young players have had to face up to rejection at that age, it's a pivotal moment, the time when you finally find out if all the hard work you've been putting in has paid off or whether your manager is going to try to soften the blow of your being released by insisting that the young player in question now has the opportunity to 'prove me wrong'. Believe me, if any manager or coach thinks a youngster might go on to do just that, then they aren't likely to be wanting to let them go in the first place! There are exceptions of course, and some very notable ones at that. Gossy, as I've already written, bombed out at both Aston Villa and Southampton whilst Norwich released Dion Dublin when he was 19 without Dion ever having troubled the first team dressing room – yet he went on to win the Premier League with Manchester United as well as play for England.

But that's a very rare exception indeed because the very great majority of those who are not offered professional terms by the time they reach their 18th birthdays rarely prove anyone wrong. Indeed, in most cases their managers, whoever they were, are absolutely spot on with the decision they've made.

I knew I had something to offer. In fact, I'd never been more certain of anything in my life. And now John Bond agreed with me.

### Things were on the up

Norwich finished the 1977/78 season in 13th place. That sounds respectable enough, but in truth it was the end result of a fairly mediocre campaign that had seen the club win just one league game away from home (that season opener at West Ham) as well as end up on the wrong end of a 4-0 hammering at Ipswich whilst exiting both the League and FA Cups to teams in a lower division. We also had the distinction of being watched by Newcastle United's lowest-ever league gate for a home match since World War One when just 7,600 turned up at St James' Park for the 2-2 draw on 26 April. That had been the game that saw John Bond give yet another young hopeful his first league start; this time it was 18-year-old Mark Halsey who'd signed his first professional contract with the club on the same day as me. I look back at that match now and wonder if I'd been close to getting the nod to play in it myself but, for all that, I didn't begrudge Mark his opportunity, even if it now seemed he had, along with, by now, quite a few others, jumped in front of me in the queue.

Mark certainly didn't have a debut to remember, at least not for the right reasons. He was, as you'd expect, keen to impress and put himself about as much as he could in order to not only show his new team-mates he was worth a place in the side but, just as importantly, give notice to an experienced Newcastle side that included the likes of Mark McGhee, Alan Kennedy and Micky Burns that he wasn't just some kid they could walk all over. You've got to give Mark credit for that; however, he went about it in a rather over-enthusiastic manner and ended up getting two yellow cards in fairly swift succession, which meant that he ended up being sent off on his debut. His actions also, sadly, made a big impression on John Bond, albeit for all the wrong reasons, and Mark only ever played two more league games for Norwich before drifting into non-league football with Great Yarmouth Town and Wroxham.

Also making his Norwich debut that evening was goalkeeper Clive Baker. Clive's birthplace was West Runton so, like me, he was a Norfolk boy who'd joined his local club as a schoolboy and had been good enough to work his way through the ranks and into the first team as a rival to Roger Hansbury. I felt a bit sorry for Roger and Clive mind you, as the man whose place they were both vying to take was one of the Norwich City greats, the one and only Kevin Keelan. Kevin had started the 1977/78 season as first-choice keeper just as he had the 1963/64 season, not one I remember particularly well as I was only three when it started, when he'd made his debut for the Canaries in a 3-1 defeat at Cardiff City. It's probably fair to say that he'd become, in that time, one of the most well-known and popular players that Norwich have ever had. But he wasn't just that. Kevin was a vital member of the team and squad, a larger-than-life personality who had the respect of his peers as well as being regarded as something of a role model for all of the younger players who came into the club – and not just the goalkeepers. Roger and Clive were the latest challengers to his status as the club's undisputed number one and, after being given his debut only a few weeks after his 18th birthday, Clive must have fancied his chances of retaining the shirt for the start of the following season.

I was pleased for Clive, of course, especially as we were both local lads, but his selection did, once again, make me wonder when I'd get my chance. No, let me rephrase that, it made me wonder if I was <u>ever</u> going to get an opportunity in the first team. I'd seen ten young players come into the side and make their debuts over the last couple of seasons, four of them had still been in their teens and, whilst Andy Proudlove was the 'veteran' of that bunch, having made his Norwich debut at the ripe old age of 22, he'd been signed from Sheffield Wednesday for whom he'd made his first-team bow when he was 20. So yes, it rankled a bit that I now seemed to be the odd one out. I was never going to kick up a fuss and ask John Bond why he was giving everyone a chance apart from me; aside from anything else, if I'd done that, he'd have pointed out the likes of Colin Suggett, Martin Peters and Graham Paddon to me and asked which one of that illustrious threesome I felt should be dropped in favour of Peter Mendham, footballing logic I could never even have begun to offer a counter argument against.

What I could do, however, was spend the summer of 1978 making sure that I was fitter than I'd ever been so that when I returned to Trowse for pre-season training I'd hit the ground running and make so much of an impression on John Bond and his coaching team that they'd have me in their thoughts from day one.

What I didn't realise at the time was that someone had already taken note of me and the qualities that I hoped to bring to the team. Martin Peters had been a regular spectator at our youth-team games over the last couple of years and I'd made an impression on him, not that I realised it at the time. He went on to refer to me as a 'real scallywag tearing up and down the right side of the pitch' before qualifying that statement by adding that he'd noticed how very dedicated I seemed to be with regards to my dream of becoming a professional footballer. There weren't many better references a young player could have received at the time than one from someone who'd achieved as much as he had in the game, a man who had not only played in a World Cup Final but had scored in one as well. So that was some testimony and I have little doubt that Martin would have talked to John Bond about me on more than one occasion, something which wouldn't have done my chances of getting a call-up to the first team any harm at all.

The summer of 1978 saw, once again, a lot of movement in terms of players leaving or joining the club and I'd be as attentive of the back pages of the *Eastern Daily Press* as any Norwich fan when it came, in particular, to new faces, although a big part of me was hoping that John Bond wouldn't be signing any new midfielders. One of the new boys was Phil Hoadley, a centre-half whom Norwich signed from Orient after Phil had got in touch with the club asking them if they'd be interested in signing him as he was coming towards the end of his contract with Orient. It later turned out that Phil's move to Norwich was the very first one to be ratified under the new freedom of contract legislation that had come in that year, with a tribunal ordering Norwich to pay £110,000 for him. Phil was joined at the club by another of those big-name signings that John Bond was so fond of, in this case the former Tottenham and England centre-forward Martin Chivers, who'd been playing for Servette FC in Switzerland.

Phil and Martin made their debuts in our opening league game of the season against a Southampton side that included former Canaries Ted MacDougall and Phil Boyer, with Martin scoring in an impressive 3-1 win. We then had a disappointing little mini run of three draws and one defeat in our following four games before welcoming Birmingham City to Carrow Road on 16 September, winning that game 4-0 with Martin Chivers one of the scorers, his fourth in six games.

We were, by now, up to sixth in the table and looking to improve on that at Bolton a week later, only to lose 3-2 after being 2-1 up at half-time, a result and, in particular, second-half performance that John Bond wasn't particularly happy with. His mood post-match wasn't helped when it became clear that Martin Chivers was injured and would miss a few games as a consequence, his enforced absence meaning a lot of responsibility and no little pressure for Kevin Reeves which was, on reflection, a little unfair on him. Kevin was a good player who might have been a very good one and he certainly proved his worth to Norwich City as the club eventually got over a million pounds for him from Manchester City. However, with Martin Chivers now out of contention for a few games, Norwich needed someone who'd take all the knocks and hold the ball up as only the old-fashioned, traditional centre-forward could – and Kevin was not that sort of player.

John Bond's solution to the problem was to sign a player by the name of Davie Robb from Tampa Bay Rowdies in the USA. Robb had previously been with Aberdeen and had excelled in the rough and tumble of Scottish football as the sort of striker who went in with his head where others would be frightened of putting their foot and was rewarded for his bravery with plenty of goals. He wasn't the most energetic of trainers and I have to say as an 18-year-old player who was yet to make his first-team debut I was a little bit nervous in his company. Yet, as well as my apprehension, I was also excited about Robb signing and couldn't wait to see him in action as we had a game against Derby County coming up.

That meant the battle-hardened Davie Robb's introduction to English football would involve him coming face to face with Roy McFarland, Derby's classy centre-half who'd played 30 times for England. It would be an interesting test for both of them and one that would, to add a little bit of extra spice to the occasion, be played out, as we later learnt, in front of the BBC's *Match Of The Day* cameras.

A big day for both the club and for David Robb in particular, who was now going to make his first appearance in England a decade after making his debut in Scottish football. What neither he nor anyone else suspected as the morning of that match dawned, however, was that the game would feature a second Norwich debutant.

I'd arrived at the ground in good time for the match as I always did, confident that we'd be able to make up for the poor performance and result up at Bolton the previous week. I did think that John Bond might have had a few changes in mind for the Derby game as he rarely hesitated to give the team a bit of a shake-up if he thought a performance had been below par. On this occasion, however, he made just two changes to the starting XI, with Kevin Keelan returning to the side in place of the unfortunate Clive Baker, who had maybe been culpable for one of Bolton's goals, whilst the injured Martin Chivers made way for Davie Robb in what was a bit of a like-for-like change with one strong and powerful striker being replaced by another. The other change affected who sat on the bench; there was only one named substitute back then with the man in possession of the number-12 shirt on the day not always guaranteed to get a run out. Only Mick McGuire and Graham Paddon, with one appearance each, had had any game time from the bench so far that season in Norwich's previous eight games. I'd expected Graham to get the nod again but, much to my surprise, it was my name up on the board against the number-12 shirt.

Neither John Bond nor the lads said much. They didn't need to. I had a few 'good lucks' as we got changed for the match but with everyone focussed on the game and their own performances (as well as going through some of their pre-game rituals), no one made much of a fuss of me. And that is, of course, exactly how it should have been. The manager had decided I was good enough to be part of the first-team squad on the day and his staff and my team-mates were more than happy to respect his judgement. I changed quietly, taking great care not to do or say anything that might have sounded or looked out of place and, once the pre-match warm-up was finished, happily took my place on the bench alongside John Bond and Ken Brown.

I say 'pre-match warm-up' but it wasn't anything like the well-organised and choreographed routines that the players go through today. A gentle jog on to the pitch, a stretch or two and maybe, if anyone was feeling particularly energetic, a shot or two hit in Kevin Keelan's direction. Mind you, it was generally agreed that it might not be best to put too many shots past him in the warm-up, just a few sweeteners to warm his hands up a bit would be enough.

Norwich's team on the day was as follows:

Kevin Keelan; Kevin Bond; Colin Sullivan; John Ryan; Phil Hoadley; Tony Powell; Jimmy Neighbour; Kevin Reeves; Davie Robb; Keith Robson and Martin Peters, with a very excited but also very nervous Peter Mendham sat on the bench!

Reading through that starting XI, there's a lot of quality there. Kevin Keelan had long been one of the best goalkeepers in the country, whilst on his day Jimmy Neighbour was a winger who could turn even the most revered full-backs inside out. Then there was Kevin Reeves, a real star in the making, and John Ryan, a left-sided attacking midfielder in the Gareth Bale mould who'd ended the previous season as the club's top scorer with 16 goals as well as being named by the fans as the Canaries Player of the Year – no mean feat when you have the likes of Kevin Keelan, Martin Peters and Kevin Reeves as team-mates.

No one would have been very surprised then when it was John Ryan who opened the scoring at a little over ten minutes after he got on the end of a nod down from Martin Peters and sent a spectacular 25-yard shot past John Middleton in the Derby goal. Kevin Reeves then put us two up not long before half-time when he headed in a Phil Hoadley cross.

As for me? Well, I had just about the best seat in the house and was loving it!

We went in at the break 2-0 up and, it seemed, cruising towards a convincing victory. Yet John Bond went to great pains at half-time to warn everyone about getting complacent (we'd been ahead against Bolton at half-time but still lost) and to keep the pressure on a Derby defence that, McFarland included, was struggling to cope with both Robb's sheer physical presence and the pace and awareness of Kevin Reeves. Then, just as the bell rang to signal the second half, John Bond turned to me and said, 'Stay sharp Peter, I'll look to give you a little game time providing the lads have everything under control.'

Which was exactly what I wanted to hear! After all, if you're a young player and you're set to make your debut, what better time to do so than late on, in a home game, when you're winning and the team is playing well. John was as good as his word as well, taking the opportunity to replace Keith Robson, who was carrying a knock, with me with about 20 minutes to go.

A lot of players either can't remember much about their debuts or, when pressed, will confess they did little but run about for five minutes or so whilst trying not to get in anyone's way! But I remember that Derby game very well because I not only found myself in a position to have a shot but very nearly scored from a header I darted in for at Middleton's near post. Being a local lad meant that the Norwich fans took to me straight away and were absolutely brilliant from the start, just as they still are to this day whenever I'm out and about and happen to bump into one or two of them. That rapport with the fans has always meant a lot to me, and I must admit I wasn't in too much of a hurry to leave the pitch when the final whistle went, with us running out as 3-0 winners after Davie Robb marked his debut with a powerful header from Jimmy Neighbour's pinpoint cross. Job done, two points (not three!) in the bag and I was enjoying every second of it as I slowly walked off the pitch and back into the home dressing room where, as you'd expect, the mood amongst the players and management was very good. But not that I went in there and started putting myself about as well, far from it. I bathed and changed quietly, listening to the banter being exchanged between the lads and offering up a quiet 'thank you' in response whenever one of them, and they did, took time out to say 'well done' and wish me all the best.

I wasn't going to go out and celebrate either. Some of the lads would have done of course – most of the first-team players had their favourite clubs or bars where they'd go for a few drinks after a win – but I didn't want to be seen out and about in the city that evening in case it made me look, in the eyes of the fans, or, indeed, any of my team-mates, as if I thought I'd made it and was coming across as a bit 'big time', something that I most certainly wasn't.

No, it was an early night for me. Plus, of course, the opportunity to watch *Match Of The Day* so I could see myself in action! Jimmy Hill duly said a few nice things about me which topped off an extraordinary day that had, in the end, exceeded all of my expectations.

I didn't do so badly out of that game financially either. As well as getting a £25 appearance bonus, I'd also get a £250 win bonus, a not inconsiderable sum of money at the time, so I was made up as you can imagine. Yet, as the weekend drew to a close, I knew that I now had to knuckle down and work harder than ever if I was to convince the manager to give me another chance and to eventually be regarded as a regular first-team player.

The game is littered with hundreds of players who have made just one or two appearances for their clubs before disappearing from football forever, and that was not something I wanted to happen to me. I therefore trained hard, ate well and went to bed early, in other words doing everything that I could to catch the manager's eye in the run up to our next game, which was also at Carrow Road but just happened to be against Liverpool, who were, at that time, the holders of the European Cup (now the Champions League) and top of the Division One table. Who wouldn't want to test themselves against such a team and players like Ray Kennedy, Alan Hansen and, of course, Kenny Dalglish?

I did, that's for certain. And I couldn't wait for the moment when the team selections for that weekend's games went up on the notice board at the end of that week, eagerly running my finger down the list of names to see if I'd made the first team or was going to get another opportunity as substitute.

No such luck. I was down to play for the youth team early on that Saturday morning, which meant it'd be back to sweeping the terraces and cleaning out the baths after the game.

But that was hardly surprising. I'd had my chance against Derby and hadn't, as far as I was concerned, let anyone down. So I'd dealt with all the pressure and expectation that went with being called up to the first team well. It was another step on the journey and my response had been noted. What John Bond wanted to gauge now was how I'd react to being put back in the youth team and going from a first-team debut and appearance on *Match Of The Day* to getting up early enough to catch the minibus to our game in the South East Counties League and, after that was out of the way, getting on with my chores. Would I make a fuss and let my standards drop or would I remain professional and put in as much effort and commitment to the day as I had the previous week?

Listen. I'd had the chance of a lifetime given to me. I wasn't going to do anything to risk losing it. So I not only played for the South East Counties side to the very best of my abilities, I also swept, cleaned, scrubbed and polished as if my life depended on it. Because I knew that I'd get another opportunity if I worked hard enough, if I showed that I hadn't let my '15 minutes of fame' go to my head and that I was as determined as ever to make my living as a professional footballer for Norwich City Football Club.

I was ready. And John Bond must have taken note for, after a disappointing 2-0 defeat at Middlesbrough, he decided he was going to shake things up for our next home game against Leeds United. I'd already had a bit of a run out in the week leading up to the game, having reported for duty at Carrow Road a few days after the Middlesbrough match as part of the Norwich City side that was due to take on an England XI for Martin Peters's testimonial match.

Such matches now are usually either held at the end of the season or involve former players who have retired or a mix of them and a few football-loving celebrities. They're rarely, if ever, held during the season and certainly now, as this one was, just three days before a league game! Yet, such was the respect that Martin had at the club and in the game as a whole, there wasn't anyone at the club who didn't want to take part in some way, even if the match with Leeds was just over the horizon. The England XI, which Martin would captain, was based on the line-up which had played West Germany in the 1966 World Cup Final a little over a decade earlier and was not far off being the same side, with the only changes in England's starting line-up being Ron Springett, Jimmy Armfield (who'd recently been manager of the Leeds team we'd shortly be playing), and Norman Hunter replacing Gordon Banks, George Cohen and Ray Wilson, with – adding a little spice to the occasion – the one and only Jimmy Greaves also down to play.

Some line-up then. But so was the Norwich one that John Bond picked to play against them, one that, to my utter delight, included me as one of the substitutes and I duly got a run out on the same pitch and in the same game as some of England's most well-known and respected players ever, including, of course, Bobby Moore and Bobby Charlton. It was all the more memorable for me as Norwich won 4-2, with Greg Downs (2), Kevin Reeves and John Ryan scoring for us and Bobby Charlton and Geoff Hurst (from the penalty spot) replying for England. What a night and what an experience for a young player such as myself as well as, of course, Greg who was still only 19 himself and had marked the occasion by scoring two goals. Greg became very well known as an exceptionally good full-back; indeed, he was part of the Coventry City back four that famously won the FA Cup in 1987. He'd started his career, however, as a striker and big things were expected of him. Testimonial or not, scoring two goals in such hallowed company wasn't going to do his career chances any harm at all, so much so that when John Bond named the team to play Leeds Greg was handed the number-nine shirt for what was his first start of the season, with me also picked for my first start and full debut wearing number ten and playing alongside Martin Peters in the centre of the Norwich midfield.

I was, as you will have guessed, excited enough about making my full debut. But what made the day and match especially memorable for me was that it was against the team I'd worshipped as a young boy, the team whose greatest players had adorned the wall of my bedroom in our Gaywood home. Nearly all of those greats had, of course, moved on by now (although I'd still had the pleasure of coming up against Jack Charlton and Norman Hunter in Martin's game) but Paul Madeley was still at the club, as was David Harvey, whilst they also had a new generation of first-team players who were very good footballers in their own right as well, such as Brian Flynn and Tony Currie.

Jimmy Armfield had only been able to play in Martin's match earlier that week because he'd recently left his job as Leeds manager. Much of the gossip surrounding what was still considered one of the top jobs in the English game, certainly as far as the press were concerned, centred on John Bond being a serious candidate for it but, if he was, he never said anything to us or any of the local press lads and we certainly didn't say anything to him. He felt, rightly as it happens, that this was a game that we could win and that he had enough faith in both myself and Greg to be part of a team that would do just that, pre-match words that did a lot for my confidence and made me want, as the saying goes, to run through the proverbial brick wall for him.

It ended up being an excellent game that included one of the more bizarre goals that Carrow Road has seen being scored. We'd played well from the start and both Greg and I were getting plenty of touches, yet it was Leeds who went in a goal up at half-time, courtesy of Frank Gray. John Ryan then equalised for us before, with about 20 minutes to go, Kevin Keelan took umbrage at a Leeds challenge just outside his box that the referee had seen fit to ignore. Kevin being Kevin, he wasn't having that and he stalked outside his area in order to have it out with the man in charge, oblivious to the fact that he was leaving both the ball and his goal unattended which meant that John Hawley had the easiest of chances to put Leeds 2-1 up. Luckily for us, Martin Peters was able to set the seal on what had been a very good week for him by scoring a second equaliser for us shortly afterwards and the score remained at 2-2, a good point won but it should have been two, and John Bond wasn't slow to tell us in the dressing room after the game. I kept my place for our next five league games as well as, in the middle of that sequence, a League Cup match against Manchester City, which we lost 3-0. One of the league games was at home to Coventry, a team whose manager, Gordon Milne, had, like John Bond, a reputation for bringing through and giving first-team opportunities to his younger players. Some of the older ones in our team must have felt as if they were playing in a youth-team match. On the day, in addition to myself and Greg in our starting line-up, we also had Kevin Reeves, Richard Symonds and Ian Davies, all teenagers apart from Ian, who was 21, whilst Coventry had four teenagers of their own, including Gary Gillespie who would go on to win three league titles and a European Cup with Liverpool.

All that youthful endeavour meant that it ended up being a game played at a good pace throughout and with the emphasis very strongly on attack. We ended up winning 1-0 thanks to Kevin Bond's first goal for the club, and in doing so ensured that John Bond was happy enough to name an unchanged team for the game against Everton a week later, a match that was as dull as the Coventry game had been exciting and which we lost 1-0. It was also my last game for a while as I went on to pick up a nasty pelvic injury which meant I had to sit things out until the following April, when I won a starting place in the side that lost 2-1 at Carrow Road to Aston Villa in a game that not only saw Justin Fashanu score but also put in a tackle on Ken McNaught that, completely legal though it was, saw Villa's defender carried off as a result of the challenge.

Justin was the latest in the exceedingly long line of young players at Norwich that John Bond was integrating into the first team. We got on very well and used to spend a lot of time together, with Bond eventually pairing us up as roommates for away trips. Although, as much as I liked Justin, he'd get on my nerves for always leaving the room so untidy even though he was always immaculate! He'd made the very most of the opportunity he'd been given after making his debut at Carrow Road against West Bromwich Albion (the *Match Of The Day* team were in attendance for that one as well) and had, by the end of the season, scored five goals from the 16 league appearances he'd made.

A memorable campaign for both Justin and myself then. But not such a good one for the club. Norwich ended the season in 16th place, and although there were never any real fears of relegation at Carrow Road we'd far from done ourselves justice. Only seven wins (and none at all away from home) for a start, but, not only that, a 6-0 pasting at Liverpool (unlucky 13 for Martin Chivers, it was his 13th and final match for the club) and a 3-0 home defeat at Leicester City, who were then in Division Two, in the FA Cup. That had been a particularly miserable day, another game for the *Match Of The Day* team to reflect on[2], and they duly let Norwich have it with both barrels as a spirited Leicester side, inspired, in freezing cold conditions, by Keith Weller, who was clad in a pair of white tights, ran us off the pitch and out of the FA Cup. It was a Norwich performance that was so bad, a furious John Bond immediately responded by putting Martin Chivers, along with John Ryan and Graham Paddon, on the transfer list.

---

2   Jimmy Hill and company would not have been at Filbert Street at all if the icy conditions that Peter refers to had not been prevalent across the country at the time. Only four of the scheduled 32 ties were played on the day, with one of them, Wrexham's 6-1 win over Stockport County, not played until nearly a month later.

Another worry for the club had been a gradual tailing off of attendances at home matches with an average home gate of just 17,874, which was down nearly 3,000 on the previous season and over 6,000 down on the average home attendance of 23,799 for the 1974/75 campaign, Bond's first full season in charge which, of course, saw Norwich playing in the Second Division. Over 23,000 had come along to Carrow Road for a game against York City during that season, yet in the season that had just finished the game against Manchester United had attracted a gate of just 20,077. This was at a time when clubs depended almost entirely on gate receipts in order to maintain a healthy business, so a drop in the average home attendance as large as Norwich's had been was something the board would have to take very seriously, an issue which would, of course, also impact upon John Bond's wish for funding in order to bring in better-quality players to the club. It should, therefore, come as no surprise to anyone when you look back at that time and reflect on just how many young players, not all of whom came anywhere near to securing a long-term career in the professional game, he introduced to the side; a case of 'needs must' at a time when, if John Bond did have £300,000 to spend, he would almost certainly have chosen to bring in a couple of established players rather than take a gamble on the likes of Phil Lythgoe, Greg Downs and myself.

Introducing Justin Fashanu to the first team was no gamble though. We all knew he was going to be something extra special from the moment he walked through the gates at Trowse for the first time and put a pair of boots on. Ronnie Brooks had seen Justin score a couple of goals in a game for Norfolk Schools. He wasn't the only scout at the game either. Word had got out about Justin, with Charlton Athletic sending along two scouts to the same match with the brief to watch Justin and do all they could to get him along to the Valley. Luckily for us, Justin was settled in Norfolk with his foster parents and was always going to sign for Norwich if he got the chance, which, thanks to Ronnie Brooks, he did. He went on to score 18 goals in just 22 matches for the youth team during the 1976/77 season and was offered his first professional contract when he was still just 17.

Our capitulation at Leicester City in that instantly forgettable FA Cup game led, indirectly, to Justin getting his first start. John Bond's patience with Martin Chivers finally ran out after that match and, when we returned to league action a week later, Justin found himself in the number-nine shirt and playing alongside Kevin Reeves in what must have been the youngest strike partnership in any of the four English senior divisions on the day. It wasn't a particularly easy game for him to come in for either. West Brom were riding high in the table and a good result at Carrow Road would have seen them hit the top, so we were up against it. The whole team played well on the day though and Justin ended up unlucky not to have marked his debut with a goal – but we all knew, as did the manager and most of all Justin himself, that they'd come.

Despite the club feeling the pinch financially, John Bond's wish for a few more experienced faces to have around the place over the summer was granted by the board. John McDowell and Alan Taylor arrived from West Ham along with Roger Brown from Bournemouth. John had proven pedigree and was the sort of player Bond loved to have around the place, someone who was schooled in the old West Ham ways, a defender who liked to have the ball at his feet and wasn't afraid to try and do something with it when he did. He'd already won England youth and under-23 caps while he was with the Hammers and you wonder if, deep down, both he and the manager wondered if a move might give him an opportunity to maybe think about getting noticed for the full England team. Alan, on the other hand, was a classic goal poacher, the type of striker who came to life in the penalty area and who thrived on half chances. He was a quite well-known name in the game as well; he'd scored both goals when West Ham had beaten Fulham in the FA Cup Final four years previously, so his arrival was seen as something of a coup and, character wise, he looked as if he would fit in well with the lads, unlike Martin Chivers who, for whatever reasons, had never really seemed comfortable after he'd joined us.

We had a brilliant start to the 1979/80 season, winning our first three league games with a total of ten goals scored and only three conceded. This included a 4-2 win at Everton on the opening day (the club's first away win in the league in 41 matches) and a fantastic 4-0 win over a Tottenham side that included Hoddle, Ardiles and Villa four days later. After our third win in a row, a 2-1 success against Leeds, Norwich went to the top of the Division One table for the first time in the club's history, that win coming via two goals from Kevin Bond who was beginning to show those who felt he was only in the team because he was the manager's son that they were very misguided. Kevin was a great right-back, he was sound defensively, as you'd want, but he also loved to bomb forward, and he had a hell of a shot on him as well, something that he showed in that Leeds game with his second goal which went in from all of 30 yards out.

I was desperate to be part of things but had no chance in those early weeks and months of the season as my groin was playing up again and I was spending most of my time with the physiotherapists. No footballer likes to be out injured and, take it from me, I hated it more than most. You soon become a forgotten man, you miss the banter in training as well as the thrill of getting ready for a match and, of course, you also miss the extra money that comes with appearance, win and goal bonuses, which really came in handy for me as my basic wage was just £55 a week when I signed as a professional. That meant the win bonus I got after the Derby game was nearly five times my weekly wage which felt like a fortune to me at the time.

All footballers talk about money and we were no exception to the general rule and, inevitably, I found myself drawn into a conversation with some of the more senior players towards the end of that first season as a full professional. They knew I was on only £55 a week and advised me to go and see John Bond to ask for an increase as I was now regarded as a first-team player. I made an appointment to see him after training one day and went up to his office, knocked on the door and, hopefully looking more confident than I felt, walked in.

'How can I help you, Peter?' said the gaffer, barely looking up as he did so. Note it's 'Peter', not 'Pete' or the even more informal 'Mendy'. This made me feel like I was standing in my old headmaster's office, which was probably exactly how John Bond, a man used to dealing with big names like Ted MacDougall, Kevin Keelan, Martin Peters and Martin Chivers, wanted me to feel.

But too late to back out now. This was my moment.

'I have come to see you for a wage rise.'

Silence. He was writing away at something or other on his desk, fully occupied with whatever he's doing. But, after what seemed like an eternity but was probably only about half a minute or so, he spoke again. Slowly, clearly and with feeling.

'Come back and see me when you have played 50 games. We will discuss it further then.'

And that was that. Clearly, there was going to be no chance of any further discussion, let alone negotiation. John Bond had said what he wanted to say and that was that. So I promptly did an about turn and left, determined, as I made my way back to the first-team dressing room at Trowse, that I'd work even harder to show him that I was worth more and realising, as I did so, that his reaction and response to me was all part of his philosophy of dealing with the younger players by testing their character and seeing how they'd respond. It had, in this case, certainly worked with me and, although I hadn't got my wage rise, I knew that a time would come when he wouldn't be able to turn down a similar request as I would have more than proved my value to both him and the team.

I had to make do with that £55 for quite a while as the 1979/80 season progressed. My pelvic injury was taking its time to clear up, and every time I felt like I was ready for a full match it'd flare up again or I'd get some soreness. Not too much but enough to mean I couldn't take part in a full training session so, of course, as a result of that, I wasn't going to get a game. The lads were doing well though, and by the end of November Norwich were securely sat in eighth place in Division One, impressive enough but still the lowest position we'd had so far that season, having dropped down two places from sixth as a result of a 5-0 defeat at Manchester United on 24 November. United looked good that day. They were managed by Dave Sexton who, like John Bond, liked his sides to play what is universally referred to as 'good' football, that is, a passing game with lots of movement and the option of no little pace and trickery from your wide players, in this case, Steve Coppell and Micky Thomas. Coppell was just about unplayable on that afternoon, as was the rather more rumbustious Joe Jordan in attack. He bullied our defence mercilessly, scoring two goals, the second of which he managed to get past Kevin Keelan despite the attentions of at least three of our players as he did so. That game did, at least, give another one of the team's younger players the chance to make his debut, on this occasion my good friend and fishing companion Mark Barham.

After such a heavy defeat, most people expected John Bond to make a few changes to the side for our next game at home to Aston Villa on 1 December, which he did, leaving out Mick McGuire and Alan Taylor in favour of me and Keith Robson with us both, I would say, chosen for the slightly more physical edge that we'd give the side. Keith certainly didn't take any prisoners when he was playing. He wasn't the biggest of strikers but he put himself about for the cause and was rarely far from the scene if the fists and studs were going in, earning himself a reputation which a reporter from the *Daily Telegraph*, no less, once summed up by sniffily declaring of Keith, '... he does not always prefer the cerebral approach.' I wasn't quite that type of player myself; however, I was more than willing, if the need arose, to battle away in the midfield and win the ball so that I could get it to our players who <u>did</u> adopt the cerebral approach. This would have pleased, no doubt, the man from the *Telegraph* in the process, as we possessed players like Graham Paddon (who had survived his public lambasting and transfer-listing after our collapse at Leicester the previous season) and, of course, the peerless Martin Peters, both of whom were very pleasing to the eye in the manner they played the game.

If John Bond had been expecting a physical encounter then he wasn't to be disappointed as it was exactly that from the start. Villa's manager was Ron Saunders, who'd previously been at Norwich and was the man who took the Canaries up to the top flight for the first time in their history in 1972. He'd left the club in somewhat acrimonious circumstances, however, and now, as Villa boss, was always keen to put one over on his former employers, especially at Carrow Road. So he and his players were more than up for the game, as, fortunately, were we and I enjoyed pitting my wits, as well as my physical presence, against a wily Villa midfield that included players like Dennis Mortimer and Des Bremner, both of whom were good players but also players who wouldn't be slow, given the opportunity, in letting some little ginger-headed kid know he was playing a man's game now!

Villa's Allan Evans was another no-nonsense player who could put himself about a bit if the occasion needed it. Unfortunately for him, one of the players he chose to, shall we say, introduce himself to on the field of play was Justin, who didn't take kindly to Evans's flailing knees and elbows and promptly laid him out (and got sent off for doing so), no mean feat as Evans was a powerfully built six-footer who normally considered opposing centre-forwards as a tasty *hors d'oeuvre*. Just prior to that incident, Evans put Villa ahead, although it's questionable as to whether the ball crossed the line. In any case, and despite our protests, the goal was given and, from that moment on, the atmosphere at Carrow Road grew positively fractious, so much so that coins were thrown on to the pitch and both John Bond and Ron Saunders had to appeal to their respective fans to calm down.

I was loving it! It was a real blood-and-thunder football match with no quarter given by either players or supporters. It was the first game I'd been involved with that had included a bit of a physical edge to it of this nature and, despite all that was going on,

I know John Bond and Ken Brown would have been keeping an eye on me, making sure I didn't shirk any tackles or lose possession. They needed to know that, as good a footballer as I was, I'd scrap if I had to and wouldn't let either them or my team-mates down. We battled on and, despite being down to ten men, continued to push forward, with the risk, of course, of being caught out by a Villa breakaway until, a couple of minutes or so before the end, one of the Villa players went in a little bit too heavily in their penalty area and we were awarded a late and maybe slightly contentious penalty.

Dennis Mortimer, who I'd enjoyed a good battle with, wasn't having it and went off on one to the referee in a big way in protest, so much so that he joined Justin in being sent off. The resulting penalty was tucked away with his usual aplomb by Kevin Bond which meant we'd won ourselves a late point, enough to keep us in eighth place and, as far as individual performances were concerned, enough to keep me in the team for the following week's fixture which was a trip to play Derby County, the team I had, of course, played against in my senior debut for the Canaries a little over a year earlier.

We drew that game 0-0 before, the following week, enjoying a 2-0 win over Bristol City which we did without Justin and Kevin Reeves, with their replacements Alan Taylor and Keith Robson scoring the goals. I played but didn't get a full 90 minutes this time as John Bond opted to take me off in the second half in order for Phil Lythgoe to get a game.

I then went on to have a nice little run in the first team, starting in 14 and coming on as a substitute in three of our remaining 22 league games as well as getting a run out in all three of the FA Cup games we had that season, one of which was a 3-0 win at Yeovil on their famous sloping pitch, as well as a League Cup fifth-round tie at Liverpool which we lost 3-1. I was now, as you'd expect, determined to get my first goal for the club and it came in, of all matches, a game at home to Ipswich Town on Boxing Day 1979. Yes, my first East Anglian derby and what a game it was, one I can still remember and look back on with great fondness to this day. Eric Gates had opened the scoring for them fairly early on before I managed to get my head to the ball and flick it past Paul Cooper after Martin Peters had headed on a cross from Greg Downs. Alan Taylor then put us ahead just before half-time and we were, at that stage, so dominant, that we should have gone on to win the match comfortably. Yet we still contrived to let Ipswich back into it and they went 3-2 up after goals from Arnold Muhren, who was a great player, and John Wark.

John Bond then took the gamble of taking Roger Brown, a defender, off and replacing him with Justin from the bench. It was a gamble and, thankfully, it paid off as Justin's sheer presence unnerved the Ipswich defence enough for Keith Robson to deflect an otherwise wayward half chance in with only a minute remaining and for us to rescue a point.

We were, of course, delighted to have been able to do so and celebrated with our fans at the end in the way that you do when you score a late goal. But John Bond wasn't feeling so happy with us when we got back to the dressing room and made that clear to us in what I can only describe as his version of the 'hairdryer' treatment that Sir Alex Ferguson was later renowned for dishing out to his players at Manchester United. And he had a point. We'd dominated the match to such an extent that at half-time, and in the true spirit of the season, Keith Robson said that the Ipswich defence were 'handing out Christmas presents'. Keith had been spot on and we hadn't been able to take full advantage of that, indeed, more to the point, we'd ended up being as generous in the gift of giving as they had been in giving away the goals that we had. Take, for example, Ipswich's first goal which came after we had spent the first quarter of an hour or so absolutely battering their back four before Town had, finally, made some sort of break out of their defence, a frantic retreat up the field (as it seemed at the time) that ended in disaster when Kevin Keelan had spilled a speculative shot at the feet of Eric Gates, who said thank you very much to 'Cat' and scored from close range.

As good as we'd been in attack, we'd then proceeded to let ourselves down at the back and had, in the end, scraped a fortunate point in a game that we should have won easily. We had our chances to win as well with John Ryan and Martin Peters both missing good chances to put us ahead before Arnold Muhren put them 3-2 up and looking as if they'd win the game. Thankfully, Keith Robson's late equaliser had got us a point that, in fairness, Ipswich didn't deserve as we had been by far the better side for all of the match, reason enough for the manager to express his displeasure afterwards in the way that he did.

Yet, as thrill a minute as that game was, it didn't come anywhere near to the excitement that the 25,000 plus in the ground witnessed as well as the many millions more who tuned into *Match Of The Day* (the BBC certainly seemed to pick their Norwich matches well) later that evening when Liverpool came to town on 11 February.

And let's face it, the incentive for the BBC was the opportunity to record yet another Liverpool win as they powered their way towards yet another league title. They'd been on a hell of a run in the weeks leading up to the game, with a run of ten wins and two draws from 12 games before they'd gone down 1-0 to Coventry City at Highfield Road. The Reds didn't take defeat at all kindly back then and we knew it was going to be a real backs-to-the-wall job when they came to Carrow Road, and with such names as Alan Hansen, Kenny Dalglish and Terry McDermott in their side you didn't exactly need to be a footballing anorak to work out that it was going to be one of our biggest challenges of the season just to keep them at bay. But it wasn't as if we didn't have previous against them. We'd headed up to Anfield back in September and had managed a clean sheet in a 0-0 draw, despite their having, as you'd expect, much of the play throughout. We'd defended well, with Phil Hoadley, in particular, outstanding. I hadn't played in that game but had been selected earlier that same season when we drew them in a League Cup quarter-final match. They'd been at their ruthless best that evening, going 3-0 up in just over half an hour before switching to cruise control for the rest of the game with our goal, scored just before half-time by Kevin Reeves, nothing more than a consolation prize.

I'd enjoyed the game despite our defeat, but how could I not have relished the opportunity of battling away in our midfield against some of the greatest players the English game has ever seen playing, as they were, in one of the greatest club sides there has ever been in England? They were all on show and at their imperious and even arrogant best. Graeme Souness, in particular, was something else, he acted as if he not only owned the pitch but all of us as well – what a player. David Johnson scored two of their goals before Kenny Dalglish dinked and danced his way into our box before scoring. They'd been hugely impressive and I couldn't wait for the third and final act of that season as I reckoned we had a chance of getting something from the game. Liverpool had, after all, lost their previous game whilst in ours we'd beaten Coventry City, the team they lost to, climbing, in the process, up to fourth in the Division One table, our eighth game without defeat in a run that had, mind you, seen rather too many draws including a 2-2 at Leeds United. That was a particularly special game for me as I'd opened the scoring for us early on, a bit of a tap-in from Alan Taylor's driven cross but they all count and I was thrilled to have scored at the ground of the team I'd supported as a boy.

My feelings of optimism were soon rewarded when Martin Peters put us ahead after just two minutes. Funnily enough, though, for all the joy of the moment and the celebrations that followed, you knew deep down that scoring so early on against a side like Liverpool was like going into a dragon's cave and tweaking its tail and that your act of total and utter audacity was just going to wind them up and elicit a response. It came just two minutes later when David Fairclough, who'd go on to have a short spell at Norwich, scored the first of his three goals on the day. His hat-trick and one apiece for Kenny Dalglish and Jimmy Case was enough to get them a 5-3 win in a terrific game that is, of course, best remembered for Justin's fabulous turn and volley at the Barclay End, the goal that made the score 3-3 and gave us brief hope that we could go on and win it.

And what a goal it was, what a goal. That, of course, and Justin's cool celebration afterwards as he simply turned and walked back to the centre circle with just the one finger held aloft in acknowledgement of what he'd just done before Kevin Reeves and Martin Peters jumped on him in celebration. If you look back at the goal now, you can see that, as we're all enjoying the moment, John Bond is out of his dugout and jumping around on the touchline, not, I hasten to add, in joy himself but in order to try and communicate to us that now we've got the game back to 3-3 he doesn't want anyone to do anything silly that might mean we go on to lose it.

### Sorry gaffer

It had been a fantastic game, a joy to play in and to watch. Yet we'd still lost, and despite all the plaudits that headed our way in the game's aftermath, especially after the nation had seen it for themselves that evening, John Bond wasn't a happy man. Again. He was, post-game, particularly critical of his son Kevin, accusing him of not battling at one point and saying that he wanted to take Kevin off and play the game with only ten men. The reason that he hadn't done so was because he'd already had to take me off when, early in the second half, I'd had to be carried off, with Mick McGuire coming on to replace me. I thought at one point my groin had gone again, and if it had that would have been the third time I'd had an injury there in less than two years. It was certainly painful enough, I was doubled up in agony and was barely able to move. Luckily for me, Dave Baldwin, who was the club's physiotherapist at the time, soon diagnosed it as a pulled muscle at the top of my thigh. There was a lot of bruising to go with the pain and I was a little bit frantic at first as I thought it would mean I would be out for a long time again. Dave, however, was confident that I was both young and fit enough to be able to play in our next match, and, sure enough, his skill and my body's powers of recovery meant that I took my place in a Norwich team that showed only two changes from the starting XI which featured against Liverpool, with Stevie Goble coming in for John Ryan and, marking the end of an era, Roger Hansbury for Kevin Keelan.

I wonder if Cat Keelan wanted his last game for Norwich to have been so memorable? I'm sure he'd have preferred a dour 0-0 draw which meant he went out with a clean sheet rather than having five put past him. Mind you, this was, again, Liverpool at their very best. They had quality throughout their squad as illustrated by Fairclough's hat-trick. He was never a first-team regular and had previously been labelled as the team's 'supersub', yet here he was, called up in the absence of England striker David Johnson, with a hat-trick that, if it hadn't been for Justin's wonderful goal, would have been all over the back pages the following day.

We might have lost the game but we enjoyed the brief spell in the headlines that it brought to the club and the players – some more than others. Phil Thompson, the Liverpool captain, was kind enough to say it was the best match he'd ever played in, adding that he thought Justin's goal would certainly be the best that anyone had scored in England that season, whilst Bob Paisley, the legendary Liverpool manager, was very fulsome in his praise, observing that Norwich had attacked Liverpool from the off rather than, as most other teams did at the time, looking to close them down and play for a draw. Even the referee felt compelled to have his say on the matter, with Mark Scott being quoted in the *Eastern Daily Press* as saying, 'I never refereed a better match and I don't think I ever will. From now on, it must be downhill.' The final word on that remarkable game must, however, go to the chairman of Norwich City, Sir Arthur South, who, when he was presenting David Fairclough the match ball afterwards, said, 'Don't do this too often, David, these cost £32 a time you know. But then it's worth it to see a game like that.'

It was even better to play in one like it!

Following that game, we were all on a bit of a high by the time we welcomed Wolves to Carrow Road a fortnight later. I was fit, having made the best use of the fortnight gap between the two games to get over my thigh strain, and took my place in a Norwich side that saw two changes, with Roger Hansbury coming in for Kevin Keelan and Steve Goble replacing John Ryan who, after 132 Norwich appearances and 29 goals, had headed off to the USA to play for Seattle Sounders.

I'd like to be able to say we carried on in the same manner we had against Liverpool and, in a way, we nearly did, and I say 'nearly' because on this particular occasion we let in one goal less than we had against the Reds, and ended up losing 4-0, with Kenny Hibbit scoring two penalties. It was a woeful performance all round and our heads were well and truly down in the dressing room afterwards, particularly as, after an undefeated run of eight matches, we'd now lost two on the trot at Carrow Road, and by an aggregate score of 3-9. Not good.

John Bond promptly wielded his sharpest axe for our trip to Middlesbrough four days later as Richard Symonds, John McDowell and Mark Halsey all got a recall to the first team and the added steel they brought to our back four meant that we were able to grind out a 0-0 draw, not the sort of result that John Bond wanted to have (he'd far rather have won 4-3 than 1-0), but it was a case of needs must on the day and we played well, with David Jones, who'd been out for a while with injury, playing particularly well.

It was a sequence of results that summed up that season really. We'd been good enough to win our first three league games and go to the top of the Division One table as a consequence of that, and we'd also been good enough to record good wins against Nottingham Forest (3-1) and Derby County (4-2) as well as win a thrilling game at Brighton by the same score. Good wins, plenty of goals and performances deserving of far more praise than we actually got at the time. But, up against all of that, were performances and results that were, in some cases, absolutely shocking, such as our 5-0 defeat at Manchester United, that 0-4 at home to Wolves and a 4-2 hiding at Ipswich at Easter in a game that ended with us 15th in the table (we'd been in or around the top six to eight until the new year) and wondering if we might end up going on the sort of run that would drag us down into a relegation battle. That, fortunately, never became the case and we ended the 1979/80 season in 12th place.

Strangely enough, the club had been thinking about our end-of-season programme at around the time of that classic Liverpool match. We'd been invited to spend part of our pre-season in China, an extremely rare honour at the time, which had only, up to then, been something that West Bromwich Albion had done. Clearly, the Baggies had impressed their hosts so much that the Chinese government decided to ask another team, which was to be us. However, it wasn't in any way a given that we'd even go. Sir Arthur South had accepted the invitation on behalf of the club, but had made it very clear that it would be dependent on whether or not the players wanted to go, especially as it was to take place from mid-May onwards, a time when we'd normally have been on our holidays, something Sir Arthur acknowledged by saying, '... it's one thing to ask the players to tour the South of France or sun themselves in Florida. It's quite another to ask them to go to Peking – and it's only right that they should have their say.'

I was certain of one thing, and that was that I wanted to go! What a fantastic opportunity it would be to visit and explore a country that, back then, was still largely a mystery to the average westerner. Sir Arthur and his board of directors would, I am sure, have shared my enthusiasm about the visit and would certainly have spoken to their counterparts at the Hawthorns about West Brom's visit to the country, which had taken place two years earlier. That trip, which had seen them play five games, was considered so ground-breaking at the time that the club's management and players were summoned to Downing Street beforehand in order to be given a briefing by the Prime Minister.

They weren't, however, the first-choice guests of the Chinese leadership, who had originally issued an invitation to England's national football team with the tour intended to work as a warm-up prior to the England squad flying on to Argentina to play in the latter stages of the 1978 World Cup. Once England's failure to qualify for the finals was confirmed, however, the FA swiftly fell out of love with what would have then been seen as nothing more than an expensive PR junket for a failed squad and the trip was swiftly cancelled, with West Brom stepping into the breach at pretty much the last minute and being described by Denis Howell, the then Sports Minister, as 'football ambassadors'.

Now it was our turn and, although a few of the older players weren't all that thrilled about the prospect of a long and arduous trip overseas so soon after the end of the season, the financial rewards on offer to the club for making the trip were too generous to turn down and off we went.

It was my first tour anywhere as a Norwich City player and I couldn't have been more excited. I'd never been abroad before, not even on a day trip, so the thought of travelling halfway around the world just to play a few games of football was, for me, unbelievably exciting. We headed out on 11 May 1980, a little over a week after playing in our last game of the season and the day after West Ham had beaten Arsenal 1-0 in that season's FA Cup Final, which meant, of course, that I got to sit and watch the match with my dad, just as I had always done. Our destination was Peking, now Beijing of course, with our schedule including four matches as well as the obligatory functions and a little bit of sightseeing.

The hotel we'd all been booked into was a short walk from the famous Tiananmen Square. I was rooming with Justin Fashanu, an arrangement which suited us both perfectly as we were both young, lively and liked to have a bit of a laugh and a joke, tendencies that some of the older players weren't so keen on. Justin was, at the time, well on his way to becoming one of the most well-known and highly rated players in the English game. He also had a real presence about him and remained, for all the attention that was being lavished upon him, one of the nicest people you could ever wish to meet.

Once we'd settled into our room, we went downstairs to meet up with the rest of the squad for dinner but arrived a few minutes late, meaning that we'd missed an announcement made to the rest of the squad by Ken Brown asking that everyone looked out for John Bond's suitcases as they'd been taken to the wrong room in error and were, at that time, still missing, meaning that the manager only had the clothes he was standing in for the entirety of the trip. We soon found out, of course, that the manager's cases were missing but had never been aware that they might have been in our room so we carried on with the tour, both of us believing that the two suitcases that had been left in a corner of our room belonged to the other person.

Sixteen days later, as we packed and made ourselves ready for the trip back to the airport and on to Hong Kong, I noticed that Justin was about to head off out without picking up his remaining suitcases, so I quickly called him back.

'Justin, don't forget your other cases mate.'

'I've got mine Mendy. I thought they were yours.'

The penny soon dropped and we both knew that we were, potentially, in a spot of bother with John Bond, who wouldn't believe, however much we would try to convince him otherwise, that we hadn't known his cases had been in our room all the time. After all, we were Mendy and Fash, wind-up merchants and jokers extraordinaire and it wouldn't have been at all out of the question that we'd have thought it might have been a bit of a laugh to keep all the manager's luggage in our room for the entirety of our stay.

Except that we would never have even thought about doing such a thing. The problem was, no one would believe in our innocence, even if it was genuine.

We briefly wondered if we should toss a coin to see which one of us should bring the cases downstairs before Justin said that he would do it and I wasn't to worry. He was, after all, the club's blue-eyed boy, a million-pound plus player if ever there was one and someone who was, now that the tour was coming to an end, shortly off to continue his education in the game by playing some matches in the NASL before reporting back for pre-season training.

Justin reckoned he could get away with it whereas my chances would not have been quite so good. He was right. There was, as we'd guessed, something of a commotion when he turned up in the foyer with John Bond's cases, but he managed to sweet talk both himself (and me) out of any trouble and was able to leave for the USA without punishment, whilst I prepared for the second part of our tour which was to take place in Hong Kong.

I'll never forget that trip to China. At one point, Justin and I went for a walk around Tiananmen Square but had hardly been outside the confines of our hotel for five minutes before we noticed a crowd of people were following us, one that was getting bigger and bigger all the time. We were, or so we thought, innocently sightseeing but in doing so had become something of a tourist attraction ourselves. Westerners were very infrequent visitors to China at that time, especially those who took it upon themselves to wander around one of the busiest parts of the nation's capital and, what with me and my bright red hair and Justin, tall, black and very charismatic, we did tend to stand out amongst the soberly dressed and slight residents of the city who were now surrounding us, all of them talking at once and asking, as they did so, an absolute barrage of questions.

Justin soon got hold of a football from somewhere and we started passing it to one another, doing a few little tricks and flicks, a keepie-uppie or two and some head tennis between us, much to the appreciation of our audience, who laughed and clapped at every opportunity and, now aware that we were members of the English football team that was visiting the country, started asking us for our autographs, something that was, for me at least, still a relatively new experience and one that I thoroughly enjoyed. Justin and I saw, at that moment, the human face of China. These were happy people with smiles on their faces, they were friendly and welcoming and were, no doubt, delighted to see Justin and I out and about ourselves. It was a rare and fleeting sign of joy and emotion in a population that was living in the thrall of a totalitarian leadership, drab dress and surroundings and also seen, by myself and my team-mates, queuing up in silent subservience as they filed past the tomb of their long dead leader, voices low and heads bowed and oblivious, it seemed to us, as we were guided to the front of the line by the state officials who accompanied us everywhere.

This included, of course, a trip to the Great Wall of China, which remains one of the travel highlights of my life, although I have to admit the long coach trip that got us there was something I'd still rather forget, especially the sheer drops down the side of the mountain that we were all able to see as we looked, if you dared, out of the windows as we made our way there. Mind you, the journey we took in order to play what was our second match was also a memorable one, albeit for different reasons. We'd already played the Chinese national team in Peking, winning that game 2-0 in front of a large and curious crowd before moving on, three days later, to play a game in the north of the country against Herbei Province. This meant a 200-mile train journey, not, you might think, that bad a mode of transport and that would have been exactly the case if the train that we were on didn't have a top speed of just under 30mph! As a consequence, it took us an age to get there which meant most of us had to make use of the train's bathroom facilities at least once. Well, they were terrifying, you'd be standing, or, worse than that, squatting there with the moving track clearly visible beneath you with only the crudest of holes in the floor provided for whatever it was you needed to do.

We were all so pleased to get there in one piece, and, despite the fact the game was played on a clay surface that would have been more appropriate to the French Open tennis championships, we ended up putting on as good a performance as we had done in a long time in front of another large crowd, winning 2-0 before heading back to Peking where we were due to play the Chinese Army XI in what was our third game in seven days. As a result of that, we didn't put in the best of performances and drew that game

0-0, much to the delight of our hosts, who must have regarded it as a great patriotic victory over their decadent visitors!

On then to Hong Kong and, with Justin heading off to the USA to play his summer football there, I needed a new roommate. I ended up with John Benson, who had come to the club as a player from Bournemouth with John Bond and was now a member of the coaching staff. The fact he was a member of John Bond's staff, together with his being nearly twice my age, meant that I wasn't really looking forward to sharing with John but, as it turned out, I thoroughly enjoyed his company and got to know him really well in that time. We played just the one match whilst we were in Hong Kong, which was against Bulova and it ended in a 2-1 win for us. The game had to be played in the early evening as the daytime temperatures in Hong Kong at that time of year are absolutely stifling, so with that and the associated high humidity, we were struggling from the start, especially as we were playing against a side who, we'd learnt, were on a very big cash incentive to win the game whilst we were on nothing more than a slice of orange at both half-time and full time. That didn't sit particularly well with any of us and, with that in mind as well as the extreme weather conditions we'd be playing in, Mick McGuire, who was our representative on the Professional Footballers' Association (PFA) at the time, approached the club management and managed to negotiate a little reward for us in return for playing the match, our fourth in 11 days, against an opposition who were now highly motivated to win it.

I can't remember what Mick ended up getting for us but I do remember that we'd collectively agreed that we wouldn't play the match unless we were to get something for our efforts as we'd now been away for nearly three weeks, and with this tour coming so soon after a long season, the lads, myself included, just wanted to get home and have some time for ourselves and with our families, especially as it was now nearing the end of May and we'd be expected back for pre-season training before the end of June! Still, at least we didn't leave Hong Kong completely empty-handed as we all ended up taking some of the very best handmade silk suits back with us after we all went to a tailor during some down time and got measured up for them. And they were a bargain!

Once we'd arrived back in Norwich and been given our instructions for keeping fit over the summer and when we'd be expected to report back for pre-season training, I sat down and almost for the first time for the whole of that campaign I quietly took stock of all that had been going on in my life over the previous ten months or so. It had been quite a ride. I'd started that season hoping to shake off a niggling groin injury that was, at one point, so bad I'd wondered if I'd ever play again. Thankfully, the combination of my own self-belief as well as the talents of Dave Baldwin, the club physiotherapist, meant I'd not only recovered but gone on to play a full part in the club's 1979/80 season with a total of 24 league and cup appearances made and scoring three goals. I'd also been part of the squad that had flown out to China on what had been a very high-profile club tour and played a full part in proceedings there. Justin was, of course, grabbing all the headlines, and rightly so. He was already a fabulous footballer who was only going to get better. This meant that, as another one of the club's younger players, I could focus on my game and becoming one of the first names John Bond wanted to put on his team sheet away from all the glare and attention that was being heaped upon Justin's shoulders. I was, as people say today, working my way up 'under the radar' and that suited me perfectly.

# CHAPTER FOUR

# On the Up

*He was a big name player, someone who'd played at the very top of the game, an established top-flight player and international and an on-pitch leader. He was worth every penny.*

AS MUCH as I'd been looking forward to having a bit of a break after our end-of-season tour to China and Hong Kong at the end of the 1979/80 season, it wasn't long before I was kicking my heels in boredom and looking forward to getting back to Trowse and in and around the lads as we started our preparations for the new campaign.

It had been a busy summer at Carrow Road, with a number of departures, the most significant of which was that of Martin Peters who left us to become player-manager of Sheffield United. Nobody thought that Martin would be gone for long, mind you, as all the footballing gossip that summer was centred on John Bond and the fact that he might have, after nearly six years, come to realise he'd done all that he was ever going to do for Norwich and that if he really wanted to prove himself as a top manager he'd soon be moving on. He'd already been linked with Leeds United and, as the speculation continued, it wasn't hard to work out that Martin would be one of the prime candidates to replace him. Had that been the case of course, it's likely that Martin wouldn't have left for Sheffield United and I'm sure I'm not the only one who wonders if he was quietly told that the top job at Norwich wasn't going to be offered to him in the event of Bond leaving, something which probably sped up his own decision to move on.

In addition to Martin leaving, we also lost the services of Alan Taylor and Phil Lythgoe as well as centre-half David Jones who was retiring due to injury. Alan and Phil were both strikers so it was clear that John Bond would be looking to bring in a new face to add to the goalscoring ranks and he didn't disappoint when he did, signing former England international Joe Royle from Bristol City. Joe duly took the number-nine shirt for our opening match against Stoke City and played his part as we, with me wearing number four, the same as Billy Bremner my idol at Leeds United, ran amok in the Carrow Road sunshine, winning 5-1, with Justin scoring a hat-trick in just under 20 minutes.

Everything and everyone clicked on that day, as good a game and team performance as I'd known since joining the club. I guess both we and the fans had hoped that it would have helped convince John Bond that he was capable of achieving great things with Norwich – and why not? Signing Joe had been a masterstroke, he'd be the perfect partner in attack for Justin and, with Clive Woods and Graham Paddon providing the sort of midfield guile that a lot of other First Division clubs would have been glad to have for themselves, we were all very optimistic about not only improving on the previous season's 12th-place finish but having a proper go in one of the cup competitions.

And you know what? Maybe we came out of that Stoke game just a little bit too cocky for our own good?

Actually, there's no 'maybe' about it. We went into our next game against Aston Villa thinking we'd need to do little more than turn up to record another win and we were woeful, losing a dour game at Villa Park 1-0. Three more defeats followed, and by the time we'd lost 3-0 at West Brom in our fifth game we were down to 20th and in the relegation places.

Now that shouldn't mean anything at that early stage of a season, especially if you're the sort of side that has something about you and has the nous to regroup and start climbing up the table, but we never did that and never climbed any higher than 17th for the rest of that ultimately very disappointing season, one that ended in relegation when, needing to beat an already relegated Leicester at Carrow Road in the last game of the season in order to have any chance of staying up, we lost 3-2, despite dominating much of the game.

John Bond was long gone by then, of course. We'd played Middlesbrough up at Ayresome Park at the start of October and had been well and truly turned over to the tune of 6-1, all – wouldn't you know it – in front of the *Match Of The Day* cameras. I wasn't playing as my groin was giving me stick again; indeed, the whole of that season was a bit of a no-go for me because of that and other injury issues. I was fit enough, however, post-Middlesbrough, to be named on the bench for our next game which was against Wolves at Carrow Road and we drew 1-1. We did so, though, minus John Bond who had been approached by Manchester City just prior to the match, an invitation that he couldn't turn down, with the appointment being confirmed by the end of the following week and a day before we were due to go to Coventry.

Most people, myself included, expected John Benson to be named as John's successor but he opted to take John with him to Maine Road, splitting up, in the process, the long and prosperous partnership that he'd had with Ken Brown who was promptly appointed as caretaker manager alongside Mel Machin. It was a choice that the very great majority of the lads were delighted with as Ken was what you would call a 'proper' football man who had, like his predecessor, learnt his trade at West Ham. He had, of course, that reputation that goes with him to this day, that he is a lovely man with time for everyone but, believe me, underneath all of that is a steely resolve and if needed a fierce temper and a hairdryer as hot as anyone's! Not that he would have needed it much though, as Mel was quite happy to play the fire to Ken's ice.

He didn't mince his words and could cut you down with ease if he felt you weren't performing to the best of your abilities. Ken and Mel took charge of us for the first time at Coventry and we responded to their appointments in the best possible way, winning 1-0, that win and the performance that went with it enough to see them awarded the jobs on a permanent basis the next day.

We were, however, a team that was on a downward spiral and for all their collective efforts, Ken and Mel were unable to prevent us from being relegated at the end of that season. It was a tired squad that needed refreshing, something they addressed as the season progressed with some astute purchases such as Dave Watson, Steve Walford, Martin O'Neill and Chris Woods, but although their presence gave us all a lift, especially that of Martin, even a run of four consecutive league wins from the beginning of April wasn't going to be enough to save us. We'd pretty much been in the bottom three since just after Christmas, and as good as the new players were they'd come on board just a little bit too late in the day.

Sadly for the club, our relegation saw Martin O'Neill exercise a relegation release clause he'd had written into his contract when he joined us from Nottingham Forest (for whom he'd won a European Cup winners' medal) in order to sign for John Bond at Manchester City. His departure was a huge blow to us. Signing him in the first place had been a real statement of intent from Ken Brown, who did one hell of a job to convince him given his quality as a player as well as the other options he must have had when it became obvious that Cloughie wasn't too bothered whether he went or not. He only played 11 games for us from the time he signed up until the end of the season but his class stood out in just about all of them, and if we'd have managed to stay up I'm sure Brown would have started to build his own side around Martin just as John Bond had with Martin Peters. But it was not to be and that, for all of us, came as a great disappointment.

Regardless of what Ken Brown might have told him about his plans for Norwich on the field, Martin's pay at Norwich must have played a big part in convincing him to sign for us, and in doing so helped soften the blow of having to leave the two-times European champions. He was, during that first playing spell at Norwich, on a contract that paid him £2,500 a game, which was an absolute fortune at the time and would easily have made him our most highly paid player ever. To put that into context, whilst Martin was earning the £27,500 (plus bonuses) he was paid for the 14 appearances he made for us up until the end of the 1980/81 season, I was on a contract that paid me just £125 a week. Now, don't get me wrong, I didn't, and never did, have an issue with the amount that Martin was being paid. He was a big-name player, someone who'd played at the very top of the game, an established top-flight player and international and an on-pitch leader. He was worth every penny.

But come on. Wasn't I now also an established first-team player? After all, I'd now played in around 50 matches for the club and had weighed in, during that time, with a couple of important goals. I never expected or even thought I should be on as much as Martin was, but at the same time I was now beginning to realise that the club were getting away with paying me a pittance and determined that I would, over the summer, look to do something about it, although I also knew that my absolute priority was to ensure that I was fit and ready to play a full part in what would now be a season in which promotion back to the First Division was the target, one that Ken Brown knew he needed to deliver in order to hang on to his job.

One inevitable departure that summer was that of Justin Fashanu. Such was his burgeoning reputation in the game by the time the 1980/81 season came to an end, it was unlikely we'd have been able to keep hold of him even if the club had managed to avoid relegation. The fact that we had ended a very disappointing campaign by joining Crystal Palace and Leicester City in Division Two the following season made his departure inevitable and we all knew it. Quite a few clubs had been linked with him, including Liverpool and Leeds United, but it was Nottingham Forest and Brian Clough who ended up signing him, with Cloughie so set on sealing the deal that he had Justin's signature on a contract before Ken Brown was able to walk into the room to join them for what he probably thought would be a lengthy negotiating process.

That wasn't Clough's way and I am sure he was able to dazzle Justin with both his plans for the club and for his footballing career. When you add that sort of pulling power to the £1 million Norwich got for their prime asset, a lot of money for a team that had been relegated, then we stood next to no chance of keeping him. I could only wish Justin well with his big move. He was a lovely lad and I'd miss him as a friend as well as a team-mate.

One story that wouldn't go away, especially in the light of relegation, was the one that made clear that the club was, again, in serious financial trouble, which was a worry. From a personal point of view, I knew that going to see Ken Brown and asking for a pay rise would almost certainly be met with a resigned look and an admittance that the club couldn't afford it. Ken would, I am sure, have loved to have spent the fee we got for Justin on some new players, but he was only given a small amount to play with, spending that on the player seen as Justin's replacement, Keith Bertschin, who joined us from Birmingham City. The fact we'd signed him from them wasn't so much a problem for the Norwich fans, it was having included Ipswich Town on his CV of previous employers! So poor old Keith was up against it from the start with a section of the Norwich support who had not only lamented the departure of Justin but were now being expected to put their full support behind someone who used to play for the enemy. Replacing Justin was going to be a difficult enough job for anyone, on the pitch and in the hearts of the fans. And Keith wasn't, in any way at all, a similar type of player.

Justin was power and grace, he was an athlete, he had balance, poise and pace but he was able to mix that with, if needed, the sheer brute strength and aggression that you'd expect from someone who was also a highly skilled boxer. Keith, on the other hand, was more of an 'old school' striker, the type who'd go into action with his sleeves rolled up and his socks rolled down.

If an opposing team's defenders were all arms and elbows, Keith would be in the middle of the melee taking the kicks and the knocks and doing whatever it took to get the ball in the opposing team's net. He'd never win Goal of the Season but he'd win plenty of battles and be there for the tap-ins else be the player who scored off his knee or backside. He was a fighter, a scrapper and just what we needed.

With Keith taking his place in attack alongside Greig Shepherd and with me in the number-seven shirt, confidence was, for all the monetary concerns at the club, fairly high as we travelled up to Rotherham for our first game of the season. Now, I mean absolutely no disrespect to them here, and we didn't at the time, but running out at Millmoor in front of a crowd of just under 9,000 people is a bit different to doing the same at Highbury, Old Trafford or Anfield. It's a culture shock and a reminder, if you needed one, that playing at the highest level of the game isn't something that I, or any of my team-mates, could take for granted. No one had expected us to go down at the end of the previous season as we were slowly beginning to establish ourselves in the First Division under John Bond. If you look back now at all the clubs who started the 1980/81 season in the top league, then you'd notice there were quite a few clubs similar in size or maybe just a little bit bigger and more established than Norwich, the likes of Ipswich (who did remarkably well in finishing second), West Bromwich Albion, Southampton, Stoke City and Brighton, all of whom stayed up. We might, reasonably, have been expected to finish ahead of Brighton; indeed, they would have been many people's favourites for the drop at the start of the season but they finished two points ahead of us as well as having a better goal difference. We'd beaten them at Carrow Road 3-1 that February; that had been the game that saw Martin O'Neill make his debut and we looked a class above them throughout the match, a result and performance that had given us the belief that we'd get out of trouble. But what is it they say about fine margins? I'm thinking of the corresponding game between the two teams at the old

Goldstone Ground in September when we lost 2-0, despite them having Neil McNab sent off. Had we won that game, we would have stayed up and they'd have gone down.

We'd let our standards drop and had paid the price throughout the season with some poor performances, of which that game down in Sussex was one of the worst. We'd now paid the price and Millmoor was the first of the 42 harsh punishments we'd be facing this new season as a result of that. We had to be up for each and every game and it started here in the modest confines of the Millers' South Yorkshire ground.

Well, they turned us over. You may have gone to that game as full of hope as we were prior to kick-off. You'd have celebrated with us as, after just seven minutes, Greig Shepherd put us ahead. Promotion here we come. It sounds more than a bit stupid coming at just seven minutes into a new season, but I think everyone believed it at that precise moment. Anyway, we switched off and that was all Rotherham needed as Rodney Fern equalised a minute later, and from that moment on, and inspired by a winger by the name of Tony Towner, they took us apart. Welcome to Division Two lads. Let your guard slip and the opposition will have you. Rotherham weren't afraid of us in the same way we hadn't been frightened of Manchester United when they went 2-0 up against us the previous season at Carrow Road, we stuck to the job in hand and got a point. Rotherham had done to us what we had done to Manchester United. We had to sort ourselves out. And fast.

At around the time of that game, the state of the club's finances was made public and it didn't make good reading as the club's accounts recorded an annual loss of £327,000, a colossal amount. That meant, of course, that, Keith Bertschin aside, Ken Brown wasn't going to be able to spend any money on new players but would have to, just as John Bond before him, trust and give some opportunities to the club's younger players, the ones who, like me, were making their way through the ranks.

That meant, as the season progressed, debuts for Andrew Hart, John Fashanu, Paul Haylock and Peter Mountford. Of that quartet, only Paul went on to have a decent career at Norwich, although John, of course, did well with Wimbledon, amongst others, after he'd left Norwich. But it was hard on some of these players who, with the best will in the world, may have ended up in the first team before they were anywhere near ready. Peter only made four appearances in total for Norwich, three of which came from the bench, whilst Andrew was a one-game wonder, his 17-minute cameo against Newcastle from the substitutes' bench on 19 September being his only appearance for Norwich and, indeed, in professional football before he drifted into the non-league game with Gorleston.

Think about it. The club has just been relegated. We're in serious debt, so much so that Ken Brown is drafting players into the first team who may not even be good enough. And we're looking to get promotion from a Second Division that, in addition to ourselves, also includes big clubs like Sheffield Wednesday, Leicester City, Newcastle United, Chelsea, Crystal Palace and Derby County. So although the pressure is on us to get straight back into the top flight (and it wouldn't be long before Ken Brown started to feel some of that pressure via the back pages of the newspapers), it's going to be just the same, if not more, at a lot of other clubs. Expectation and pressure isn't a modern phenomenon in football, not for players and especially not for managers. Ken may well have been lucky to have kept his job when we went down in 1981, but he probably wouldn't have held on to it if we didn't look as if we were serious about getting back to Division One at the first attempt. By the middle of February 1982, it looked almost certain that we wouldn't be doing so. We'd gone up to Oldham to play them, they were then in or around the top two and looking a pretty good bet to get the promotion that we seemed to be doing our best to avoid. And they outplayed us in a fractious game, winning 2-0, the defeat dropping us down to 12th in the table.

There had been, up to then, all sorts of rumours about Ken losing his job. Martin Peters was being linked with his position, as was Geoff Hurst, the man who'd scored a hat-trick for England in the 1966 World Cup Final a little under 15 years earlier. He'd previously been in charge at Chelsea, who were then in the same division as us (how times change!) and had just missed out on taking them up in 1980 before coming close again the following season before being sacked in April 1981. So whilst he didn't have a promotion on his coaching CV, it certainly looked as if he knew what it took to get a club in the right place at the right time. He'd also made the club some money through player sales, a quality that was always going to appeal to the Norwich board, but most of all he was a big name and the prevailing logic must have been that his presence at the club might attract players as well as commercial possibilities that hadn't, up until then, been realised.

I had a lot of time for Ken and didn't want to see him lose his job. Yes, we'd had some bad results that season but I, along with the rest of the lads, felt that we were in a false position in mid-table and that we were a much better side than our league placing suggested. But we weren't the only ones. Way back in August, in fact, right after the first game of the season, the one that had seen us lose 4-1 to Rotherham, Millers manager Emlyn Hughes, once of Liverpool and England, had said we were a good side and we'd be there or thereabouts in May. We just had to prove him right but we were making it very difficult for ourselves. That is until Martin O'Neill returned to the club. He hadn't settled at Manchester City, who were, at that time, having the sort of financial crisis that made our own pale into insignificance. John Bond had gone there because he fancied being at the helm of a bigger club with a bigger budget, but he was, in the middle of the 1981/82 season, being forced to reduce his wage bill and to cut costs on the playing side as much as possible. Their financial woes were so acute that they hadn't even been able to make some of the payments on the money they owed us from the Kevin Reeves transfer, something that the club used to its advantage when Ken enquired about the possible availability of Martin and whether or not he'd consider a return to Norwich?

There was no need for Martin to come back, of course. He had, after all, left Norwich because he didn't want to play in the Second Division, something he'd made very clear to Ken when he signed in the first place and the reason why the opt-out clause on relegation was included in his contract. So would he be interested in returning? It seemed improbable. It wasn't as if we were top of the table and clear of the pack, we were struggling to even establish ourselves in the top ten. Plus, of course, Martin didn't come cheap, he'd been paid a fortune in his first stay with us and would, unquestionably, be our highest earner again if he came back.

So neither I nor any of the other lads thought anything of it until, surprise surprise, there was Martin back again at Trowse one morning, ready to train and a Norwich player again, all for the sum of £125,000, which the club had knocked off the amount we were still owed for Kevin Reeves. Ken had sold his vision of the club and where he wanted to take us and it gave us all a boost of self-belief that maybe hadn't been there before and, following that drab defeat at Oldham, we went on a run of just two defeats in 16 games, including, at one point, six consecutive wins in the league, the sixth of which, a 2-0 win at home to Orient, meaning that we'd only need a point from our last game of the season at Sheffield Wednesday to seal an unlikely return to the First Division. Martin had played a big part in our good form, but, as we soon found out, was quite content to go out and do his own thing between games – and by that I mean he wasn't out on the golf course, or, as me and some of the lads would have been, Marky Barham included, down at Barford Lakes doing a spot of fishing. No, Martin was that rare thing for a professional footballer, he was a bit of an intellectual and liked to spend his time off with a book or a day trip to a place of interest. When we played Barnsley up at their place, he tried to persuade Mick McGuire to accompany him on a trip to look at the house where the Yorkshire Ripper used to live. Martin was fascinated by stories relating to crime and human misdemeanour, but it wasn't an interest shared by any of the other lads and Mick turned down his invitation, preferring to stay at our hotel and put his feet up!

Typically for my luck at the time, I was missing out on the late season surge. I'd played and scored in a 2-0 win at Shrewsbury before breaking my toe in a tackle and having to come off. That was it for me for the season and I became a frustrated spectator for the remaining games, the most impressive of which was a 4-1 win at Leicester City, a game that saw another of Ken's inspired purchases, striker John Deehan, or Dixie as everyone called him, open the scoring.

We took 10,000 fans up to Sheffield with us for that last league game, but they, and we, went through the proverbial mill on a very warm afternoon. We didn't get the point we needed but with Leicester, our nearest rivals, losing their game we ended the day in third place and had, against all the odds, won promotion back to the First Division at the first attempt, justification for the faith that the board had, eventually, put into Ken as well as Keith Bertschin. Keith, a fellow angler, had endured quite a bit of stick when he first joined us, but he'd worked hard and ended the season with 12 league goals, two more than Dixie. I'd had, toe injury aside, a pretty good season myself, 29 appearances all told in the league and six goals scored, one of the sweetest of those coming in a 2-1 win over Chelsea, an early first time shot from distance that I reckon Steve Francis knew nothing about until he heard it hit the net behind him.

Once we'd returned from a quick end-of-season trip out to Jamaica, everyone went their separate ways to go on holiday and do what all professional football players do during the summer, which is let their hair down – and then some. I was, by then, in a relationship with a lovely girl by the name of Gabrielle, who I'd met in a wine bar in Norwich which meant it was a very happy pre-season for me even if I had to combine relaxing and enjoying spending lots of time with her by keeping my fitness levels up. And just as well really, as all too soon it was time to return for pre-season training, and with that our first game of that pre-season, which was at non-league Corby Town, a game that ended up being abandoned at half-time due to torrential rain, no bad thing really as we were losing 1-0 at the time.

We then had a couple more friendlies at Southend United (won 4-0) and Bournemouth (won 3-1) before playing the first of three fixtures in something called the Football League Trophy. We didn't do too badly in that, beating Northampton 3-0, Peterborough United 6-2 and Mansfield 3-1. It's the sort of pre-season form that gets fans just a little bit excited about what might lie ahead and maybe there were a few people at the club who in the wake of the Mansfield game might have thought we were a little better than we were. But that's not a good way of thinking. We were, after all, playing lower league teams in a competition that no one was taking particularly seriously. It's easy to look good under those circumstances, just as it is easy to get complacent after a couple of wins. And, yes, we'd beaten those teams convincingly enough. But we would soon be playing teams like Manchester City, Arsenal, Everton and Tottenham in Division One, a different level altogether with opponents who had far better players than any we'd so far faced in pre-season, something Ken Brown wouldn't have hesitated to remind us of – and on more than one occasion.

Pre-season training is usually a chance to meet and get to know any new faces about the place, the result of a club strengthening its ranks prior to another season of hard slog. We didn't have that pleasure, however, as, due to the club's ongoing financial woes, Ken wasn't able to bring in anyone of note. One player who we never saw again was record signing Drazen Muzinic who was released. Big things had been expected of him when he'd arrived in Norfolk, a player who'd impressed at the highest level for both club and country but, for whatever reason, it never even came close to happening for Drazen in Norwich. He was a nice enough chap and his quality showed in training, but he never got to grips with the language, or, for that matter, living in England and I think his departure was, in the end, a blessed relief for all concerned. One player who had been looking good and who continued that form into pre-season though was Ross Jack, who hit a hat-trick in the win over Peterborough. He'd cost the club just £20,000 when he joined from Everton and looked worth every penny and more, so much so that for a while we wondered if he'd end up moving to a big club for a large fee. That would, at least, have given Ken a little money to spend, but Ross stayed put and duly found himself, perhaps to his surprise, on the bench for our first game of the season, which was a rather tasty looking one against Manchester City, managed, of course, by former Norwich gaffer John Bond.

If we'd needed a reality check, then we got it in that game. City were ahead after just two minutes when David Cross, another former Canary, headed in the opener and worse was to come when, right on half-time, Paul Power turned a Ray Ranson cross past Chrissy Woods. They were, to be fair, a decent side, or so it seemed at the time. But so were we and we were confident of coming good. The lead-in to that match hadn't really helped anyone mind you, as with the big story of John Bond returning to Carrow Road (and I don't know why, as we'd played them both, with Bond as their manager in the 1980/81 season, and hardly any fuss had been made about it then), Anglia TV tried to set up an interview that featured the two of them together, something that never came off as they both allegedly refused to be sat in the same studio as the other. Bond then said something along the lines of how Ken was still angry about the circumstances of his departure from the club which was, in honesty, a bit beneath him and not what I would have expected. But, gent that he was, John was big enough to apologise to Ken after the game and that little spat was over as quickly as it had begun.

Three days later we headed down to Highbury to play Arsenal, a team who were, at that time, full of attacking flair and goalscoring possibilities. You could mark one of those goal threats out of the game only to let another one in. Alan Sunderland, Tony Woodcock, Lee Chapman and Graham Rix were all quality players that you simply couldn't give even the tiniest of space to. Woodcock in particular was a good player and he was fast, like a certain something off a stick fast if I'm honest. We'd done well to keep them to 0-0 going into the last 15 minutes or so of the game when, bang, he ran into an empty space before we had a chance to react and put them ahead.

Things weren't going so well for me either. I'd played for the whole 90 minutes against Manchester City but found myself getting taken off by Ken in this match as he replaced me with Peter Mountford. Peter was, like me, a midfielder who liked to cover as much of the pitch as possible, and in doing so make his presence felt to the opposition and perhaps unsettle them a little. So it was pretty much a like-for-like swap. I never liked being hooked in any game and my main concern on this occasion was that if Peter played well then Ken might have opted to start him in our next game at Swansea, which would leave me on the bench. As far as this particular game was concerned, we did well to get back into the game almost immediately, when barely a minute later Dixie (John Deehan) scored from a header, not a typical type of goal from Dixie but one that went down well with us and the Norwich fans there on the night as we held on for a 1-1 draw.

It was enough to send us on our way to Swansea for our next game with a little bit of impetus running through the camp. They'd had a fairly decent start to their season, drawing with Notts County (then a top-flight club, one that beat both Manchester clubs, Everton and Aston Villa that season but ended the 2018/19 campaign relegated to non-league football) and Coventry. So, like I said, decent enough, albeit against fairly modest opposition – they'd played Notts County and Coventry whilst we'd had to contend with Manchester City and Arsenal. So, even if we'd just got one point from six up until our afternoon at the Vetch, we went into the game confident of getting something. I was particularly happy as Peter Mountford had done nothing to convince Ken he was worthy of a starting place ahead of me after his cameo at Arsenal (he only featured once more that season before joining Charlton) which meant I started, wearing the number-11 shirt, in a more than handy Norwich side that read as follows: Woods, Haylock, Smith, McGuire, Walford, Watson, Barham, O'Neill, Deehan, Bertschin and Mendham. You can't argue that there aren't some quality players in that starting XI; three of them went on to play for England at senior level whilst Martin O'Neill had spent the summer in Spain, not on holiday but playing for Northern Ireland in the World Cup.

Well, we were atrocious. Terrible. Swansea had some decent players as well, one of whom was Bob Latchford, the former Everton and England striker who proceeded to make us look like a Sunday league team as he helped himself, to a hat-trick, with Robbie James adding another to give them a 4-0 win, one that lifted them up to second in the table but saw us drop down to 19th. Latchford was quality and, as much as it hurt on the day, I enjoyed watching him that afternoon as, indeed, I did any good player who I was on the pitch with. He was 31 then, not exactly near to quitting time but certainly not in the first flush of youth either, and he might have thought his career was on the wane when he left Everton, but there was no sign of it that afternoon. He was head and shoulders above every other player on the pitch.

That was all very well and good, but it meant that after playing three games we had just one point and had conceded six goals. I felt for Colin Smith, a defender who we'd signed from Nottingham Forest who was playing just his second game for us that afternoon. His arrival at the club was, in a way, symbolic of the financial play of things at Norwich back then; Ken had been very keen to sign some new players and integrate them into his first-team squad that summer, but no money had been available so, still needing to bolster the numbers, he took a chance on Colin who'd been released by Forest at the beginning of the year. Colin had, by then, played a few games in Hong Kong as well as having a trial with Huddersfield, who were then in Division Three. That hadn't worked out either and the story went around that Colin was about to sign on the dole before Ken made him an offer. It must, I guess, have taken Colin by surprise when that happened;

Hong Kong was pretty much a footballing backwater at that time, whilst Huddersfield were a middling Third Division side who at the end of that season only just escaped relegation to the bottom tier by four points. So, after his trial with them didn't work out and with Colin set to be handed his UB40 card, he might have been forgiven for thinking a career in professional football wasn't going to happen for him at any level.

Then, just as he is least expecting it, he gets an offer from the manager of a First Division club. He'd done well enough, to be fair, at Arsenal but then, as a debutant, he'd been eased through that game by Dave Watson and Steve Walford. But they couldn't keep an eye on him in every game and at Swansea Colin was, as were we all, made aware of his responsibilities and expected to get on with it, which meant, on this occasion, having to deal with Bob Latchford, an ex-England striker with the smell of blood in his nostrils. We all struggled that day, but Colin did more than most and it came as no surprise to anyone, least of all, I suspect, Colin himself, when he was replaced by Greg Downs in our next game, which was at home to Birmingham City.

Looking back, I do wonder if in Colin Ken Brown was trying to make a point to the Norwich board. He'd just won us promotion to Division One and was expected to make do with the squad that had ended the previous season winning that promotion by just one point and, over our 42-game league season, winning just 22 of them, so just over half of our games. So we were a good Division Two side but not an outstanding one, like, for example, Luton, who finished as champions, 17 points ahead of us. So we needed quality additions, two or three top-class players who would be able to make a difference, players who the likes of Chris Woods, Dave Watson and John Deehan would look over in training and think, 'yep, he'll do', just as we had when, for example, Martin O'Neill pitched up for the first time.

Colin was a decent lad and a competent-enough player, but he wasn't ever going to make the grade at the highest level. Cloughie and Forest had known that; they'd released him without him even playing a game for them. Even Mick Buxton up at Huddersfield, a so-so player himself who went on to become a highly respected coach, had, after seeing Colin on trial, decided he wasn't good enough for them. So what had Ken Brown seen that Brian Clough and Mick Buxton hadn't? I wonder if this was Ken's way of saying to the board that on the budget he had it would be players like Colin he'd be bringing to the club, the type of players who weren't quite good enough and who would, at the very top level, likely struggle, just as Colin had done at Swansea.

Subtle. But a telling way of letting the people who mattered know that if he wasn't able to bring the sort of players he wanted to Norwich City, then the club was set for another season of struggle and a relegation battle, a third in under a decade, that no one at Carrow Road wanted.

### *Especially the board*

I'm not saying that Colin was brought in as a bit of a sacrificial lamb and that he was expected to fail because he didn't. He was a good professional, but as I have already said he didn't have the quality needed to compete for a starting place in a team that was looking to re-establish itself in the top division of English football. He wasn't the first to have been given a chance by Norwich to do so and most certainly wasn't the last either. The list, for example, of promising young players of whom big things were expected at Norwich, who, nonetheless, didn't make it with us, or even in the professional game, is a long one and it will get longer by the year and well into the future. Football is merciless. There are many different reasons why football can chew you up and spit you out, and this is just one of them. But regardless of whether or not he meant it, or thought there was a chance the signing wouldn't work out, his arrival and rapid departure from Carrow Road showed that if we wanted to stay in this league then, financial difficulties or not, Ken needed to be able to sign players of proven quality rather than, as he had with Colin, being forced to take a gamble.

Following that heavy defeat at Swansea, the last thing we needed was a reunion with another one of our ex-managers at Carrow Road. John Bond's arrival with his Manchester City side on the opening day of the season had been a story in itself, one that Anglia TV had been only too pleased to hype up as a battle between John and Ken Brown, two former colleagues that had fallen out and who were now not even on speaking terms.

It was an approach you might have expected one of the less reputable red-top newspapers to take rather than our local television station, who were, if I am honest, more well known for shows like *Sale of the Century* ('It's the quiz of the week') and *Tales of the Unexpected* than the sort of controversy they'd tried to whip up with John and Ken. Fortunately for everyone, they didn't take the same approach for the arrival of Birmingham City on 8 September. Their manager was Ron Saunders, who had been, of course, John's predecessor at the club. Mind you, Ron didn't suffer fools gladly and I am sure that if someone had shoved a camera in his face and tried to get a reaction about his return to Norwich then they would have got one – but not the sort of response they wanted.

Ever the gentleman, Ken Brown made a point of welcoming Ron in his programme piece for the game, championing the successes he had enjoyed at Norwich as well as recalling his first meeting with him which had been when Ron was in charge of Yeovil, and Ken, coming towards the end of his playing days, was at Torquay United. Ron, who knew a good player when he saw one (some of his signings for Norwich, notably Graham Paddon and Jim Bone, are testament to that), offered Ken the opportunity to come and play for him at Yeovil, one that Ken, after some thought, turned down as he didn't want to end his career playing non-league football. He went on to add that they'd remained in touch and the two of them had been good friends ever since.

Typical Ken. He'd been lured into a bit of a media honey trap when John Bond had arrived with his Manchester City side at the start of the season, something which he neither enjoyed nor approved of. He wasn't going to let that happen again, and even if he and Ron had never worked together (although they came close to it down at Yeovil), the fact that Ron was an ex-Norwich manager was enough to get a few people excited and want to build it into something it wasn't. Ken was right, of course. Football is a game where the nature of the work is very transitory. That applies to both players and managers, yet, with regards to the latter, no one seemed to mention that Birmingham were the club that we'd signed Keith Bertschin from other than the Norwich programme editor who slipped in a little piece where Keith mentioned playing his old mates. Managers and players will always return to their former clubs, and in recent years Norwich have welcomed both Paul Lambert and Chris Hughton back with the clubs they went on to take charge of after their time with the Canaries came to an end. With Paul there has always been a bit of friction whenever he arrives at Carrow Road with another club, something that came to a controversial head when Norwich played his Ipswich Town side in February 2019. These games are tense enough without the rival manager having previously been 'one of your own', but for all the usual exchanges between the two sets of fans the person who got the most wound up during the game itself was Paul, who ended up being sent off for his troubles! I'm not sure that there was ever the slightest chance of that happening to Ken whenever we went to play West Ham, the club he served as a player from 1953 to 1967; they love him down there now as much as they did when he was playing alongside the likes of Bondy and Bobby Moore, so that was never going to be an issue.

Ken hadn't held back in training in the days after the Swansea game and he didn't hold back on letting us know what he'd thought about that match and our performances that season so far either. Greg Downs came back in to replace Colin Smith, and with him on one side of the back four and Paul Haylock the other we had a little bit of extra width which he intended to use against the Birmingham defence, which, full of experience as it was, with players like Dave Langan, Mark Dennis and Pat van den Hauwe, didn't have an awful lot of mobility. Ken felt we could get at them and should do from the start, reasoning that Ron would have them set up in a rigid 4-4-2 that would look to get a point first and foremost with anything else a bonus.

We did that and were 3-1 up and cruising at half-time, thanks to goals by Keith Bertschin and a couple from Martin O'Neill (a prime example of the sort of quality we needed), the second of which he hit from distance with all the skill and confidence of a player who was right at the top of his game. Brilliant. Martin ran the show that day as we won 5-1 with Keith getting another late on, in addition to one from Mark Barham.

We all knew what everyone would be saying at the end of the game. Fans, manager and coaches, the reporters from the local papers – why haven't you been playing like that since the start of the season?

It should have been both the result and the performance that lit the yellow and green touch paper for the rest of our season. We'd been far too good for Birmingham on the day, we'd passed them off the pitch and down on to Riverside and beyond. There was no reason we shouldn't have carried on in that manner. Martin O'Neill was in imperious form; Keith Bertschin and John Deehan were as good a strike force as any in the division, whilst at the back we had two future England internationals in Chris Woods and Dave Watson as well as Steve Walford plus Mark Barham in a wide position, and, of course, me, chasing and harrying and doing my best to get into good positions playing the pass that got people like him, Bertsch and Dixie into attacking positions. We were a good side. We just needed that little bit of extra quality, someone to take some of the responsibility away from Martin and, to a lesser extent, Mark Barham.

The problem was, we'd just beaten Birmingham City 5-1. With a starting XI who were all, without exception, at the club the previous season. So maybe that result didn't do us any favours in that the board would have been looking on and thinking we didn't need to waste any money we didn't have on good players as the current bunch had just gone out there and convincingly beaten a side that <u>had</u> been able to spend a bit of money over the last few seasons or so. There was no argument to be had, not that I think Ken would have had much luck in winning it even if he had been able to sit down with the board and argue his case.

Our form after the win against Birmingham was not good. By New Year's Day, which saw us lose 1-0 at Stoke, we'd played 22 league games and won just six of them. We were 19th in the table and had a squad so sparse in numbers and quality that Ken had been forced to play John Deehan at left-back in that game – and it was Dixie, our best striker, who'd made the error that allowed Sammy McIlroy to score the only goal. Ken had, at least, been able to play a few new faces in the time leading up to then. Seven to be exact, of which four were 'graduates' from the youth team, namely Phil Alexander, Mark Metcalf, Matt Crowe and Louie Donowa. Dennis Van Wijk had also joined the club from Ajax, not that we paid any money for him as he'd originally signed on a non-contract basis. Joining them was Mick Walsh who arrived on loan from Everton and another Mick, albeit a rather more well-known one, a certain Mick Channon.

He is, of course, best remembered for the two spells he had with Southampton as well as the games and goals he played for England, the latter always being marked with his famous 'windmill' celebration. Mick was 34 when he joined us. He'd been seeing out time really with Bristol Rovers and probably never thought he'd play in the First Division again, but Ken knew he could make a difference and he did. His legs might not have been as good as they were but his footballing brain was as cute as anyone's – here was a man who knew his stuff. He was never going to take life at Norwich too seriously; indeed, he compared playing for us on more than one occasion to turning out for a kick-about for a village team and just having some fun with his mates. He made his debut for us the day after Boxing Day, a tasty festive clash with Ipswich. We won that game 3-2, one I will never forget as I scored our first two goals, the first of which was a header, something of a collector's item in the Mendham scrapbook. Russell Osman and

Paul Mariner popped in a couple of goals for them which meant it was 2-2 going into the last couple of minutes and a bit tense for the 30,000 or so packed into Carrow Road. But we were never going to lose that game, and with time nearly up Martin O'Neill curled an absolute beauty past Paul Cooper to seal the points and the Christmas glory for us.

It was one of the high points of a fairly dismal season that had genuinely, at one stage, looked as if we were going to have a real struggle not to drop back into Division Two. The low point was probably a 4-0 defeat at Southampton on 5 February. Things down at The Dell didn't get off to the best of starts when Dave Watson had to go off with a head injury, and with only one substitute to call on back then the fact our number 12 on the day was Greg Downs meant we didn't have a lot of height in the back four all of a sudden, something Southampton immediately benefitted from as they opened the scoring with Dave off the pitch and with Ken Brown, at that time, not knowing if he would need to replace him or not. It summed up our day really – we were caught short and paid the price with a heavy defeat that dropped us to just one place off the bottom.

We were saved in the end by a run of four consecutive league wins in April, one of which was at Liverpool and their only home defeat of the season. How was it we could beat them at Anfield and Carrow Road plus put five goals past Birmingham and four past Swansea and then Birmingham again (who must have been sick of the sight of us, that was 9-1 on aggregate!) yet also let in five against Swansea as well as another four at Manchester City when they did us 4-1 on 15 January? Blowing hot, cold and ever colder, that was us throughout the season, and although that little run of wins at the end eventually helped to lift us up to a finishing place of 14th it wasn't good enough and we all knew it.

There was, at least, some good news when it was announced that after the enormous financial loss the previous year (the one that had so restricted Ken Brown in the transfer market) the club was able to post a working profit in that year's accounts. So things might have been looking up all of a sudden, maybe Ken would have some money to spend in the summer of 1983. That news all coincided with the election of a new chairman, a man by the name of Robert Chase. It was a name that was to become very familiar to Norwich City fans over the next few seasons.

*The Mendham children: Steve, self, Lynne and Paul. Peter Mendham-private collection*

Nº 6297      *Peter Stanley Mendham*

Name of Schoolboy

This is to certify that you have this day been registered as an Associated Schoolboy with The Football

League Ltd. for the......*NORWICH CITY*............Football Club.

Date......*6/2/75*............        ........................................

To be signed by a responsible official of the club

L. Form 9      This portion to be completed by a responsible official of the club and handed to the player at the time of signing      UPS36523 12.73

*My schoolboy registration certificate at Norwich City. Peter Mendham-private collection*

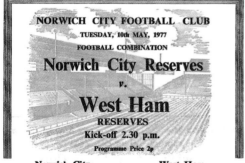

*A reserve team programme – some good players on each side. Peter Mendham-private collection*

*Ken Brown, a man who had such a great influence on my football career*

*A souvenir from
a pre-season game
against Bulova
in Hong Kong.
Photo courtesy of
the* Lynn News
& Advertiser

*Fighting for
possession with
Stoke City's
Paul Bracewell.
Photo courtesy of
Archant Publishing*

*Summer in New Zealand spent with Miramar Rangers. Peter Mendham-private collection*

*Mark Barham and I up against Ray Kennedy of Liverpool.*

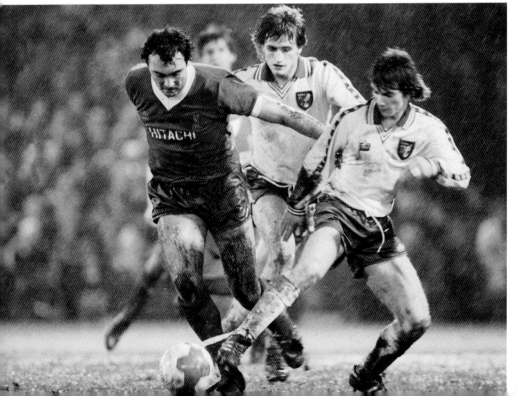

Promoting QPR's artificial
pitch along with Tony
Currie. Peter Mendham-
private collection

Norwich City pre-season line-up 1983/84. I'm third from right on
bottom row. Norwich City Football Club

Training at Bisham Abbey with Mel Machin and John Devine before our FA Cup game against
Tottenham on 28 January 1984

**SCHEDULE**

a) The Player's employment with the Club began on the . . . . . . . . . . . . . . . . . . . . . . 25 JUNE . . . . . . . . . . . . 19 76 . . . . . .

b) No employment with a previous employer shall count as part of the Player's continous period of employment hereunder.

c) The Player shall become or continue to be and during the continuance of his employment hereunder shall remain a member of The Football League Players' Benefit Scheme (and a member of the . . . . . . . . . . . . . . . . . . . . . . . . . . . . . . . . . . . . . . . . . . . . . . . . . . . Pension Scheme) and as such (in the latter case shall be liable to make such contributions and in each case) shall be entitled to such benefits and subject to such conditions as are set out in the definitive Trust Deed or Rules of the Scheme.

d) A contracting out certificate is not in force in respect of the Player's employment under this Agreement.

e) Basic Wage.

£ . . . . . 400 . . . . . . . . . per week from . . . . . . 1.11.85 . . . . . . to . . . . . . 30.6.88 . . . . . .

£ . . . . . . . . . . . . . . . . . per week from . . . . . . . . . . . . . . . . . . to . . . . . . . . . . . . . . . . .

£ . . . . . . . . . . . . . . . . . per week from . . . . . . . . . . . . . . . . . . to . . . . . . . . . . . . . . . . .

£ . . . . . . . . . . . . . . . . . per week from . . . . . . . . . . . . . . . . . . to . . . . . . . . . . . . . . . . .

f) Any other provisions:–

FOOTBALL COMBINATION WIN AND DRAW BONUS TO BE PAID AS PER RULE.

A ONCE ONLY SIGNING ON FEE OF £13,000 WILL BE PAYABLE IN EQUAL ANNUAL INSTALMENTS AS FOLLOWS:–

£4,333.33 LESS TAX ON 1ST DECEMBER 1985
£4,333.33 LESS TAX ON 1ST DECEMBER 1986
£4,333.33 LESS TAX ON 1ST DECEMBER 1987

FOR ADDITIONAL PAYMENTS SEE SCHEDULE ATTACHED.

Signed by the said . . . . . . P S MENDHAM . . . . . . . . . . . . . . . . . . . . . . . . . . . . . . . . . . . . (Player)

and . . . . . . N S PLEASANTS . . . . . . . . . . . . . . . . . . . . . . . . . . . . . . . . . . (Secretary/Manager/Chairman)

in the presence of

(Signature) . . . . . . . . . . . . . . . . . . . . . . . . . .

(Occupation) . . . . . . . . . . . . . . . . . . . . . . . . . .

(Address) . . . . . . CARROW ROAD NORWICH . . . . . . . . . . . . . . . . . . . . . . . . . .

. . . . . . . . . . . . . . . . . . . . . . . . . . . . . . . . . . .

4

*Part of the new contract I signed at Norwich City in 1985. Peter Mendham-private collection*

*Helping Paul Haylock celebrate his 22nd birthday at Carrow Road (note burnt down City Stand in background) which would coincide with our Milk Cup Final clash with Sunderland on 24 March 1985.*

*Gazing down at my Milk Cup winners' medal after our 1-0 win over Sunderland at Wembley. Archant*

*Celebrations in full swing after our Wembley triumph – Mick Channon is enjoying himself!*

*Celebrating with John Devine after the match!*

*Milk Cup homecoming in Norwich – an unforgettable night. Archant*

# Norwich City
## Football Club Limited

Registered Office: Carrow Road, Norwich, NR1 1JE
Telephone: (0603) 612131 3 lines

Company Registration No. 154044 England    VAT No. 105 4810 04

Milk Cup Winners 1984–85

KB/ALB

28th October 1985

Mr P Mendham

Dear Peter

This is to inform you that you have been fined the sum
of £75 for failing to turn up for the recent team trip
to Trinidad.

Yours sincerely

K Brown
**Manager**

*Not the sort of letter you like getting! Peter Mendham-private collection*

*Pre-season portrait. Archant*

*Our bonus system for our participation in the 1986/87 Full Members Cup tournment – we lost to Charlton in the semi-finals. Peter Mendham-private collection*

*In the thick of it in a game against Brighton. Archant*

*John Toshack, then manager of Real Sociedad in Spain and I after my testimonial match against them. Peter Mendham-private collection*

*The new player manager of King's Lynn FC strikes a confident pose.*
Lynn News and Advertiser

*With Richard Keys from Sky Sports at Carrow Road*

*Celebrations
with Diss Town*

EASTERN COUNTIES

DISS TOWN FOOTBALL CLUB
WINNERS

PATRICK

DISS TOWN FC

*Another open-top bus homecoming – this time with Diss Town! Archant*

*With the East Anglian Air
Ambulance – a job I loved!
Peter Mendham-private
collection/EAAA*

*I love my fishing – this rather lovely
carp was caught at Barford Lakes
near Norwich. Edward Couzens-Lake*

*HMP Prison Norwich.*

*Happy days! Celebrating with Steve, Lynne and Paul at Lynne's 50th. The future is bright!*

# CHAPTER FIVE

# Joy and Despair

*He was already on a high wage; in fact, I'll go as far
as saying he may well have been, at that point in time,
the best paid player in Norwich's history.*

WE'D ALL gone into the 1982/83 season on a bit of a high. Promotion had been won and with a playing squad that was very much the classic mix of youth and experience that any football team requires if it fancies itself to go places. So we all thought we'd have been able to give it a real go back in the top division of English football. That belief wasn't born out of entitlement or arrogance either, just a deeply felt conviction that we had both the players and management team to do well and look to seal at least a place in the top ten the following May.

It wasn't as if the club had never done it before. Following our promotion under John Bond in 1975, the club had gone on to finish in tenth place at the end of the 1975/76 season, so we all, realistically, felt that was something to at least equal and maybe even surpass, which all meant that a brief but alarming encounter with the relegation places and final placing of 14th wasn't satisfactory to anyone at the football club.

As far as my own life was concerned, though, I was blissfully happy. I was playing for my local football club alongside some great players, many of whom were amongst, and remain, my greatest friends. And, whilst the massive disparity between my earnings and those of Martin O'Neill had given me fair cause to grumble, my own personal remuneration was never that much of an overriding issue as I was just happy to be playing for Norwich City.

Living the dream as they say. Living the yellow-and-green dream.

I was, by now, married to Gabrielle, and on 17 September 1983 we celebrated the birth of our first child. It was a busy old day really! I rushed Gabrielle into the maternity block at the Norfolk & Norwich Hospital just after her waters broke, but just before, as this was a Saturday, I was due to meet up with the rest of the Norwich City first-team squad for our pre-match meal at the Oaklands Hotel on the Yarmouth Road in Norwich prior to our game with Nottingham Forest.

It was a cracking game, one for the neutrals I suppose, but not for Canary fans as we lost 3-2. Forest played well on the day and, despite having some big names in their team, the likes of Colin Todd, Ian Wallace, Peter Davenport and Steve Hodge, won courtesy of a hat-trick from one of their less-heralded players, midfielder Colin Walsh.

I'd usually stay behind after a match regardless of the result, but nothing was going to stop me rushing away as soon as I could after the final whistle as I wanted to see my son being born. Unfortunately, I changed and got away so quickly I got caught up in all the other post-match traffic leaving the ground and got to the hospital later than I would have hoped. But all was well. Gabrielle was still in labour and I tried to make myself as useful as possible, although I don't know how useful the father-to-be can be in such circumstances, but I did my best! Then, wonder of wonders, at 10pm Ross William Francis Mendham made his entry into the world, the greatest gift anyone could have or hold. What a moment. Thus, with both mother and baby doing well, I met up with Judy, Gabrielle's mother, and Tony, her stepfather, in order to wet the baby's head.

When my second son, Jamie Oliver Henry, was born, I was also present and within seconds of his birth was bathing him. Words will never describe how I felt on those two days, being there at the birth of my two sons and welcoming them into the world. It's a feeling, of course, that all parents will be familiar with and they will all, like me and Gabrielle, have memories of those special days. I was now looking forward to when Ross and Jamie would be old enough to watch their father playing for Norwich.

The true scale of life's responsibilities and priorities really hit home for me after Ross had been born. I've already said how happy I was with my lot and that the sheer joy of playing for a football team that I loved meant that I had never been that concerned about what I was being paid, and I was, as a consequence, one of the lowest-paid members of the first-team squad. But now, with a family to support, I began to wonder if my loyalty was being taken for granted by the club?

This really came to the fore for me when during the 1983/84 season I was made aware that Norwich had, in the preceding few months, received some enquiries about me from other clubs who were looking to see if I would be interested in joining them.

I wasn't looking for a move. I loved the club and I loved living in Norfolk, a special place which I often think should have a big brick wall built all around it in order to protect its people and communities from the ravages of the outside world. So I'm glad no motorway comes anywhere near to Norfolk. It's a place you have to want to go to rather than one you idly pass through, and I like that. But that didn't mean I wasn't aware there might be other places and opportunities to explore in life. So when I found out that other clubs had made approaches for me and that I hadn't, on every single occasion, been told about it, I was very upset. Why, I wondered, had that been the case? The club would have been aware of how happy I was at Norwich, but at the same time that didn't give them any entitlement to decide about my career and future. Yet it seemed they'd done exactly that and taken my happiness as a sign that I wouldn't even want to consider going anywhere else.

Even so, I did think they could have made me aware of any interest in me. It's almost certain that, had they done so, I'd have thanked them for letting me know but said I wasn't interested. End of story.

It wasn't as if the club fought tooth and nail to keep hold of its players when there was interest from other clubs either. I'd already seen Kevin Reeves and Justin Fashanu sold for big money, while it was no secret that Dave Watson and Chris Woods, among others, were already attracting admiring glances from other clubs and that the club's ongoing financial difficulties meant that if a big enough bid came in for them then they'd be off.

So why brush off similar interest in me?

I now know that one of the clubs who made more than one enquiry about me was Leeds United, then managed by Eddie Gray. This was the club I'd supported as a boy and Eddie would have been one of the players whose picture I would have had stuck on my wall, him and all the other greats of that all-conquering Leeds team from the 60s and early 70s. Would I have wanted to meet with Eddie to discuss playing for such a great club? Of course I would. Does that mean I would have left Norwich to sign for them? No it doesn't. But I would have liked to have been afforded the courtesy of talking to them, and the club's apparent disregard for what I might have wanted at this time was both, in my opinion, unfair and unreasonable. What if, for example, I'd gone off somewhere to have secret talks with the manager of another club without telling anyone at Carrow Road?

I'd have been in no end of trouble had that ever happened, and rightly so. So this was, for me, a very clear case of double standards. It wasn't as if the club had even told me about the interest but added that I was a valued member of the first-team squad and under contract so they wouldn't have sanctioned a move. I'd have found that reasonable enough. It was the fact that I wasn't told anything at all about these enquiries that was really getting to me.

One thing I was certain of was that knowing other clubs wanted to talk to me would have worked to my advantage when it came to my salary. As I've already said, I was way behind most, if not all, of the other senior players salary wise, and for a while that hadn't bothered me too much, at least when I was young, single and making my way in the game. But that was no longer the case. I was an established first-teamer who up to the start of the 1983/84 season had made 115 competitive appearances for the club. So hardly someone who still needed to prove himself to anyone. Things were different now. I was 23 years old, married and I now had a family. And, whilst a move to another club would hardly have made me a millionaire overnight, I would almost certainly have got a substantial pay rise with it as well as a signing-on fee, money that would have been very useful to a man with new responsibilities in life.

Maybe the fact I was on such low pay is what made the club so desperate to keep hold of me. If, after all, they'd have sold me to Leeds or whoever, the pressure would have been on for Ken to sign a like-for-like replacement. So not only would Norwich have had to find someone who was capable of playing 30-plus games in Division One, they'd also have wanted someone who was content enough to be on a similar wage to me, or else they'd have ended up out of pocket. And when you consider the sort of players who were similar to me, both positionally and in the way they played the game at the time – for example, Geoff Pike at West Ham, Robbie James at Swansea or Ricky Hill at Luton Town – then it's not only extremely likely that, had their clubs even considered selling them in the first place (and if they'd have wanted to come to Norwich anyway), not only would Norwich have ended up paying out more for them than they received for me, they'd, in all probability, have had to double the wage I was on, at least, to get them to agree terms in the first place.

I ended up fretting about the whole thing for quite some time until eventually Gabrielle told me I shouldn't let the issue hang over me and that I should get over to the club and speak to Ken Brown about it. But the opportunity to make my discontent clear came, fortunately, before I got the chance to do that and it revolved around, of all things, an end-of-season tour.

We'd had a busy end to the 1982/83 season. Our last game was at home to Brighton on 14 May, which we won 2-1. I wasn't playing as I'd had a knock in our game against Arsenal a month earlier, one that was bad enough to rule me out for the rest of the season. So I was at the last games more as a fan than an injured player, even though, at that time, the sense of injustice about my opportunities to move on were still at the back of my mind, even as the final whistle went in our game against the Seagulls. Normally that also signals the start of a few weeks' holiday for all the players and staff, but not on this occasion, as two days later we all headed off to Norway for a mini-tour there that involved playing four games in five days. It's not normally something any player welcomes: you've just finished a long and physically demanding season, one that saw four of the lads play in 50 or more games, with quite a few more not far behind that. I'd played in 33 but given I'd had a few injury worries, as well as the fact that Gabrielle was five months pregnant, I was quite keen on a bit of a break myself.

But these tours, which are usually related to sponsorship or some sort of tie-in with a business, are not something you can opt out of as a player. Attendance, if required, is mandatory, written into your contact, so if two days after the season ends you're told to meet up as a squad to fly out to Norway you go, it's as simple as that. Not all such jollies are a trial, of course. You'd have had to lock me up somewhere to prevent me being part of the travelling party that flew out to China in 1980. But this felt different, an obligation rather than an adventure and I wasn't the only one who wasn't enthusiastic at the prospect of heading out there.

Mind you, I'm sure our very own Norwegian, Aage Hareide, was delighted to be popping home for a few days! We duly got on with what we had to do, and two of the games we played were, if I am honest, were a waste of time as we won them 17-1 and 11-2 – the sort of matches that make it very clear to you that your presence is for anything and everything you can think of other than football. Thankfully, it was a bit of a get in, do the job, get out again type of affair, and less than a week after we'd headed out there we were on our way back again, a little under ten months after the first match of pre-season at Corby, to finally have a holiday.

I still wasn't happy though. Being at home for a few weeks gave me all the time in the world to sit and brood about how the club had treated me over the preceding few months, and again Gabrielle suggested that I went in to see Ken Brown or, better still, the new chairman in order to have my say. But I had a better idea, one that I knew would get me a lot more attention from the powers that be than merely having a chat with Ken or Robert Chase.

It concerned the club's pre-season (as opposed to post-season) tour, another jolly which, on this occasion, was a four-game tour of Kenya, which was scheduled to commence soon after we'd reported back for pre-season training at the beginning of July. I therefore put all of my concerns to the back of my mind for a few weeks, enjoyed the time that Gabrielle and I had together before reporting in for pre-season and sweating my nuts off with the rest of the lads at Trowse for a few weeks. But as far as Kenya was concerned I wasn't going and, after telling Gabrielle of my decision, I added that I was putting in a transfer request as well.

I didn't have the option of not going, of course. I had to, and refusing to take part in the tour was a breach of my playing contract with the club, an offence that, had they felt so inclined, Norwich City would have been within their rights to sack me for. But I didn't care. I wasn't, as it turned out, the only player to be in dispute with the club at the time as I then learnt that Steve Walford had also refused to take part in the tour, something which was ultimately resolved when Steve left to join West Ham just before the start of the season. He'd done what needed to be done and had got the result he wanted, now I was hoping that my actions in boycotting the Kenya tour would eventually get me what I felt I deserved.

But it wasn't going to be made easy for either of us. I was at home on the day after the rest of the squad had flown out to Kenya when the phone rang. It was Ken Brown, who got to the point quickly by saying that none of the players wanted me to leave the club and that it might be best if both me and Steve got out there as soon as possible so our respective issues with the club could be quickly resolved. I quickly got in touch with Steve, who was adamant that he wanted to get back to London but added that maybe both our cases would be heard and dealt with more quickly if we did what the manager asked. There was another consideration of course in that, if we both wanted away, we didn't want any prospective new clubs to think we were possible troublemakers so I hastily packed a few things and met up with Steve in order to take a flight out to Nairobi.

It wasn't the most enjoyable of flights but we got there and I even ended up playing in our first match, which we lost 3-1. Yet in a way the stand I had made and effort the club had put in persuading me to fly out there after they'd already arrived made me feel as if I'd made my point.

More importantly, the fact that in that telephone conversation Ken had said that none of the lads wanted me to leave, well, that made an enormous difference to how I was feeling. I still wasn't entirely happy with the terms of my contract but vowed that, rather than continue to make a fuss, I'd knuckle down, work hard and earn the sort of contract I felt I deserved. Yes, the thought of a club like Leeds United being interested in signing me had been an intriguing one but, looking at it from my place on a sun lounger on the east coast of Kenya, I realised that with Gabrielle about to give birth, the prospect of moving house and all the trials and tribulations that go with it wasn't the best of ideas at that precise moment in time, so I ended up telling Ken that I didn't, after all, want to leave and would continue to do my best for him and the team. He was delighted of course and deep down I was relieved the whole issue had been resolved. I'd made my point and was quite sure that when it came to discussing a new contract Mr Chase would be only too aware of how poorly I'd been paid up until then and do everything he could to get me on a salary that was more deserving of a first-team player at Norwich City Football Club.

Ken Brown had, of course, handled the whole situation beautifully. He knew that I wasn't being paid enough now, not after what I'd achieved and how I'd come on as a player since I'd signed my last contract, and I am sure he would, given the opportunity, have made his feelings clear when he met up with Mr Chase when they first sat down together, manager and chairman. So I knew he would always be on my side. He must also have realised, however, that once he'd persuaded me to change my mind and fly out there, my attitude would soften. The lads had made it very clear that they didn't want me to leave, and in such beautiful surroundings it was difficult to feel angry with anything and anyone for very long. The beaches out there were pure white sand, whilst having the opportunity to swim in the beautifully warm and clear waters of the Indian Ocean after a hard morning's training was an experience about as close to pure bliss as I'd ever had.

That tour ended up being really enjoyable, much more so than I had expected. Wally (Steve Walford) enjoyed it as well but he remained focussed on getting away from Norwich. It was nothing personal with him – he said he'd enjoyed his time with us but he wanted to get back to living and working in London – so West Ham was a perfect opportunity for him and he left with everyone's best wishes, with his place in the team and squad being taken by another ex-Arsenal man, Willie Young. He was one of two former Arsenal players that Ken was able to bring on board, signing on a free transfer from Nottingham Forest just two days before the end of the season, along with John Devine, who arrived in June. John had quite a footballing CV for someone who was still only 24, having represented Arsenal in the 1980 FA Cup and UEFA Cup finals as well as having already played for the Republic of Ireland at youth, under-21 and full international level.

John arrived too late to have a chance of joining us in Kenya, but that might have been a blessing for him really, as whilst we were out there pranks and wind-ups were very much the order of the day. One victim in particular was Greg Downs who ended up being more than generous to all of his mates on that tour. The club was really looking after us and had worked with our hosts to ensure that we could have whatever we wanted, all we had to do was sign for it and job done, it was ours. So we all decided to sign Greg's name for whatever it was we ordered at the bar, in the restaurant, on the beach – everything and anything, it all went on to Greg's tab. Mind you, one of the reasons that we picked him out to do so was that we knew he'd take it well and there wouldn't be a ruckus as a result of our largesse, something which would most certainly have been the case had we signed everything away to some members of the squad who were out there!

We hadn't long been back from Kenya before we were heading out to Norway again for our second trip there in three months. More games and three convincing victories in five days meant that we headed home ready to top off pre-season with games at Wokingham, Grimsby Town and Cambridge United with the sun, sand, sea and signing everything in Greg Downs's name nothing more than a fading memory, especially at Cleethorpes which, for all the good things it boasts as a coastal resort, is never going to match the resorts on the Kenyan coast.

But I'd only permit myself to think that for a second or two because it wasn't the sort of attitude you should have had, in my opinion, as a professional footballer. We'd all enjoyed the summer but it was now time to put all the hard graft into practice and get ourselves fine-tuned for the fast approaching 1983/84 season. That meant Blundell Park in Cleethorpes, home to Grimsby Town, was now, for 90 minutes at least, the epicentre of my footballing world. Game face on, get out there, put on a show and convince the manager and those Norwich fans who have made the trip that I was fully committed to the club and ready to play my part.

Naturally enough, it all went well as Grimsby Town, who included a precocious 23-year-old striker by the name of Kevin Drinkell in their ranks, proceeded to beat us 2-1!

After our poor start to the previous season, we were all determined to make amends this time around and get the new season off to a flier. We drew 1-1 at Sunderland in our opening fixture, a game we should have won, really, after Keith Bertschin put us ahead just before the hour mark, but rather than tightening things up and seeing out the game, we sat back a little and that was all Sunderland needed, a slip by Willie Young who looked to be struggling anyway, letting Colin West in to equalise. Four days later, we welcomed Liverpool to Carrow Road, an opportunity, we hoped, to catch them cold early on in the season before they'd had a chance to get into the sort of rhythm that had seen them win the title the previous campaign by 11 points. But who was I kidding? Liverpool didn't need to get into any sort of rhythm, they simply carried on where they'd left off in May, beating us 1-0, thanks to a goal from Graeme Souness. They put out a quality side that evening and, to be fair, we did well to keep it going as a contest. Neal, Lawrenson, Hansen, Dalglish, Rush and Souness, amongst others, in their starting XI? How do you even begin to plan against a team like that? We'd managed, somehow, the previous season, when we did the league double over them. They weren't going to let that happen again and won far more easily than the scoreline suggests.

With Steve Walford gone, we did lack a little bit of strength and mobility at the back for much of that season, qualities that Wally, who was a very underrated player, provided for us in abundance. And regardless of the accompanying fanfare that came with his arrival, Willie Young was never up to the job of replacing Steve at the heart of our defence. But it's easy to say that in retrospect. No one was questioning the decision Ken had made in signing him. Young had made nearly 300 league starts at the highest level for Tottenham, Arsenal and Nottingham Forest, a proven player and a well-known one as well. You could almost go as far as saying that for a club that had been close to being on its financial uppers in recent years, he was a bit of a marquee signing, something that Ken alluded to in his programme notes when he admitted, 'I'm surprised he was available as his reputation speaks for itself.'

As good a player as Willie had undoubtedly been, however, he was clearly past his best and it showed both on the pitch and in training. There is a famous story surrounding him with regard to the latter which occurred after Ken's assistant, Mel Machin, a man who didn't take any nonsense from anyone, took us all out for a run one morning, something which prompted Willie to protest, 'We didn't do any running at Arsenal.' Mel wasn't having that and after a few choice words sent Willie in from training as if he was a naughty schoolboy. His time at Norwich was always going to be brief after that little outburst, and he left us in order to sign for Brighton, where, perhaps, they didn't do any running, shortly before Christmas.

We were also missing Martin O'Neill, who'd left us to join Notts County. Martin had been, not unlike myself, unhappy with the remuneration he was getting at the club and was looking, again not unlike me, for some kind of material acknowledgement for what he had contributed at the club since he returned to us from Manchester City.

He was already on a high wage; in fact, I'll go as far as saying he may well have been, at that point in time, the best-paid player in Norwich's history. Unfortunately for Martin, and not for the first time in his career, he found Robert Chase to be rather more of a challenge than he was maybe expecting so he welcomed the chance to return to Nottingham, where, in all likelihood he became, again at that point in time, the best-paid player in their history as well.

Overall, the 1983/84 season was another frustrating one for us. There were some high points, notably our 3-3 draw with Manchester United on 1 October when, after being 3-0 down after an hour, we fought back to draw 3-3 with Louie Donowa scoring the equaliser in the last minute. It was a result that gave us a lot of confidence, so much so that after a 1-0 win at Birmingham on 10 December we found ourselves up to sixth in the Division One table. We then managed to stay in or around the top ten until early March, when a dreadful run of just one win from our last 12 league games meant we ended the season in a very disappointing 14th place. That one win had been, incidentally, our biggest of the season and remains Norwich's biggest in their top-flight history, a 6-1 thrashing of Watford which perfectly illustrated how good a striker Dixie Deehan was as he scored four in that game. From my own perspective, it was the best season I'd had at the club, starting in all but one of our 42 league games, the one I missed being a good game not to be involved with, as it was our 2-0 defeat at Ipswich on 23 April. One thing that disappointed was my goals return that season – just two in total, one in the league in a 2-2 draw early on at Luton, plus the second in a 3-0 win over Aston Villa in an FA Cup third-round replay on 11 January that, according to my co-writer Ed, was on *Sportsnight* as he remembers rushing out and away from his usual place in the River End to see it all over again on television later that evening!

We had fairly decent runs in both domestic cup competitions that season, reaching the fifth round of the FA Cup before going out to Derby whilst making the quarter-finals of the League or Milk Cup as it was then called, before losing 2-0 at home to Aston Villa who, in the process, got some sort of revenge over us after we'd dumped them out of the FA Cup six days earlier.

Another up and down season. If only we hadn't had that terrible run of results from early March onwards in the league, a total of just nine points from the 36 on offer. If we'd even have made that a vaguely respectable 18 from 36, say two more wins and three draws, then we'd have ended the season with 60 points and probably finished in the top ten, which had been our target all along. But there's a saying isn't there, about how if your auntie had balls, then she'd be your uncle. Everyone plays the 'what if' game in football. What if we'd won that game? What if that penalty hadn't gone in? What if so-and-so hadn't been injured or suspended? What if we'd have done this instead of that? What if our opponents hadn't got that lucky decision that went for them? And so on and so on. You can turn yourselves from relegation candidates to promotion certainties if you played that game long and hard enough. We'd finished where we did in the league because, ultimately, that is where we deserved to finish.

It was very frustrating. I knew we had the makings of a top side at Norwich and no, that wasn't my yellow-and-green-tinted spectacles speaking. Look at the playing squad that we had for that campaign and tell me it was lacking in quality? Mark Barham for one was full of pace and probably the most technically adept player in that squad, one who I was certain would go on to bigger things. Keith Bertschin and John Deehan were up front, and these were, remember, the days when nearly every team played two up top and they were as good as any. They'd scored 62 goals between them over the previous two seasons yet, despite more than proving themselves, were never in with a chance of an international call-up. Why was that? Did England permanently have 20 to 25 players available at that time who were all better options than Bertsch and Dixie?

You could say the same about Chris Woods. He signed for Norwich in 1981 and was outstanding in goal for us from day one, yet he didn't get his first full international call-up until 1985. He made four appearances for England while he was a Norwich player, but was hardly tested in any of them as they were in games against the USA (who were nowhere near the decent international side they are today) plus Egypt, Israel and Canada, all of which were games that he came on as a substitute.

Hardly the sort of situations where Woodsy would be put under pressure and have the chance to prove to the world outside of Norwich and Norfolk what a top keeper he was. He signed for Rangers in July 1986 and you can guess what happened next – all of a sudden he was getting games for England against the likes of Yugoslavia and Spain even though he wasn't, while he was in Scotland, playing against top-class opposition every week, something which he had certainly been used to at Norwich over quite a few seasons.

Dave Watson was another who impressed anyone and everyone who watched him. Dave was as consistent as they come, he'd put in an 8/10 performance on a regular basis; in fact that was standard for Dave, one he rarely, if ever, dropped below. He'd formed a very decent defensive partnership with Steve Walford while Wally (who was such an underrated player, he had so much quality it was unbelievable) was with us, and following Steve's departure to West Ham we spent the whole of the 1983/84 season looking to replace him but with little to no long-term success. Willie Young was meant to be the natural replacement for Steve but that never worked out; Ken also tried Aage Hareide alongside Dave (Watson) and that pairing was looking like it might have had something going for it, only for Aage to unexpectedly leave the club that April in order to return to Norway.

Plenty of quality then, which meant I got to the end of the season feeling frustrated that we hadn't, again, been able to prove just what a good side we were by either having a good run at the top six in the division[3] or by, at least, having a decent run in one of the domestic cup competitions. We had, as I have already written, got to the League Cup quarter-finals that season but were never really in it against Aston Villa at Carrow Road in that game after Dave Watson had to go off early on. With only one substitute to call on at that time, Louie Donowa replaced Dave, which meant Aage had to rely on me and John Devine to fall back and cover in Dave's place and, good players that we were, centre-half wasn't a natural role for either of us, especially me. That meant Villa's team on the night, which was full of tough and gnarly players like Des Bremner, Peter Withe and Steve McMahon, were able to outmuscle us and in the end win quite easily.

I wanted the 1984/85 season to be different. I wanted us to finally show the rest of the footballing world what a good side we were and I wanted us to go at least one step further in each of

---

3   Peter is not being at all unrealistic here in his aspirations for the Canaries at the time. Clubs that were regarded as 'unfancied' or just as plain unfashionable were regularly finishing in the top-six places in Division One at that time. QPR had ended the 1983/84 season in fifth place while Southampton had ended it runners-up. The previous season (1982/83) had seen Watford finish as runners-up whilst Ipswich (second) and Swansea (sixth) had similarly defied expectations to massively over-achieve in the 1981/82 season.

the domestic cups, to make a statement and make people sit up and take notice rather than drift around in mid-table and be told, endlessly, what a nice football club Norwich was, lovely people, lovely city in a lovely part of the world and all the rest of it. All true by the way. But it was time to be remembered for what we did on the football pitch and I threw myself into pre-season training with the sort of energy and commitment that I maybe hadn't in a while, hoping, as I did so, that my team-mates would be looking across at me and wanting to take things as seriously as I was.

From day one.

And you know, I do believe that Ken Brown had been thinking along the same lines as me. For a start, he managed to get the board, now led by Mr Chase, to let him have some money to spend that summer. Evidence of that arrived when Steve Bruce, perm and all, turned up at Trowse not long after we'd started pre-season training, having signed for us from Gillingham for £135,000.

Steve had been getting quite a name for himself at Gillingham over the past few seasons and, although it was no secret that a few clubs were after him that summer, it was a bit of a coup for us to have got him to Norwich when teams like Spurs and Leeds were also said to be interested in him. He'd been signed, of course, to fill the gap at the centre of our defence and play alongside Dave Watson, and I am sure that when he spoke to Ken and Mel Machin that summer they'd have told him that was exactly what their plans were for him. No waiting around, no settling down period or spell in the reserves to acclimatise himself at Norwich. Steve would be straight into the side alongside Dave, with the two of them only having our pre-season games to get used to each other.

Our pre-season schedule in the summer of 1984 was as tough a one as I can ever remember having at Norwich. We not only headed out to Norway (again) at the end of July to play five games but then flew on to Sweden for another five before heading back for what was our only pre-season game in England, which was a 3-0 win at Cambridge United in the Cambridgeshire Professional

Cup. So a nice piece of silverware for Dave to lift before the serious stuff got under way.

I loved the trips we used to take out to Norway during the close seasons, tours and games that have provided me with some very happy memories. Match wise, the standard of our opposition wasn't always as good as it might have been; we found the sides that we played were certainly very fit but lacked the sort of technical ability that we had, and over 90 minutes that usually told in a most emphatic manner, with us winning a lot of our games by a big margin. As the years (and tours) came and went, however, you could see that the standard of Norwegian football was greatly improving, something that soon became very evident to a wider audience when Norway beat England 2-1 in a World Cup qualifying match. By 1982 Norwich had a Norwegian player in their first-team squad, Aage Hareide, who went on to become a very good friend of mine. Aage played in central defence and, as well as doing very well for us there, had previously impressed at Manchester City who'd initially signed him from FK in his native country. The Manchester City manager who'd signed him incidentally was none other than our former gaffer John Bond, who knew a decent defender when he saw one, having been a very good right-back himself in his playing days.

When we went out to Norway with Ken Brown and Mel Machin it was anything but a 'jolly' – at least as far as the football was concerned. Training was taken very seriously indeed and you weren't expected to slacken off in any way just because we were away from home or anything like that. Mind you, the old maxim of working hard and playing hard often applied, and once we'd done our work for the day we found ways to amuse ourselves, even if it was just getting away in the evening for a few drinks and dinner together. It didn't really feel as if we were having a night out because we were in Tromso at the time and it never got dark which sort of took a lot out of the normally vaguely illicit thrill gained from going out and sneaking back in the early hours of the morning!

My greatest memory of being away in Norway with the lads was all about a wind-up that wasn't! I was sharing a hotel room with Mark Barham at the time (May 1983) and we were in the process of getting ready to head off for a game against Molde when the phone rang. I answered it, fully expecting it to be one of the lads mucking about, that or Ken Brown asking us to get a move on, only to hear a very clear and proper-sounding voice announce that, 'This is the Football Association in London, please can I speak to Mr Mark Barham?'

I handed the phone over to Mark who, after listening for a few seconds, put the receiver back down, claiming, as I'd initially suspected, that it was just one of the lads on a wind-up. Hardly surprising really, we played tricks on each other all the time and at a time when telephones weren't quite as ubiquitous a part of our everyday lives as they are now a lot of prank potential came with them. But I wasn't so sure on this occasion.

'Marky mate, that sounded a genuine call to me. I think it really was the FA.'

But he was adamant.

'No way, it's one of the lads pratting about.'

But then the phone rang again. I answered, got the same message and, once again, handed the receiver to Mark who, on this occasion, spent a little bit longer talking to whoever was on the other end. When, after five minutes or so, he put the phone down for a second time, he had the biggest smile I've ever seen on his face. It was the FA who were ringing him in order to let Mark know he'd been selected for the senior England squad for their forthcoming tour of Australia and New Zealand.

Marky was a good player at the best of times, but, boy oh boy, he celebrated the news by having a 'worldy' against Molde that evening. We won 5-2 and he was absolutely unplayable. It was great news and everyone was really happy for him. How tragic, therefore, that Mark's career was so often interrupted by injury as I am convinced that had he not been so unfortunate with his fitness he'd have got a lot more caps for England than the two he won on that tour and, in all probability, ended up playing for one of the top clubs in the country. A happy memory for me from Norway and, I am sure, a wonderful one for Mark. I'd like to go back to Norway one day. It's a lovely country, one where the standard of football has continued to impress, both in the men's and women's game with players like Ole Gunnar Solskjaer, Tore Andre Flo, John Arne Riise, Hege Riise and Ada Hegerberg all becoming household names. I'm sure plenty more will follow.

Great trips and great memories. But, as I have already said, we worked hard. If, for example, you look back at the matches we had in Norway from the end of the 1983/84 season to the beginning of the 1984/85 season, we played, in just over three months, a total of 14 matches, which is not far off how many we might have played in that period of time over the course of any season. It did, of course, give Steve Bruce plenty of time to 'bed in' to the way we did things at Norwich so, even if he was a new face to all of our fans in our opening match of the campaign, we felt we all knew him pretty well by then but, more importantly, felt that he was a quality acquisition and would waste little to no time in proving it.

This is probably a million miles away from what our fans were thinking after only two minutes of our opening game at home to Liverpool on 25 August when Steve misjudged a long ball and, rather than clearing his lines in the manner which Norwich fans, spoilt by some quality centre-halves over the years, would have expected, managed to power a spectacular own goal past a startled Woodsy to give Liverpool an early lead. It was the sort of opportunity you never gave the champions, not if you wanted to escape being given a hiding, and that is exactly what looked to be on the cards 20 minutes later when Kenny Dalglish put them 2-0 up. That might, I think, have led to lesser sides folding and ending the day on the wrong end of a 0-5 or 0-6 scoreline but, and I'll say it yet again, this was a Norwich team full of quality players and we proved it that afternoon by fighting back and earning a point in a 3-3 draw that even saw me have the honour of scoring our first 'proper' goal of that campaign when I shot past Bruce Grobbelaar from just inside the penalty area.

We even missed a penalty when Dixie blazed it high over the bar in front of the Barclay but we managed to convert one late on to equalise when Mike Channon, still full of running, made the most of a fairly light challenge to go down as if he was one of his race horses falling at Becher's Brook. Mike took on the responsibility himself and showed Dixie how it was done in the process, a thrilling end to one of the most entertaining and truly end-to-end games I've ever had the pleasure of playing in.

We didn't start the season too badly and by the time we took a break from all the league action in order to play Preston in a League Cup second-round game on 25 September, had played seven games with a record of W2 D3 L2, enough to put us comfortably in mid-table. Our first win, incidentally, had been against West Brom on 5 September, a 2-1 win that saw me score the winner, my second goal in just four games which meant I'd already equalled my goal total from the previous season, which especially pleased me and made me think, yet again, that this had the potential of being a good season all round for both me and the club.

That League Cup game against Preston didn't do much to excite the fans, however, as it was attended by just over 5,000 fans at Deepdale on the night. It might, I expect, have been seen as a great opportunity for Ken to give some game time to some of the younger players in the squad at that time, people like Paul Clayton, Mark Farrington and Jeremy Goss, but managers took both cup competitions very seriously back then and Ken put out a more-or-less full strength team that night, one that managed, somehow, to throw away a commanding 3-1 lead in the last few minutes to end the game at 3-3, Preston having done to us what we'd done to Liverpool on the opening day.

Ken Brown wasn't too happy about how we'd let the game slip out of our hands as it meant we'd have to be at our best in the second leg at Carrow Road to have a chance of going through as Preston would have more than fancied their chances of a cup upset, something which the Norwich fans would have been heartily fed up with, having been on the end of quite a few of them in the last few years. It was tough going as well and, even though we were 2-0 up at half-time, no one sat in the home dressing room thought that the game was over. Fortunately for us, we had a new face sat there amongst us, someone who, like Mick (Channon), had pretty much been there and done that in the game. It was, of course, Asa Hartford who was having the proverbial blinder in midfield, dictating the flow of the game as well as contributing a couple of goals as we eventually won 6-1. But Asa wasn't the only debutant for Norwich in that game as we also had one in goal after Woodsy had gone down with a bit of a knock that saw him miss three games. The keeper in question was, like Asa, a big name in the game, the ex-Manchester City and England number one Joe Corrigan. Typical Ken Brown, he hadn't, when we knew Woodsy would be missing a few matches, gone out and brought in the first goalkeeper he could lay his hands on but had taken his time and, no doubt with the help of his massive contacts book, got one of the most respected and experienced keepers in the English game. It showed, for me, the approach both Ken and the club were taking at this time. Yes, we only needed someone to cover Chris for three games so maybe it didn't matter too much who we got in as long as they knew what they were doing. But for Ken that wasn't good enough. He wanted to replace quality with quality so went out and did exactly that.

We seemed to be taking things very seriously at Norwich City and it was great to be part of that new approach.

Unfortunately we let that slip, as far as playing matters were concerned, for our next match in the competition, which was against Aldershot Town at home. We knew we'd be in for a bit of a battle as, pre-match, their manager had said he was going to make sure his players humped the ball forward at every opportunity and generally did their level best to get in our faces and put us off our game. It was an approach that nearly paid off for them as, forced to come down to their level, we toiled our way to a very dull 0-0 draw, with Len Walker promising us we'd be in for more of the same in the replay at their place a week later.

And he was right. Aldershot got in and amongst us from the start, just as they had at Carrow Road, with the only surprise being if anyone who was at the game, Len and Ken Brown included, saw very much of it at all. That was because we played it in the thickest fog I've ever seen, let alone played in, thick enough on the field of play for me to be able to hear our supporters but not actually see them. Quite how the match wasn't called off, I'll never know but it's just as well that it wasn't as we eventually overcame their spoiling targets to take control of things and won 4-0, with yours truly netting the final goal in the last minute of the game, which meant that, all of a sudden, after four games and 13 goals scored, we were on the verge of another decent cup run.

It hadn't, as is sometimes the case, distracted us from our league fixtures; indeed, after beating Luton 3-0 on 10 November, we found ourselves up into tenth place in the league. That ended up being one of our best wins in the league that season. We dominated Luton from the kick-off which was no mean feat as they had some decent players in their side, Ricky Hill and Brian Stein being two of them as well as the former England defender Colin Todd. But they couldn't live with us on that day, one that was pleasing for me because, once again, I got on the scoresheet with our opening goal.

We were back on the League Cup trail shortly afterwards with a home match against Notts County. We dealt with them at the first time of asking with a convincing 3-0 win with goals from Mick Channon, Dixie and Louie Donowa. That win meant that, without really being aware of it, we were now all of a sudden in the quarter-finals of the competition and, potentially, only three games, of which at least one would be at Carrow Road, from Wembley, a venue that Norwich hadn't visited for ten years. That had also been a League Cup Final and had been a disappointing day all round as John Bond's much admired side had lost 1-0 to Aston Villa. We now had a chance to go one better and were, at least initially, encouraged when the quarter-final draw matched us with Grimsby Town, the fourth consecutive time we'd been drawn against lower league opposition (the other six clubs in the competition at that point were all fellow Division One teams) meaning that we couldn't help but start wondering about those famous Twin Towers and a coach trip up Wembley Way.

If any complacency was lurking in and around Trowse at that point, mind you, Ken Brown and Mel Machin would soon have let us know about it – and, as regards Mel, in no uncertain terms. They didn't want our form in the league to be affected by any thoughts of cup glory and for the most part it wasn't as, between the Notts County and Grimsby games, we had some good results, including a 4-2 win over Everton and 1-0 wins over West Ham, Arsenal, West Brom and Southampton, meaning that by the time the Grimsby game rolled around we were still sat in tenth place in the Division One table and looking as if we would be more likely to push onwards and upwards as our league form, buoyed by our cup run rather than distracted by it, kept our spirits high.

A trip up to Cleethorpes to play Grimsby Town in any match might, on the face of it, have seemed a fairly straightforward job. Granted, they had a few decent players in their ranks, one of whom was Kevin Drinkell, who would, of course, eventually sign for Norwich before going on to play for Glasgow Rangers, but on the whole, although we respected them, we also felt we had more than enough to come away from Blundell Park with a win and a place in the semi-finals, which would be played over two legs.

One thing we hadn't allowed for was the weather on the night! It was absolutely freezing cold as the whole of the country was in the grip of an icy spell of weather that had, the night before, covered the Grimsby pitch with four inches of snow, more than enough, you would think, to get the game called off as, indeed, was every single other match that was due to be played in England that evening. But they're a doughty lot up that way and there was no way they were going to have their big cup night cancelled.

Not, I hasten to add because Norwich were in town. We were no big deal as far as Grimsby were concerned; indeed, they'd already knocked Everton out of the competition so their incentive to play wasn't to see us but to continue their good cup form, knock us out and get that cherished semi-final place. The fact that the weather was bad with snow in the air and a cold wind blowing was even more incentive for them as they fancied that we might not be too happy to play in those conditions, so were there for the taking.

But if they thought we'd be a soft touch then they were wrong. I know that Dave Booth, their manager, played the radio coverage of their win over Everton in the previous round to his players just before kick-off, and the PA at Grimsby did exactly the same thing in order to get the fans whipped up as much as Booth clearly hoped he would the players. And maybe, just maybe, some of their players thought the game was already won. But, as Martin Tyler said early on in his commentary, we'd got ourselves a good reputation as a solid First Division team now, and although previous Norwich sides might not have fancied playing in the ice and snow[4] it didn't bother us, whilst the fact that their support seemed to think they'd already won the game just served as, not that we needed one, a further incentive to put on a good performance and win the game, bad conditions (and the pitch was in an absolutely dreadful state) or not.

It helped us that Kevin Drinkell wasn't playing. He was their best player and talisman and would, no doubt, have given us a few problems. They still had two good strikers on show, mind you – Gary Lund, who'd recently won England under-21 honours, and Paul Wilkinson, who'd scored their winner against Everton. He was being watched on the night by a number of scouts from Division One clubs so would have been well up for the battle. As was I. It was my sort of match really. Away from home, tough conditions and against a side that were going to get in our faces from the start. The sort of challenge I loved, rest assured I had no problems geeing myself up for this one. It was a game we'd have to

---

4   None more so than the Norwich team that John Bond took to Leicester City for an FA Cup third-round match in January 1979, another played in cold and snowy conditions that some of his team clearly, on the day, didn't fancy at all with Norwich losing 3-0 as a result.

play without Dave Watson, big Dave had a slight knock and was getting over that which meant Ken Brown wasn't going to risk him on an icy pitch. Dennis Van Wijk came in for Dave and, with Asa Hartford back in our midfield after missing a few games himself and, no doubt, expecting me to do his running for him, we were pretty much, minus Dave of course, at full strength.

Did I tell you it was cold? I think it might just have been the coldest I have ever felt whilst playing a football match. It doesn't last for long of course, as you soon warm up once the game gets under way, but, for all that, every time the wind cut across from the North Sea and across the pitch, you knew all about it. Our fans were magnificent that night, they'd turned up in high numbers and, from what we'd been told, had endured all sorts of travelling difficulties en route, such was the bad condition of the roads. The terrace they were all huddled on to was open as well, so it must have been a very uncomfortable evening for them indeed. So it's just as well we won really, doing so via a first-half goal from Dixie Deehan, who got his head on to the end of a typically lethal Mark Barnham cross. It silenced the Grimsby fans to a certain extent. I think all the pre-match hype had led them to believe they were going to win the game without too many problems, so our going ahead wasn't in the script at all. It was enough to win the game and we headed home, back on those icy and slippery roads, delighted to be in the semi-finals of the competition, while at the same time looking forward to taking on Liverpool at Anfield a few days later.

We hadn't missed Dave Watson that much at Grimsby, but we most certainly did at Liverpool. Dave would have been very disappointed at missing out on playing against his former club, as were we at the end of the game as they beat us 4-0 without really breaking out of first gear. Dave was back in for our next league game which, due to the big freeze that was gripping the country at the time, came a fortnight after the Liverpool game.

That was another defeat, 0-1 at home to Nottingham Forest, which meant, for the first time that season, we'd lost two league games in a row, something which was hardly good preparation for our next match, the first leg of our League Cup semi-final, which, of all clubs, was to be against our closest and most bitter rivals, Ipswich Town.

At least the first leg was to be at Portman Road. As a player, you preferred to get the away game in these situations out of the way as it meant that whatever you needed to do in order to win a tie on aggregate you were able to do so on your own pitch and in front of your own fans. We knew that Carrow Road would be absolutely rocking for the second leg, which meant all we had to do in the first leg game was avoid defeat or even sneak a 1-0 victory, meaning all the pressure would be on Ipswich at the very last place on earth where they'd want to go in order to get a result.

Having said that, it was pretty lively down at Ipswich with 27,000 packed into Portman Road, the very great majority of whom would have had the famous Twin Towers on their minds when, after just six minutes, George Burley floated in a free kick that Mitch D'Avray met with all the time and space he needed to head it past Woodsy. Pandemonium ensued and, if I'm honest, they might well have had the impetus at that point to give us a bit of a battering as we were all over the place for a few minutes and could have gone further behind. But, as we had already proved on more than one occasion that season, we could tough things out when we had to and that's exactly what we did, keeping them at bay for the rest of the game and heading back to Norfolk reasonably confident we could turn that result on its head in the second leg. Looking back on that game now, we should really have been dead and buried by full time with the second leg nothing more than an academic exercise as they were rampant, but we'd dug in deep and held on, somehow, and it was the sort of performance and luck that makes you think that, as the saying goes, your name is already on the cup.

People talked about little else other than the second leg over the next couple of weeks, which was a bit of a distraction from our league programme that saw us play just the one game, a 2-2 draw at QPR that, again, saw us go a goal down early in the game when Steve Wicks scored in under a minute. Thus, again, we found ourselves under a lot of pressure from the home team and it probably came as no surprise to anyone when Wayne Fereday put them 2-0 up. Luckily for us, Mike Channon was on his game and flying; he pulled it back to 2-1 shortly after Fereday had scored, with Dixie making it 2-2 five minutes before half-time. At that point, everyone was expecting more of the same in the second half but both clubs seemed satisfied with a point at that stage, so that's how the game ended.

A thrilling game and hard won point with it but, wouldn't you know it, we were barely back in the dressing room at Loftus Road after the final whistle when thoughts, inevitably, turned to the massive game coming up against Ipswich, one that was now only four days away and would be, for most of the Norwich squad, myself included, the biggest and most important game we'd ever played in, even if it was going to take place in a ground that now looked very different to how it had done at the beginning of the season.

The reason for that was the fire that had swept through the club's main stand the previous October. That stand, which backs on to Carrow Road, was completely destroyed in the blaze, meaning the club not only had to fork out nearly £2 million on a new one (which remains in place today) but also had to face up to the decrease in matchday revenue that would come about as a result of the stand, which also, incidentally, included the directors' box and boardroom – so not much opportunity for pre-match schmoozing either, for either Norwich City or their guests on the day. The club also lost a lot of its history, with the fire claiming the Canaries trophy cabinet and the myriad honours it contained. A sad day for everyone but one which was, for us, enlivened the next day when John Deehan, ever the joker, turned up dressed as a fireman asking all and sundry where the fire was!

Too late Dixie mate. What a character he was. Our first home game after the fire was against QPR who, as we'd also lost the dressing rooms in the fire, had to get changed in The Nest, which was the pub built into the River End at the time. Quite fitting really, as they were sponsored by a well-known brewery back then! It was a funny old game to play in, what with one side of the ground empty and derelict but the spirit amongst the lads and fans was fantastic and we ground out a 2-0 win, courtesy of goals from Mike Channon and Dixie.

It wasn't ideal, therefore, going into one of the club's biggest games for at least a decade at a ground where you'd normally expect home advantage to be worth a goal start as it would, with the exception of the few Ipswich fans who made the trip on the night, be crammed full of raucous Norwich fans on all four sides. But if anyone had any fears that the match atmosphere might, somehow, be reduced after the loss of the stand, those worries were swiftly put to bed. There were over 23,000 there on the night and what a game it was, one I am sure I have absolutely no need to go into too much detail about as you were either there or have watched the highlights, especially Steve Bruce's winning goal, over and over and over again!

Yet it was a game and an occasion that I nearly missed out on. On the morning of the match, I was suffering from a lot of pain in my mouth which led to my booking an emergency appointment at the dentist who had to give me some treatment for an abscess. What a time to have a toothache. Still, he sorted me out, even if my mouth was feeling a little bit tender afterwards, enough, at least, to take my mind off the game until we were all set for kick-off – and, by then, I was too focussed on the game to worry about anything, let alone any post-dental throbbing that was still going on. I was, like all of my team-mates, thoroughly absorbed in what was to come, the opportunity to not only beat our closest rivals in front of our own fans but, in doing so, to get to Wembley for what would only be the club's third appearance at that great stadium.

Ipswich had a good team at the time mind, lots of quality from one through to 11 and it soon told when they went close early on. If they had have scored at that point, then going 2-0 up on aggregate would have put them in a very strong position indeed, we'd have had no option but to commit to pushing forward, and they would have had every chance of scoring again on the break. And 3-0 would have meant that the tie was as good as over. We weathered that early storm, however, and went in at the break 1-1 on aggregate after Dixie stuck one away at the River End, albeit with the help of a deflection off an Ipswich player. But that didn't bother us, and as we sat in the portacabin that doubled up as a changing room at half-time all Ken Brown needed to say was to keep playing as we were, using width and the pace of our wide players, particularly Louie Donowa, and the goal would come.

Ken believed it, we believed it and I am sure that the fans all believed it. But Ipswich held on and, as the clock at the Barclay End ticked remorselessly onwards, the mood in the stadium was changing from celebratory to somewhat nervous …

… 83 minutes, 84, 85, 86 …

… 87 minutes. Corner. Up at the Barclay End and at the corner where the Snakepit is, both teams were exhausted now, except for, it seems, Marky Barham, who trotted up to take it as if it was the first minute of the match, rather than the 87th. He proceeded to float over an absolute diamond of a corner that saw the ball not only have Brucie's name on it but, in all probability, his full address, telephone number and date of birth. No one in blue saw him, no one picked him up and he met that ball with such power and precision that it would probably still have gone in if he'd been a further five to six yards back than he was. Yes Brucie, have some of *that* Ipswich!

Pandemonium. And, just a few minutes later, utter bliss. We're at Wembley. This is why I play football, this is the sort of moment I wanted from the game when I started out, that feeling of joy, pure and utter joy, when you achieve something special with your mates and everyone around you has a smile on their face as big as your own. I'd tell any young player today to just take time out if it happens to them, to stand and take stock of what you've achieved. The temptation is, of course, to run off and have a bundle with your mates, but before you do, drink it all in, have a few moments on your own so you can create the sort of memories you'll always have. I remember looking at Nathan Redmond after Norwich had won the 2015 play-off final at Wembley, the final whistle had just gone and, amidst all of the yellow and green noise and fury, he ran on to the pitch, looked up at the skies for a few seconds and pulled his shirt over his face. He was taking it in, only for a few seconds as the temptation to look for his mates would have been overwhelming, but I wouldn't mind betting that those few seconds Nathan Redmond had on his own right after the final whistle provoked the emotions he remembers the most.

It was just the best feeling ever. It's great as a fan, of course. Try magnifying that a hundred times, that is what it feels like for a player. And more than that, if, like me, you were a Norwich fan. How it must have felt for the Ipswich lads, well, I don't even like to think about it today. I caught sight of them walking up the steps to their portacabin and as they did so Terry Butcher put his fist through the door. That defeat must have hurt Terry more than most. He wasn't born and bred in Suffolk like I had been in Norfolk (Terry's birthplace was Singapore) but he'd spent his childhood in Lowestoft before signing for Ipswich (and turning down Norwich in the process) as they'd been his favourite team as he was growing up. So it would have hurt Terry, hurt him big time. Maybe that was one of the reasons he left the club the following year to join Rangers – he wanted winners' medals and on a regular basis, something he knew he was never going to do with Ipswich. I bump into Terry on occasion, and whenever we meet up he always wants to talk about that game as he still feels disappointed that they lost and makes sure I know it! But then that's the sort of player and professional he was, a man who competed to win and hated losing, no matter what he was doing. It could have been a game of I-Spy for Terry, he wanted to win at everything. I don't blame him for putting his fist through that door, nor his reaction to losing as I am sure I would have felt exactly the same way. Mind you, the club would have billed me for the damage I did to the door! He didn't do so bad in his career though; indeed, I wish

I'd had even half the career that Terry had. He won 77 caps for England and went to three World Cups, the sign of not only a good player but an exceptional one.

On this particular occasion, however, he had to endure the bitter taste of defeat – and against us, of all clubs. That must have hurt. No winners' medal for you this year, Terry.

We, on the other hand, now knew we had a chance of winning some for ourselves and, I am afraid to say, thoughts of Wembley became so strong, both before the final against Sunderland and immediately after it, that we let our concentration slip a little bit in our subsequent league games, something which, in the end, meant that none of us ended the season on the sort of high we might previously have expected.

Which is something I'll come back to shortly.

You won't be surprised to hear that whenever I meet up and have a chat with some supporters of Norwich City Football Club, one of the first things they'll mention is that day at Wembley on 24 March 1985. 'We were there Pete,' they'll go, adding, 'What a great day it was.' I can only agree with them, how could it have been anything else? It wasn't, and even the most diehard Norwich fan will admit to this, the most exciting game that the old Wembley had ever seen but that never matters when you are the winners on the day.

They remember it all, every second of every minute of every hour of that amazing day. As do I! And do you know who I have to thank for that? My old team-mate John Devine, that's who. I spoke to him about his memories of playing in an FA Cup Final for Arsenal (1980) and his words to me reflect those that I mentioned earlier. 'Pete,' he said, 'take it all in and enjoy every second of the day because it will all be over in a flash.' And he was right. But I did as he suggested and it ended up being a day that I will never forget.

I can picture the scene now. I just need to close my eyes and it all comes flashing back to me, clear as a bell and in vivid technicolour – even if it was a grey old day that saw a lot of rain!

I was sat on our coach as we slowly approach Wembley and what a sight it was, those iconic Twin Towers looming in the distance, one that hundreds of footballers had witnessed over the years, a stadium that some of the greatest players of all time had graced. Now it was going to be my turn, an ordinary lad from Norfolk who was living the dream and, in doing so, making, he hoped, his parents proud. I remembered, again, what John Devine had said and, not for the first time, gazed out of the window to look at the thousands of Norwich and Sunderland fans making their way to the game, the Norwich fans, naturally enough, waving their scarves at us and giving us the almightiest of cheers as we crept past.

It was, of course, a great occasion – no, let me put that another way. It was already turning into a great occasion and we hadn't even started the match yet. And we were enjoying it, who wouldn't? But at the same time there was a very serious resolve about the lads, even those like Gary Rowell who knew they wouldn't be taking part on the day, as we realised that, as magical as the day was, we had a job to do. And that was to win!

A quick word about Gary Rowell. He was something of a legend to the Sunderland fans, a local lad who'd signed for the club as an apprentice when he was 16. He went on to make 293 senior appearances for them, scoring 102 goals, of which 24 were penalties. Yet for some reason he became part of a bit of a clear-out up at Roker Park in the summer of 1984, which led to us being able to sign him on a free transfer. I've no doubt a lot of Norwich fans were as pleased to see him signing as I was, a proven goalscorer for nothing, what a great bit of business by Ken Brown. He made his debut in a reserve-team game and scored after barely a quarter of an hour had gone before having to go off with an injury, the start of a desperate run of bad luck on the fitness front for him that meant, ultimately, he only made six senior appearances for Norwich, scoring one goal in the process. That came, true to form, on his full debut in a game against Aston Villa at Carrow Road a fortnight before the Milk Cup Final, a goal that he must have thought gave him a good chance of being part of the 12-man squad on the day. Sadly for Gary, that didn't end up being what happened, but, for all of his disappointment in missing out on a game against his former club as well as, of course, at how his Norwich career had turned out, he was with us on the day, suited and booted and as keen for victory as any of us were, even if the game was against his childhood team and the one he'd always supported.

Gary's attitude was typical of the whole squad at the time. It's a bit of a footballing cliché to bang on and on about how any good playing squad has a mix of youth and experience, but we really did, and in abundance. You had the energy and verve of the younger players like me, Louie Donowa, Tony Spearing and Dale Gordon plus the know-how of the older pros like Mike Channon and Asa Hartford, a perfect mix. We did our best to help the older players feel young whilst they, whenever it was needed, could be counted upon to make sure we didn't get too carried away with ourselves. It was a good mix that had got us in or around the top ten for most of the season and now, with the busy footballing month of April fast approaching, a major cup final at Wembley, with a chance of playing in European competition if we won.

To be honest with you, the coverage and attention we all got as players in the weeks and days leading up to the final was something that took a bit of getting used to. For a start, lots of local businessmen who normally might not have been interested in having anything to do with the football club took a real interest in things and got involved in myriad ways that would have meant them putting their hands in their pockets whilst another business, Wensum Clothing, provided us with our very smart Wembley suits, with Rombah Wallace supplying our shoes.

So we didn't only feel good, we looked the part as well. Mind you, the less said about the tops we wore as we walked out on to the pitch before kick-off the better. They were, as some of you will remember, a rather out of character, for us, light blue and white top that didn't look too unlike the hoodies that are popular today. Still, it would have all been part of the massive commercial exercise that the club had got involved with prior to the final and if wearing them had made a few quid for the club then who am I to argue?

That was us then, but what about our fantastic support? We had no fears there, we knew they'd be in place, as colourful and loud as always, courtesy of the fantastic job that Duncan Forbes, a true Canary legend, would have done, up before dawn no doubt in order to prepare and organise the countless coaches and buses that we were taking down to London, picking up fans from meeting points all over the county including, of course, Carrow Road itself, where hundreds of fans would have been patiently waiting on that damp Sunday morning for their coaches to arrive. Duncan's army of fans included my parents, who travelled down on a bus from King's Lynn as well as my co-author on this book, Ed, who was on one of the Sanders coaches that travelled down from Fakenham, all part of a mighty yellow-and-green army making their way south from all points in Norfolk – as well as quite a few in Suffolk!

I was really happy to know that my mum and dad would be there at Wembley to watch me play. They'd always been there for me, going the extra mile on more than one occasion to make sure I'd make it to whatever game I was playing in – even if, on occasions, they might have gone a bit further with their support than I'd expected! Take, for example, the day I was playing for Gaywood Park School against our big rivals in King's Lynn, King Edward School (KES). I suffered quite a nasty injury in that game but instead of, and as I'd expected, one of our teachers running on to the pitch with his bucket of icy water and the old 'magic sponge', the first person on the scene was my mother, who was fussing over me as only a mother could! I was extremely embarrassed and told her that she was never to come and watch me play again. Very harsh I know, sorry Mum! Still, I'd forgiven her by now and knew she'd enjoy the match, even if, had I been injured, she might have found the temptation to run on to the Wembley pitch to see how I was an overwhelming one!

In addition to knowing that Mum and Dad would be amongst the 100,000 people attending the match, my wife Gabrielle was also going to be there, having left Ross and Jamie, our two sons, in the very capable hands of their godparents Bill and Sandra Smithson, who were very good friends of ours. So it was a real family day for me, the local boy who'd worked his way up the ranks at the club and who was now so very proud to be playing at such a famous stadium in a big game in front of a massive audience that included, of course, three of the most important people in his life at that time.

We just had to win to make the whole day perfect!

I had been enjoying the build-up and the coach drive to Wembley, but as we drove through the big wooden gates and into Wembley's interior my stomach started to tighten and I began to feel extremely nervous, a state of emotion that I had to do my best to keep under control as there was still nearly one and a half hours to kick-off at that point.

Even nervous energy can take it out of you and I didn't want those nerves to drain me physically even before I got on to the Wembley pitch. Resolving to try and treat the day as I would any other match, I walked into our dressing room, the same as the one used by the England team[5], and had, as it was that big, a bit of a look around. The actual changing area was large enough but then there was also a bathing area that included a communal bath as well as several individual baths and showers in what was a fairly spartan and old-fashioned set-up to some of the changing rooms I'd been in and, of course, light years away from the facilities that clubs provide for their players today. Yet all of that didn't seem to matter because this was Wembley and I think players and fans alike had almost grown used to the rapidly decaying conditions all around them because of where they were.

I also noticed there was a control switch in the dressing room that enabled you to either turn up or turn down the sound of the

---

5   England's last game at Wembley prior to that season's League Cup Final had been a 5-0 win over Finland in a World Cup qualifying game on 17 October 1984. The England starting XI on that day was Shilton, Duxbury, Butcher, Wright, Sansom, Williams, Robson, Wilkins, Barnes, Hateley and Woodcock.

crowd inside the stadium via the speakers that were provided near to where we would change. I couldn't decide whether it was a good thing or not – and certainly not if you've lost the match and don't want to hear all the celebrations going on outside, although you could, of course, opt to turn it off.

It was getting close to kick-off by the time I'd finished my little wander around the changing room, lost, as so many of my team-mates were, in my own little pre-match routine. Now it was time to look over to the wooden benches where we'd be seated whilst Ken Brown gave his pre-match team talk, and there it was, my bright yellow shirt, number five, hanging there waiting for me to put it on. Just below that was my shirts and socks, and resting on those was a telegram from Brian Saunders who worked with Russell Allison, the head groundsman at Carrow Road. They did a great job on our pitch, considering they had nowhere near the level of technology available to the modern-day groundsperson, who is as much a scientist and technician as he is a man whose job is to 'just' look after a bit of grass! I'd had a few run-ins with Brian and Russell in the past as we'd occasionally train on the pitch at Carrow Road, something that they were not particularly keen to see us do at any time, but especially if we had a home match coming up and the weather forecast wasn't looking too good. What all of that meant to Russell and Brian, of course, was that those bloody footballers would end up kicking divots out of their precious pitch before clearing off and leaving them to make good all the damage we'd done. We were not popular and they'd often let us know, especially Russell, who was a great character and might, had he got his way, forbidden any kind of matches, including first-team ones, to have been played on 'his' pitch.

Yet here was Brian, taking the trouble to send me a telegram before the match, one that contained a very lovely personal message – Brian mate, if you are reading this, thanks to you and all of your family, you were, and remain, very special and true friends, and I love you all.

I then checked my kit was ready to wear before taking a walk on to the pitch, a perfect playing surface which I knew would be particularly slick early on as it had been raining on and off throughout the day. It was, at that time, being marched upon by the massed bands of HM Royal Marines, who were striking up some stirring tunes to help get everyone in the right mood for the match. The Norwich fans were, by now, starting to pack out their end of the stadium which was behind the goal at the opposite end to the tunnel, and as I walked closer to where they were I spotted a few friends taking their seats in the main stand, their presence helping to turn that end of Wembley into a wave of yellow and green of scarves, rosettes and banners with very few, if any, replica shirts on show.

I knew now that whatever happened on the day we could never say we were short of support or that our fans had been too quiet. They were here in noisy abundance and were enjoying their day, something which made me, and, I am sure, my Norwich City team-mates want to make even more complete by winning the trophy for them.

After taking in the scenes for one last time, I went back to the dressing room where I spent at least 20 minutes doing some stretching exercises, making sure that my body was as warmed up and flexible as possible before kick-off, a little routine I went through before every match and one that I found was extremely helpful. I wasn't alone of course, all of the other lads would have been fully focussed on their pre-match warm ups by now, including Mick Channon, who would, I am sure, have made sure he had a copy of the *Racing Post* with him, alongside the Sunday papers so he could check up on how well his horses had done in the previous day's meetings!

Ken then had a few words with us, nothing too complicated, just telling us to enjoy the day and to take it all in, but, most importantly of all, to play the match rather than the occasion and to play the game we liked to play and, in doing so, let the opposition worry about us rather than the other way around. That all sounds rather trite now I suppose, but that was Ken's way, an insistence we kept our game simple, passed the ball around and kept it near enough to pitch level, nothing too elaborate. It was a system that had served us well for much of the season so far, except, ironically, in our last game before this one, which was, believe it or not, against Sunderland at Carrow Road the previous weekend. They'd caught us cold on the day, winning 3-1 at Carrow Road. It was a bad day all round but we all got off relatively lightly compared to Greg Downs who didn't have the best of games, one that included his scoring an own goal. With Steve Bruce also missing in that match and certain to regain his place in the team for Wembley, it wasn't looking good for Greg, who must have feared the worst as far as his chances of starting the final were concerned but would, perhaps, given his versatility, have hoped to at least get his chance on the bench. But no, he didn't even get the number-12 shirt, which went to John Devine, meaning Greg, who'd been with the club for a decade and who was a very popular member of the squad, missed out altogether.

People thought that Ken Brown was a nice man and, of course, he was all of that and more. Yet he wouldn't hesitate from making the big decisions and, for him, sentiment never came into consideration. Greg had played badly in the league game against Sunderland and, fearing that our opponents, thinking his confidence was still low, might target him down the right-hand side of the pitch in the final, Greg was removed from the matchday squad completely and joined Gary Rowell, both of them dressed in their best suits. A courageous decision for Ken to make but not one, for him, that he would have found difficult and he didn't hesitate to make it.

As we walked out of our dressing rooms and into the area that led into the tunnel, the emotion of the day finally started to show for both teams as, in those never-ending few seconds of waiting until we got the go-ahead to walk on to the pitch, everyone, on both sides, started shouting encouragement to their team-mates. They had a good side, Sunderland, and I was particularly aware of the danger that Clive Walker would present us. He'd joined them from Chelsea at the end of the previous season (I don't know how true this is, but there had been talk Norwich had been amongst the teams interested in signing him at that time) and was having a great first season with his new club, a fast and tricky player who always seemed to be amongst the goals, either scoring them or making them for other players. Keeping an eye on him was one of the responsibilities I had on the day and I kept half an eye on him as we walked out on to the pitch, determining, at that point, that I wouldn't now let him out of my sight until the match was over.

The noise that greeted us as we left the tunnel and entered the inside of the stadium itself was absolutely unbelievable. You did get the feeling, before you walked out there, that yes, there was a bit of an atmosphere building up but it didn't seem anything special – well, if that was the case, it was because you were relatively cocooned inside the stadium because when you got out there, wow, the noise and energy from the crowd hit you square in the face, it was so loud and completely overwhelming that, even today, I wonder if the shock of suddenly being exposed to it affected some players so much that they ended up having a bad game as a result. It was, simultaneously, deafening and spine-chilling and remains a moment that I will treasure forever.

By now we all just wanted to play. I'm sure all of the Sunderland lads did as well. But the pre-match arrangements weren't quite over yet as we all now had to be introduced to the chief guest for the day who was Sir Stanley Rous, CBE, the honorary life vice president of FIFA. When I shook his hand, I couldn't help but think of how far I'd come, from the little lad tearing about the makeshift pitches in Gaywood to meeting one of the most respected figures, as he was, in the world game, fleeting as it was.

Kick-off, and a cautious start from both sides. One that, if I am honest, prevailed throughout the match. It wasn't the best game you'll ever see, something I'll freely admit to. It might have been a lovely day out for the supporters of both sides as well as their respective sets of fans, but that didn't mean we just wanted to enjoy it and not be too bothered whether we won or not. Both sides clearly did and treated each other with a lot of respect from the off, focussing, perhaps a little bit too much, on keeping things organised and maintaining their shape without taking any undue risks. I soon got into the game, winning a lot of my 50:50 challenges and doing what I did best, taking play forward and finding a team-mate to lay the ball off to, pass and move, pass and move, the Norwich City way that had been imbued into the club's philosophy by John Bond.

Our goal came at the start of the second half, one I'll never forget as neither will, I know, any of the Norwich supporters who were there on the day as it unfolded before their very eyes. There was young David Corner, in for injured Sunderland defender Shaun Elliott, looking to shield the ball away from danger down by the corner flag, only for Dixie Deehan, always looking for the half-chance, to rob him of the ball. He did that and found Mike Channon who tried to take a shot only to lose the ball as he was tackled. Luckily for us, it fell to Asa Hartford whose shot looked to have been covered by Chris Turner in the Sunderland goal, only for it to take a deflection off the chest of Gordon Chisholm and into their goal.

### Joy ensued

I think some of the Norwich fans looking on were so shocked at what they had just witnessed that their celebrations came a split second after the ball went in as they all stood or sat there and took in what they had just seen. They didn't hold back once they'd done that though. Dixie stood facing them and raised his fist in the air in celebration whilst I ran past Mike Channon in order to get to celebrate with Asa first, with Mike and Louie not far behind me. What a moment that was. The noise was deafening but, for all that, one of the loudest noises of both those few minutes and that whole afternoon could be heard from the Sunderland fans who, having seen their team go a goal down, proceeded to chant 'Sunderland Sunderland Sunderland' in an effort to lift their spirits.

They didn't have to wait long. Sunderland put a move together that saw Barry Venison make inroads into our penalty area from the right-hand side only to be met by Dennis Van Wijk, our young but very talented left-back. Dennis might, I think, have been aware that the space Venison had run into was where we might have been expecting him to be, so, in his efforts to atone for his positional error, his tackle on Venison was a little on the enthusiastic side, so much so that, as he tried to move away with the ball, he pushed it out of the way with his hand. It was as clear a penalty as you'd ever see.

Dennis was distraught. It probably didn't help matters for anyone who happened to see Woodsy's reaction as our normally unflappable goalie put his head in his hands in horror as referee Neil Midgley pointed to the spot, mimicking Dennis's action as he did so. Woodsy knew that he'd be facing Clive Walker and, confident as he would have been of saving it, he also knew Walker was a top penalty taker who hit the ball low and extremely hard. He was a player I'd have loved to have alongside me at Norwich and he'd had a good game that had included a clear run on our goal early on which might even have ended in a penalty itself.

We shouldn't have worried. Walker did hit the ball, low and hard, to our keeper's left. But Woodsy guessed right and just got his finger to it, pushing the ball behind for a corner which, strangely, Midgley didn't give. Maybe he didn't think Woodsy touched the ball? I'm telling you now he did. The faintest of touches but enough, just enough, to preserve our lead.

It was a few moments of excitement in an otherwise fairly dull (other than Marky Barham's flying volley near the end which would have, had it gone in, been one of the best goals you'll have ever seen at the old Wembley) game which summed up football perfectly. We took our chance, they missed theirs. And we won.

We won. Unbelievable. A winner at Wembley. I was in a bit of a daze when the whistle went and immediately afterwards. There's a famous photo taken after the presentation of the trophy which shows me staring at my winners' medal, and people have commented that I look as if I can't quite believe what I'm seeing. They'd be right. I couldn't. It really did feel like a dream, one that included me finding Mum and Dad amongst our fans and giving them both a big hug before following Watto and the rest of the lads up those famous 39 steps to collect the trophy.

Dave Watson collected the trophy but the Man of the Match award went, very deservedly, to Steve Bruce. Yes, that very same Steve Bruce who, barely seven months earlier, had headed Liverpool into the lead after just two minutes of his debut for us. He'd turned things around a bit since then! He'd had a great match but he'd also played his part for us throughout the season and it was no surprise when he won the club's Player of the Year trophy at the end of the season. He was great in the air, you took that as read, but he was also good with the ball at his feet, a shoo-in, I felt, for a long and distinguished career with England, something that, inexplicably, never happened for Steve, even when he was putting in eight and nine out of ten performances for Manchester United every week.

Steve and all the rest of the lads took part in the lap of honour before heading back to the dressing room to continue the party. But I couldn't tear myself away from the scene of our win and stayed out on the pitch until all of our fans had left the stadium, taking it all in alongside Roger Harris, a lovely man who (as well as being a very good angler!) was the club photographer, just the two of us, in that cavernous bowl of a stadium, drinking it in still and, even then, still not quite daring to believe what had happened. I think one of the reasons I stayed out there for so long was that at the back of my mind were very genuine thoughts that I might never get another chance to play at Wembley, and if that did indeed turn out to be the case then I wanted to make the very most of it.

But you can never stand still in football. If you do, either as a player or as a club, the game moves on without you. Quickly and with no mercy shown whatsoever to those who have failed to keep up. And, looking back now, I wonder if we all bathed in the light of that success for longer than we should have done? You hear of how the great sides, Liverpool being an example, took success in the most humble of ways. They'd throw the winners' medals in a box before the players were told to help themselves if they thought they deserved one.

They'd win the league or a cup, enjoy the moment but then, in an instant, it'd be gone, with their entire focus on doing it all over again the following season. If anyone rested on their footballing laurels, or thought they'd made it, they'd be brought down to earth very quickly – or even bombed out of the club altogether. It was ruthless but it meant they were always looking forward, never back. We got back to Norwich and all took part in the civic reception which was hugely enjoyable, but in truth maybe that should have been that, as, unlike winning a league title, as Norwich did in the 2018/19 season, when you can truly let your hair down and celebrate as the season is over or for that matter the FA Cup, we still had another 13 league games to play and should have been focussed on them, our Wembley win forgotten.

Yet the party continued when we played Coventry at Carrow Road a week later. The trophy was paraded around the pitch and, in a joyful, almost complacent, atmosphere, we beat the Sky Blues 2-0, Micky Channon scoring both the goals whilst Mark Barham had as good a game as he'd ever had up to then. His confidence was high and it showed on that afternoon. An easy win in a happy stadium, one that lifted us back up to tenth place in the table.

But then we started to let ourselves down.

A 1-1 draw at Sheffield Wednesday in our next game wasn't a bad point, but following that game we lost five in a row, a terrible run of form that ended with a 3-2 win at Stoke on 24 April. We were down to 15th by then and, although no one was tipping us for a relegation struggle, we'd done well to win that game and our lack of form showed again when we lost our next three games, before, in our penultimate league fixture, we drew 0-0 at home to Newcastle in a game that we dominated. Yet there it was. From a place in the top ten and qualifying for Europe at the end of March to, around six weeks later, in danger of relegation. We thought we'd done enough when we won 2-1 at Chelsea in our last league game as it meant we were now eight points ahead of Coventry who now needed to win all of their last three league matches to save themselves and, in the process, send us down, which, of course, they did. But the manner in which they were able to do so was absolutely farcical as their last game was against Everton who had already been declared league champions so had absolutely nothing to play for, but, worse than that, picked several players who had supposedly been out celebrating their title win and were, shall we say, a little under the weather as a result. There was only one way that game was going to end and Coventry duly did what they had to do, winning 4-1 and, in the process, sent us down.

It was beyond sickening. Yet, for all that late season heartbreak, we did, at least, still have the prospect of European football to look forward to. Yet even that was taken away from us, and, just as it had been with our relegation from Division One, our fate was completely out of our hands as regards the European adventure we were still looking forward to. So, with a few weeks off to look forward to, I took myself fishing at East Tuddenham on the evening of 29 May, switching on my radio after a while so I could take my mind off the carp for a few minutes in order to see what the score was in the European Cup Final that was being played between Liverpool and Juventus.

The news I heard shocked me to the core. I didn't want to fish any more. Crowd trouble and the deaths of some Juventus fans. I packed up my gear and headed home to watch the events of the evening continue to unfold on television. It all ended, of course, with the decision being made to ban all English sides from playing in Europe, even in friendlies, with near enough immediate effect and with no end date set. It therefore meant that we wouldn't be playing in Europe in the 1985/86 season after all and that our wonderful fans, who were always so well behaved on their travels, were being punished, as were Norwich and the remaining 90 league teams in England for something that had absolutely nothing to do with them and for which they were completely and utterly blameless.

From an unbelievable high to the depths of professional despair in just a few short weeks, the biggest disappointment of my entire career. All we now had to look forward to was another season back in Division Two and a battle for promotion that would not only involve us, but some very good sides like Sunderland, who'd dropped down with us, plus Charlton, Portsmouth, Crystal Palace, Sheffield United and Leeds.

Would we be up for it after experiencing not one but two major footballing setbacks in such a short time? I have to admit, a little bit of me had serious doubts that we would.

# CHAPTER SIX

# Osteitis Pubis

*He was telling me, as kindly as he could, that, in his professional opinion, my career as a professional footballer was over, with immediate effect.*

DESPITE ALL the disappointments that had overwhelmed the club in those closing weeks of the 1984/85 campaign, I started pre-season training determined, contrary to how I'd been feeling a month or so earlier, that I was going to try and enjoy my football, even if, deep down, I was starting to wonder if I had a long-term future at the club. As far as the club were concerned, there had been some strong and occasionally painful doubts as to how we would cope with that double whammy of relegation as well as being told we couldn't, after all, play in that season's UEFA Cup competition, but they'd mellowed a little and I wasn't the only one who believed that we had a managerial team and playing squad that would take us back to Division One football at the first time of asking.

No one at the club wanted yet another long slog with promotion the end goal. We'd wanted to establish the club as a near-enough permanent member of the top division. Yet here we were again. You could see how maybe a few people might not have been as motivated as they could have been.

It had certainly been a hectic summer as far as player comings and goings were concerned, with four new faces in the starting line-up for our opening league fixture at home to Oldham Athletic. Of those, former Grimsby Town striker Kevin Drinkell was perhaps the best-known name. We'd also signed midfielders Garry Brooke from Tottenham and Mike Phelan from Burnley, all of whom caught the eye early on in training as well as in matches, although it took Drinks a few games to get off the mark for us, goal wise, which he eventually did in a 4-0 win over Sheffield United. David Williams was the other new name in the side and you would have been forgiven for not knowing who he was when he joined. But what a signing he was. Dave had previously been with Bristol Rovers and had ended his decade-long service with them by, briefly, being the youngest manager in the entire Football League when he took over from Bobby Gould in May 1983 – when he was still just 28 years old! Now, a little over two years later and after making 356 league appearances for Rovers, he'd gone from being the youngest manager in the league to the oldest player (at 30) on Norwich's books at that time.

He was, like Mike and Garry, a midfielder, but he was a completely different kind of player to them. Mike liked to use the ball when he was in possession, to get forward, play little one-twos and look to run in on goal whilst Garry was all action, a player who maybe wasn't that dissimilar to me in that he made himself busy, constantly worrying opponents and looking to win possession and passing the ball to another yellow shirt, a real 'pass-and-move' player who'd had a good upbringing at Tottenham which meant he'd have no problems fitting in with us. Dave, however, was a little different. You could almost have described his playing style as languid as he always seemed to have that little bit more time on the ball than anyone else, which meant he could dwell on it just a little bit longer and not have to rush things. But, whilst he might have looked laid back on the pitch, he was anything but that as it was his adept footballing brain and speed of thought that gave him more time than the average player and we all, very soon, started to appreciate his vision and range of passing, as, I know, did the Norwich City fans.

But for all that, the best bit of business that the club did that summer was keeping hold of Chris Woods and Dave Watson. There's no doubt that, following our relegation, a large number of Division One clubs would have been more than willing to sign either Chris or Dave who might also have been sorely tempted to not only continue playing at the highest level of the game but to see a substantial increase in their salaries at the same time. Yet both were happy to stay put, as were the Norwich board to resist any enquiries that were made.

A lot of credit is therefore due to Woodsy and Dave as most players in their positions would have taken the first opportunity to move on. But they thought differently and wanted to be part of a Norwich side, one that should never have been relegated, that would climb back up to the top flight at the first time of asking. Which meant that, by the time we took to the field for the Oldham game, we had a side packed full of quality in all the right places.

It was a game we should have won easily. No, let me put that another way. It was a game that we should have won by more goals. I put us ahead after just under half an hour with a rare (for me) header but it should have been more. Garry Brooke hit the post with his penalty and we also struck the woodwork on at least two more occasions. Still, at least it was a win, and with Ken Brown hinting that there'd be a few more new faces on the scene before too long, the overall mood in the squad was a good one.

Yet, and as I alluded to at the start of the chapter, I wasn't feeling too happy about how things were progressing for me at the club at that time. I was, once again, way behind some of my team-mates when it came to my salary, so much so in fact that, and as I soon learnt, Mike Phelan, who'd joined us from Burnley, a club who'd ended the previous season relegated to Division Four, was on a much higher wage than me, someone who had already made 200 senior appearances for Norwich City, with many of those played in Division One. Yet here was Mike, newly signed from Burnley, who was earning three times my yearly salary. I never expected to be one of the club's highest earners. This was about parity with new signings who had, previously, been playing a lower level of football than me. It just felt as if the club were maybe taking my loyalty and the fact I was a local lad for granted so I illustrated how I was feeling by not turning up for a PR trip to Trinidad and Tobago that the club had, along with Luton Town, arranged to go on for a few days that October. That decision cost me a fine of £75.

Crazy isn't it and unthinkable today. Not my refusing to go I mean (after all, I already had 'history' with regard to downing tools when it came to club trips abroad) but the fact that, almost immediately after our 4-0 win at Carlisle on 12 October, the playing squad, coaching team and a few of the directors flew out to Port of Spain to play a couple of matches before heading back again in time for us to play Shrewsbury a week later. The club had, no doubt, been made a very good offer to head out there, inconvenient as it was, so off everyone went – except me. And, given the fact the whole trip lasted for less than a week, there was no chance, as had happened when I'd refused, for similar reasons, to go out to Kenya, of me being persuaded or asked to change my mind.

I went to see Ken Brown as soon as he and the rest of the squad had returned. I wasn't happy and I made sure he knew it. Why was it, I asked, that local home-grown talent like myself gets left behind time and time again when it comes to what they are being paid, especially in comparison to new players who have arrived from a lower league club and who hadn't, as was the case with Phelan, unlike me, played a game at the highest level? He had, at least, got one season of Division Two football behind him, albeit one that had seen them, after being promoted in 1982, immediately relegated. Hardly auspicious stuff. Plus Mike hadn't played against Liverpool, Arsenal, Manchester United or

Nottingham Forest⁶, nor had he played in, and won, a major cup final at Wembley, let alone been picked as a starter in all but one of a team's top-flight campaign a couple of years earlier that had seen them reach the top six.

He hadn't even come near to doing any of that. Yet he'd still done enough, as far as the suits at Carrow Road were concerned, to be earning three times my salary. Now I wasn't, and never have been, motivated by money. But I did think I'd been missed out and thought, not unreasonably, I might have had an increase in my own salary so I was at least on the same as Mike and the other new boys.

Ken Brown sat quietly whilst I had my say. Then he spoke, calmly and rationally, as he always did. He was honest enough to admit that his budget, as far as players and wages were concerned, was pretty much gone at that moment in time, but added that it was always under review – if he needed to get someone in, for example, or if we sold a player or two and, with that in mind, he promised to review my situation later on in the season. Was that good enough? I don't know. Maybe I should have told Ken that I didn't accept that and asked for a move. I knew there'd been serious interest in me last time I'd been in this situation with the club and didn't doubt that there would be again but, for all that, I was still a Norfolk boy and a Norwich fan and the club, deep down, knew that my loyalties to them, as stretched as they were at this point, would hold firm. So I thanked Ken for his time and decided that the best way to respond was not to ask for a transfer, nor to kick up a fuss but, instead, to play my heart out.

It was a good decision! I'd made my mark by scoring in the Oldham game and had, by the beginning of December (1985), added another four to my personal total, three in the league plus one in the League Cup in a 2-0 win at Luton where we made a little bit of history in becoming the first team to beat them on

---

6  Forest were quite a big footballing noise at the time. They'd waltzed their way to the Football League title in 1978 and had followed that up by winning the European Cup (now the Champions League) in 1979 and 1980.

their plastic pitch. Christmas came and went and by the time we'd won 1-0 at Fulham on New Year's Day we were top of the league and, even at that still early stage, odds-on favourites to go back up as champions, helped, no doubt, by some very effective on-field communication methods introduced by Mel Machin who'd taken note of a tactic Luton Town had used to very good effect in their home matches. Mel had seen (and heard!) how the Luton players, rather than using what you might call traditional in-game calls to their team-mates, such as 'flick it on', 'hold it' or 'man on' where you then added the players name – i.e. 'flick it on, Tim' or 'hold it, Mal' – we'd turn the whole thing around and just refer to a name when we wanted to give an on-field instruction to a team-mate. So, for example, if I called out 'Jack', that meant 'flick it on'; 'Bob' meant 'hold it' and 'Fred' was 'man on'. We ended up having a very long list of men's names that we'd call out in a match. Each one meant something but, of course, our opponents were never able to cotton on to what we were doing. This worked really well for us, thanks to Mel taking note of what was happening between the Luton players and, rather than just dismissing it as a load of nonsense, as I am sure most coaches would, took the time and trouble to find out what was behind this apparent random calling out of names.

We'd gone top of the table for the first time that season a few weeks earlier, following a 3-1 win at Oldham, a position the club didn't relinquish for the rest of the season. There was the occasional hiccup, such as our 1-0 defeat at Charlton, but even that setback didn't particularly concern us, as we'd played well enough to give ourselves a decent cushion of points ahead of our nearest challengers, Charlton included. It was a great position to be in and I was looking forward to the run-in following that game with, all being well, our title celebrations due to be held at Carrow Road after our last game of the season which was, fittingly, going to be against Leeds United, the club I'd supported as a child.

It all seemed straightforward enough. But my life is rarely anything other than the unexpected.

Ask anyone who knows me what I like doing in my spare time and they'll let you know all about my passion for gardening and outside work in general. Which is exactly what I was doing one morning just after that Charlton game, doing some little bits and pieces and generally pottering about in the garden at my home when, all of a sudden, I felt a sharp stab of pain in my abdomen. I stopped what I was doing for a moment before starting to work again but, no, there it was again and, if anything, even more acute than before.

I called for Gabrielle, asking her to call the doctor; he came around quite quickly and within a few seconds of examining me called for an ambulance. I'd ruptured my appendix! This meant immediate surgery at the Norfolk & Norwich Hospital followed by a spell of convalescence at home, all of which meant there was no way I was going to play any part in our remaining seven games of the season.

I was massively disappointed about this but knew that there was absolutely nothing I could do about it. The lads duly clinched promotion in a 2-0 win at Bradford City on 12 April before, in the last match of the season, demolishing Leeds 4-0 at Carrow Road before being presented with the Division Two trophy on what was, for everyone there, an unforgettable day, especially for Kevin Drinkell, who not only scored his 23rd goal of the season for us during that win but was also awarded the Barry Butler Trophy as Norwich's player of the season pre-match.

He'd been a shoo-in for the trophy really, much like Teemu Pukki had been at the end of the 2018/19 season, another campaign that saw, of course, Norwich win the Division Two, or, as it's now known, Football League Championship trophy. It wasn't a good time to be at home and missing out on all the celebrations, but I hadn't been completely left out as Ken Brown had given me a call after the Bradford game to congratulate me on my part in our success that season as well as to thank me for all of my efforts up until that game. Oh, and one other thing. He also said I was going to be rewarded with a nice new contract that reflected, at last, how much the club appreciated and valued me as a player. So, all in all, a disappointing end to the season on a personal level but, professionally, with a generous rise in my salary now confirmed as well as a return to top-flight football in August, I had a lot to look forward to.

Or so I thought.

I'd started in every one of Norwich's matches that season up to, and including, the match at Charlton. But, despite that, making that starting XI in some of them had been a bit touch and go at times. I had, for a while, been suffering from pain and stiffness in my pelvis and hip area, something I now understand had come about as a consequence of all the effort and strain I was putting on to the right side of my body during a game, whether that was winning the ball, making a pass or even having a shot on goal. Because, bit by bit, and over the months and years, those repeated actions were putting one hell of a strain on my pelvis. I pretty much ignored it at the beginning. Most professional footballers play with a little discomfort in their bodies – it's one of the great consistencies of the game and is something that doesn't discriminate, regardless of whether you are a top international player or someone eking out a living from the game at a much lower level. Take, for example, Bryan Robson. When the former Manchester United and England captain was at his peak, he was one of the best midfielders in the world, no doubt about it. Yet for how much of that time was he, I wonder, fully fit and free of pain, certainly in the latter years of his career?

I remember him being part of a very strong England squad that went to the 1986 World Cup in Mexico. But he wasn't there for long. In only England's second match, against Morocco, he was forced to come off with the reoccurrence of a long-standing shoulder injury which ruled him out for the rest of the tournament. The look of anguish on his face as he came off in that game was one I'll never forget; he was a hard man on the field, one who could, and would, take kicks and elbows all match but never flinch. Yet, as he came off during that game against Morocco, he was very clearly in a lot of pain – and for pain to visually show on Bryan Robson's face, well, it must have been on a level that would have been beyond what most of us mortals can endure.

Robson gave absolutely everything, both in training and during a match. And, over time, his ultra-committed approach was catching up with him. Little niggles and strains turned, eventually, into more long-term injuries which meant he played less and less. Naturally, in order to prove both his critics and the medical profession wrong, he'd work even harder to get back to full fitness but, whilst he was doing that, he was, of course, putting his body through even more stress and strain. So it was never one major injury that eventually forced Bryan Robson to retire from the game, more a case that lots and lots of separate ones had, over a long period of time, become worse and worse until, quite simply, his body couldn't take any more.

Now I would never compare myself, as a player, to such a legend of the game as Robson but what we did have in common was the fact that, as we'd both been playing competitive football regularly from a very early age, our bodies were, over time, going to become more and more prone to injury, especially in those areas that we worked the hardest. For me, as a competitive, 'terrier'-type midfielder, it was all about twisting and rotating my body in order to win the ball, to shield it from an opposing player and to suddenly be able to turn and run into space, all actions that, over time, were, and not to put too fine a point on it, seriously knackering my pelvis.

This meant that, for me, even being fit enough to take part in training sessions leading up to and into the 1986/87 season became a real challenge. But it wasn't as if my injury was a one-off. It was more a consequence of 11 years of wear and tear; of doing some barbaric (indeed, some of the training methods we used are now banned) fitness sessions that included running up sand hills that were littered with rabbit holes. If you ran into one of them then a twisted knee or ankle was almost certainly the end result. It was those sort of repetitive and physically demanding exercises that wore down my hip so much that, after I'd had surgery on it in 2006, the surgeon went into great detail about how badly damaged it was. Running up those hills certainly made us fit but, for me, the stress and long-term damage that and similar exercises did to my joints was catastrophic.

I was in pain for much of the time, so much so on occasion that it wasn't possible, as it might have been in the past, to simply have a pain-killing injection before the game and to simply get on with playing and worry about the after-effects later because those after-effects were now here and preventing me from playing at all, no matter how much hydrocortisone the club's medical staff pumped into me.

This meant I made just five appearances for the club during the whole of the 1986/87 season, three of which were in the league, with the other two, one of which was as a substitute, both in the League Cup. My first of those appearances came when I replaced Mark Barham late on in our 4-1 win over Millwall in a League Cup third-round match, a game and result highlighted by David Hodgson, who we'd signed from Sunderland, scoring a hat-trick on what was his full debut. It was a much changed Norwich City team and dressing room to the one I'd been used to. With promotion back to Division One accomplished, Chris Woods and Dave Watson had departed for Rangers and Everton respectively, whilst we'd also seen the last of John Deehan (Ipswich, in return for Trevor Putney), Paul Haylock (Gillingham) and Dennis Van Wijk (Club Brugge), five familiar and friendly faces all gone in addition to those who'd left prior to the 1985/86 season, most notably Mike Channon and Asa Hartford. Plenty of new faces then, in addition to Putters, including Bryan Gunn in goal as well as Shaun Elliott, who'd joined from Sunderland and Ian Crook, the latest player to take the relatively short trip up the A11 from North London and Tottenham Hotspur.

In a way I suppose I was a bit of a new boy myself. My last game for the club had been on 31 March 1986 and now, nearly nine months later, I was working my way up to match fitness in training around a lot of players who'd never seen me play and had been used to being part of a Norwich City team that had been doing rather well without me. Norwich had started the 1986/87 season exceptionally well and by the end of October were in second place in Division One (sponsored, at the time, by the long gone and forgotten *Today* newspaper) after an excellent run of results that had included a 4-1 win over Aston Villa at Villa Park and an equally impressive 2-0 win over Newcastle at home.

That made my return to Division One football on 1 November 1986 all the more painful as, full of optimism, we made our way to Anfield to play Liverpool, only to be on the very wrong end of a 6-2 thrashing. Now that hurt – but not as much as my pelvis did after the match. But I'd got through it and was now determined, having forced my way back into the team, to get a run of games together, hoping, at the same time, that doing so would, over time, ease the soreness around my joints. I managed to retain my place in the side for our next two league games, a 2-1 win over Tottenham at Carrow Road in which Gunny made his debut plus, a week after that, a 0-0 draw at Manchester United who had recently appointed Alex Ferguson as their manager. I guess a 0-0 at Old Trafford sounds quite a credible result these days but we should have won that game and very nearly did when Wayne Biggins hit the bar with just nine minutes left. That point saw us drop to sixth in the table whilst, believe it or not, the Red Devils climbed one place up to 21st! How times have changed since then.

My last game for Norwich was just four days later in a League Cup fourth-round match against Everton at Goodison Park. We felt we had every chance of getting a win and started well but had to change our shape when Tony Spearing had to go off. It was just one sub in those days, which meant Tony, a defender, was replaced by Mark Barham, a winger. This left us rather exposed at the back and Everton capitalised on that, winning 4-1 in a game that we ended up playing so badly in, and Mel lost his temper and was booked by the referee for dissent.

I'd played in some games but hadn't been at my best and my hip was now giving me constant pain. I could barely sleep as even lying down made me uncomfortable whilst adjusting my position in bed served only to provoke more pain in my entire pelvic area. It was becoming increasingly clear that the wear and tear to that part of my body had now reached a critical juncture, something that was never going to just go away through conventional treatment means, be it massage, physiotherapy or more pain-killing injections. I was going to have to face things head on and, with that in mind, made an appointment to see Mr Hugh Phillips, who was the club's surgeon, a little over a week after the Everton game.

Tim Sheppard, who was the club's physiotherapist at the time, accompanied me to his consulting rooms in Norwich where, I have to say, we had a long and very frank discussion about my ongoing physical problems which he had diagnosed as osteitis pubis. Hugh Phillips was able to give me a little more insight into the problem which is, as he explained, a painful inflammatory condition of the symphysis pubis. That is the name given to the cartilaginous joint that sits between and, quite literally, holds the pubic bones in place. It is prone to inflammation when there is repeated traumatic stress applied to the area which is, of course, exactly what had been happening throughout my football career.

It's a condition that is more common in women than it is in men as it often occurs after pregnancy when the ligaments in that part of the body relax in order to allow gestation to progress. However, it also, as I was now learning, occurs in people that have either served in the military or played an active sport to a very high standard as the pubis will inflame as a reaction to recurrent and excessive training or stretching with the standard treatment, even today, the prescription of either anti-inflammatory or analgesic medication.

I'd already gone beyond that as Hugh had already performed an operation on the area (which is why I missed the beginning of the 1986/87 season) but, as he admitted at our meeting, it had given me little benefit and, with that in mind, he didn't think

I would be able to compete effectively for a first-team place at Norwich City anymore as it was clear to him that there was little to no chance of the condition ever improving. There was, as he went on to explain, one further option which would be for me to have further surgery that would fuse the cartilage and, in theory, give it back some of the strength that it lost whilst also reducing my symptoms. It was not, he added, a procedure that was without risk and there was certainly no guarantee that it would alleviate my symptoms enough for me to resume my career as a professional footballer, especially to the standard that I had been playing.

He was telling me, as kindly as he could, that, in his professional opinion, my career as a professional footballer was over, with immediate effect.

I'd feared the worst for a while. But I'd always had hope that, somehow, I'd have been given an option that meant I could continue playing. I wasn't, after all, the only professional footballer who'd been in this situation. Some would, I am sure, have listened but not really taken it in, they'd have been in some sort of denial, thinking straight away that the docs had got it wrong and that they'd get a second opinion, a third, a fourth even and keep on doing so until they got the news the treatment they required was out there which meant they could carry on playing as if nothing had ever happened.

I'd had that hope. But that was before I sat down with Tim, with Hugh Phillips. By the time we left his offices, with me limping alongside Tim like an old man, I knew my career as a professional footballer was finished.

The great irony of it all was that this had happened during my benefit season. The club's board had, in November 1985, agreed to my being awarded a testimonial match at some point during the following (1986/87) season which would be regarded as my benefit season for the club and feature a number of events that would be arranged and co-ordinated by a testimonial committee. It seemed perversely fitting, therefore, that my benefit season was now going to be the one that saw me bow out of the game altogether and, with an uncertain future now ahead of me, the testimonial match itself now took on a much greater significance.

I was, of course, devastated to know that I'd never kick a football at any sort of competitive level again. It was all I had ever wanted to do with my life, something that I knew would <u>be</u> my life when I was kicking a ball around back in Gaywood until I heard my dad's voice penetrate the gathering gloom of the end of another day, demanding I get in and '... get in now, you've got school tomorrow.'

I'd had the dream and I'd been living it. Now it was gone.

But I couldn't sit around feeling sorry for myself. I still had a testimonial match to arrange and, now that I wasn't playing anymore, I could, at least, give a lot more time to that than I had initially thought I would. Gabrielle and I had formed a testimonial committee that was headed up by Mr Norman Potter from the Pointer Motor Company. So there was work to do there. I was also asked by Ken Brown what my intentions for the future were and if, with that in mind, I'd be interested in joining his coaching team? What a wonderful offer, one I was never going to turn down. It was an honour to be asked and I told Ken exactly that. He'd been a wonderful mentor to me as an up and coming player, now he'd be doing the same for me as I commenced, albeit a little bit earlier in my life than I had initially thought, my career in coaching. Sadly for both me and especially Ken, it never happened.

We'd often talked about the sort of role I might have had and things were moving in the right direction when, and very unexpectedly, Ken was sacked as Norwich City manager shortly after a 2-0 defeat at Charlton in November 1987, a decision taken, much to the surprise of a lot of people, by Mr Chase, which not only ended Ken's long association with the club but put paid to any chance I had of starting my new career as a coach at Carrow Road. One door closes and another one closes, as I was beginning to think.

My testimonial match took place on 8 August 1987 with a game against the Spanish side Real Sociedad who were, at the time, managed by the former Liverpool and Wales striker John Toshack. I'd been extremely fortunate to secure the services of such a well-known side for what was a really emotional night for me, one that ended with Robert Chase presenting me with a cheque for £14,000, a more than generous amount that I wanted to invest in property, although, having said that, I didn't do so straight away and decided to also get some professional advice as how I could best make the money work for me which, after listening to and working my way through the options available, decided, a little reluctantly, to invest the whole amount in unit trusts.

Those of you who know how such things work might already have guessed what happened next. And believe me, it happened quickly. I got a phone call on 19 October 1987, the day that went down in history as 'Black Monday' when stock markets all around the world crashed in spectacular fashion. My first question was, of course, how did this affect my investment and how much of it did I stand to lose? The reply shook me to the core – 90% of the money had gone, lost overnight, due to the fact we had, against what we might have otherwise not opted to do, had the money put into the high-risk end of the market when I had, all along, been told they were all low-risk products.

Within a few months, I'd not only lost my career but now, on top of that, had lost all of the proceeds that had been raised as the result of all the hard work and effort that my testimonial committee had put in over the last 12 months. I was at rock bottom and ended up unemployed and having to sign on. There's no disgrace in having to do so of course, but it was the last thing I was expecting I'd ever have to do at the end of the 1985/86 season when my focus was solely on getting fit and over my injuries and resuming my career as a professional footballer. That had long gone, as had, thanks to the decision of Mr Chase to unceremoniously sack Ken Brown as manager of Norwich City, my chance of commencing a career in coaching at the club.

A few months before Ken was fired and with me still hoping that I'd be offered a place on his coaching staff, I was, in June 1987, and quite unexpectedly, offered the position as manager of King's Lynn Football Club.

Shocked and surprised? You bet. After all, I had little to no experience of coaching at that time, let alone management, other than a short spell out in New Zealand in the summer of 1981 when I'd spent some time with a club called Miramar Rangers as their player-coach. That had been an enormously enjoyable experience shared with some lovely people but had never been anything more than an opportunity for me to play some games so I'd return to Norwich for pre-season training 100 per cent fit and match ready.

Luckily for me, Ken Brown had a friend called Ian Wells who had connections with Miramar, and he'd mentioned to Ken that the club were struggling and needed a lift. It didn't take Ken long to work out that I'd be as good for them as they would be for me, a temporary footballing match made in heaven. And, let's face it, how often does anyone, let alone a 21-year-old who, in the nicest possible way, is still a little bit wet behind the ears, get an opportunity as good as this one was? Yes I was nervous. I couldn't, after all, run off home if things weren't working out. I would have to make it work and I did. It was a fantastic experience, one that saw me meet a lot of lovely people with Wellington, in particular, holding many great memories for me.

While I was there, I stayed with a great couple, Costa (who played for Miramar) and Debbie Leonadis, who made me feel very welcome. That was for the first part of my two-month stay 'down under'. For the second month, I did some coaching in some of the schools on the North Island with the support of Ian Wells, who was part of the *Dominion Post*, which was a morning paper that covered Wellington. And let me tell you this. The standard of football down there was of a really high quality and much better than I'd originally expected, with one consequence of that being the fact that the New Zealand national team were good enough to qualify for the 1982 World Cup finals where they played Brazil, Scotland and the USSR.

One of their players nearly ended up joining Norwich City. That was Wynton Rufer, who, along with his brother Shane, played for Miramar. Wynton went over for trials at Norwich and so convinced the club of his quality, that they made him an offer and even went as far as circulating photos of him in his Norwich strip. Sadly for Wynton, as well as Norwich, the move never happened as the Home Office, when considering his request for a work permit, decided that as he was from New Zealand he couldn't possibly be good enough to play the game in England so, just like that, they refused his application point blank. Wynton was able to prove them wrong, however, and after spending some time playing top-flight football in Switzerland he joined German Bundesliga club Werder Bremen where he ended up playing in, and winning, a European Cup Winners' Cup medal in 1992, scoring in the final as Werder Bremen beat Monaco 2-0.

Not bad for someone who the Home Office had decreed wasn't good enough to earn his living from the game!

So, all in all, it was a great couple of months for me and I returned to England in time for the start of the 1981/82 season as fit as I'd ever been. Ken Brown must have been impressed as he picked me for our opening-day game which was against Rotherham up at Millmoor. We lost that game 4-1, a result and performance that swiftly brought me down to earth after my adventures on the other side of the world. But oh my, they were wonderful times and created memories I will treasure forever. It had certainly, even at that young age, made me keen to want to go into coaching and, if possible, management when my club career ended, even though I thought it wouldn't really be something I'd consider until I was well into my 30s, given how much I enjoyed playing.

Now, six years later and as a result of my enforced retirement it was something that, naturally, had come into the forefront of my mind again, which is why I'd asked Ken Brown if I could become part of his coaching team. That wasn't going to happen now, which meant I was left pondering the possibility of getting my face and CV out and about in order to see if there were any suitable roles going for me. I was quite happy to consider going overseas if necessary. Miramar had given me a taste of what living away from home was like and I'd enjoyed it. However, when the first offer came along it came from a club that was right on my home doorstep!

CHAPTER SEVEN

# Back at the Walks

*So do the maths. Little to no money to spend, a squad
of players who, for the most part, weren't good enough
and a never ending battle trying to persuade even
half-decent ones to consider signing for us.*

### King's Lynn FC

Yes, my local club wanted to give me the opportunity of taking
over as their player-manager in June 1987. A club that was, and
remains, close to my heart for all sorts of reasons. They had, after
all, been the first football team I'd ever gone to watch, courtesy
of my lovely grandparents, who first took me to The Walks when
I was just six years old, when a chap by the name of Reg Davies
had been their manager. The Linnets have had some great players
over the years, including Mick Wright (who made 1,152 first-team
appearances for the club, a British record for any one-club man or
woman), Keith Rudd and Freddie Easthall and I'd be there most
weeks, clad in my blue-and-gold scarf and with my rattle in my
hand, making sure I always stood in the same spot on the terrace.
Now, two decades on from my being one of their youngest but
most devoted of fans, I was being invited to succeed Bill Cleary
who'd taken on the job in a caretaker role after Freddie Easthall
had departed the second hottest seat in Norfolk.

It was an opportunity that came along at both a good and bad time in my life really. A good time because I obviously needed to do something with my life, and the chance to learn the managerial ropes at a club with which I felt a strong connection was a compelling reason. And bad because I was still not only coming to terms with having to quit as a player but, in addition to that, having to cope with the fact that Norwich didn't, at that time, seem to want to have anything to do with me. And that hurt. They weren't honour-bound to give me a job of course, I understand that, but on the other hand I'd given the club absolutely everything over the time I was there, so much so in fact that the sheer repetition of all that physical effort I'd put into training and matches had caused the injury that meant I had to retire.

That may sound a little over-dramatic now, but it was how I felt at the time. It was clear, however, that there would be no job offer coming from Carrow Road, which meant accepting King's Lynn's offer was an easy choice to make in the end. It didn't worry me (and clearly wasn't much of a concern to the club's board of directors either) that, other than my brief stint in New Zealand six years earlier, I had little to no coaching experience and, of course, absolutely none as a manager, and looking back it might have been a little bit more sensible if I'd declined their invitation and waited for a position where I was part of a coaching team somewhere rather than being parachuted into the manager's role, with all the responsibility that goes with it, at just 27 years of age. But then would a chance like this ever come my way again?

It didn't take me long to realise that the club's financial position wasn't a particularly healthy one. In addition to that, I had virtually no staff to call upon apart from Bill Cleary who was staying on. So it was going to be a battle from day one. What was encouraging, however, was that, despite the fact the club wasn't in a good place, the people of King's Lynn wanted to get behind us and I got, early on, some great support from some of the local businesses who wanted to be involved in some way or other as well as the fans who, whenever they saw me, made sure they let me know how glad they were I was in charge and how good it was to have a 'local lad' leading of their team.

With backing like that you begin to think you might have a chance of turning things around.

Squad wise, it wasn't the greatest. Like me, most of the players were local and either came from the town or from fairly nearby. Some of them weren't really up to the standard required but they at least gave it everything they had in training and games, something I appreciated more than most as it was how I'd always played the game myself. So they were triers, I'll give them that. It wasn't that easy to replace them either as, even though I'd been doing everything that I could think of to add to the squad, the fact that King's Lynn is stuck out on a bit of a limb, geographically, meant that the costs for any would-be players in getting here, as well as the time it would take, made it difficult to sign new ones.

So do the maths. Little to no money to spend, a squad of players who, for the most part, weren't good enough and a never-ending battle trying to persuade even half-decent ones to consider signing for us. I was on a sticky wicket right from the start and it showed in terms of our performances and results, none more so than when we were knocked out of the FA Cup by March Town who were lower down the league tier than we were – so it was, in effect, a bit of a giant killing, not that it made *Match Of The Day*!

We should have won. Not could, should. We were at home and, for all of the issues both I and the club were having to deal with at the time, March Town should not have been a team that gave us too many problems. I'd prepared the players and we'd gone through our game plan time and time again. I'd taken it as seriously as any Division One match I'd played and hoped my enthusiasm would rub off on the players. It was, after all, and I'd told them this, the FA Cup. One of the greatest, if not THE greatest, domestic football competition in the world. So let's see how far we can get in lads, how about that? First round proper, that's not an unrealistic proposition. Third round? Well, why not? The Linnets had a decent record in the competition;

indeed, it was one of the best in the entire country in terms of games played, and won, in the FA Cup. Back in 1962, the Linnets had got to the third round and ended up drawing Everton at Goodison Park. They'd lost 4-0 but that hardly mattered; the publicity and, of course, additional income that cup run had brought the side was invaluable. So, not surprisingly, the board had budgeted for a good FA Cup run this time around for exactly the same reasons. Could we mark the 25th anniversary of that famous run in the competition that had taken us all the way to Goodison Park?

Clearly not. Though things were looking good for us at one point. It was 1-1 when Mark Howard, one of my best players, scored with a 30-yard screamer. What. A. Goal. But no, one of our players was given, incorrectly, as just offside. It was a body blow. Still, we can regroup and get at them in the replay, I thought. I'll give them a bit of a bollocking, remind them of what this competition is all about and that there is a chance, however small, of going to places like Everton or Liverpool, Manchester United, Arsenal. If players, and it doesn't matter what level they're at, aren't excited or motivated by the possibility of something like that happening in their careers, then why bother?

Why bother at all? Because March Town bombed straight up the other end and got a winner. And that was that, dumped out of the competition at the earliest possible stage we could exit it (we'd been spared having to play in the preliminary round) and with it our only genuine chance of making some money for the club that season.

But the fallout of our defeat didn't end there. I was incensed that our winning goal hadn't been allowed and had very good reason to be annoyed. I'd recently been an attendee on the FA's course for the Preliminary Football Coaching Certificate where we'd had a visit by a referee who had given an extensive talk on the rules of the game. Invaluable really, especially when you consider the fact that, even today, a lot of managers and coaches still don't seem completely familiar with them!

Anyway, he stressed during the talk that he would always give a goal if a player who was offside was not interfering with play, a ruling that still applies now. I'd taken note of that and had, immediately after the March Town game, had a few words with the referee as he was walking off the pitch, querying his decision and asking him why he'd simply gone with what his linesman had done and paid attention to his flag rather than applying the laws of the game and allowing the goal to stand before telling his linesman of his decision.

That makes it sound as if I'd had a quiet and rational conversation with the referee. But I hadn't. I was so frustrated by that point, I let all of my frustrations out with a torrent of foul language directed at that unfortunate linesman who'd chosen, incorrectly, to raise his flag. It was so out of character and so very abusive that I'm not going to reproduce what I said here, but suffice to say the referee, quite rightly, asked for my name to which my only response was to go into the home dressing room, where my players were waiting for me, and to slam the door in the referee's face.

The FA soon got involved and a month or so later I received a letter that had also been cc'd to the King's Lynn secretary which stated I had been found guilty of misconduct and was not only going to be fined £10 but suspended for a month into the bargain. I immediately put in an appeal to the FA stating my case which at least got the suspension delayed pending the result of my appeal. It didn't stop me getting into trouble again a fortnight later when I was, again, reported to the FA by a referee, although, in my defence, I do wonder if, looking back at his report, he was just looking to book me and to be able to say to his mates that 'I booked that Peter Mendham today'. I've still got his report to the FA and the incident in question is recorded as follows:

Having awarded a free kick to Bury Town, P. Mendham, stated that 'That was never a free kick referee' and I therefore cautioned him.

A booking offence? I'll leave you to decide that one. With regard to the other incident, it's interesting looking back at the FA's records at the time with regards to their disciplinary procedures. I'd been fined £10 and suspended, pending appeal, for 28 days for 'directing foul and abusive comment at a linesman', whereas an official of Runcorn FC, who was charged with 'directing insulting comment at the referee after the match' was fined £15 and 'warned to his future conduct', whilst another official, this time from Darwen FC who was 'guilty of directing foul and abusive comments at the referee after the match' was fined £50 and 'warned as to his future conduct'.

So there didn't seem any consistency at all with regard to these matters. I was later advised my hearing would be held at Carrow Road on 17 November but I never attended it as, on the day after it was heard, I handed in my resignation as manager of King's Lynn which the club, via a letter to me a week later, acknowledged, according to the chairman, 'with some sadness'. He then went on to state that my outstanding bonuses and expenses would be paid at the end of the month.

The bookings and subsequent FA actions didn't really have a lot to do with it though, what had been bothering me was that I hadn't, up to then, been paid by the club and had got to the stage where I felt the only option I had was to resign and to then seek some sort of restitution through the courts which is what eventually happened. But then things got complicated as King's Lynn decided that as I'd agreed to turn out for Wymondham Sunday FC on 22 November I was in breach of my contract, which gave them no option other than to dismiss me. This, of course, gave them the opportunity to withhold what was due to me financially, which was what led to the whole rather sad affair ending up in the hands of solicitors.

Fortunately for both parties, a mutually satisfactory resolution to the issue was eventually reached which meant that it didn't go all the way to court, something neither I nor King's Lynn FC would have wanted. It meant that my first experience of management had ended on something of a low note and made me wonder if it was something that I would ever want to get involved with again, given how my first taste of it had ended up.

CHAPTER EIGHT

# Twin Towers Encores

*My move back to Diss Town didn't come*
*without its problems.*

WHAT I missed most of all was playing. I ended up doing so for a little while with Watton Town as well as exploring some playing options in Sweden with Hammarby and NAC Breda in Holland but nothing substantial came from either and I joined Diss Town in June 1991 before moving to Wroxham in November 1992. This was a move that suited me at the time (although, as it turned out, I wasn't finished with Diss Town and I'll be talking more about the Tangerines later) as I had, back in April of that year, accepted a position at my first footballing love, namely Norwich City.

Unlike the offer I'd had from King's Lynn, this was a role that I'd heard about and was very much interested in applying for. I didn't realise, however, quite how long and drawn-out the application process would be. It would be a new appointment at Carrow Road with the title of football in the community officer (FITC) which, whilst it wasn't a purely coaching role, would be one that would give me the opportunity to work in the Norwich and wider Norfolk community in order to create and nurture a sense of connection for supporters with the club, whether by organising and attending soccer camps for children, getting involved with other community groups to work on a wide variety of projects or arranging to visit local schools with a few players. It was, in essence, not a scheme that was set up to purely make money, but, rather than that, to illustrate how grateful the club was to the city of Norwich and Norfolk as a whole for its support and to try and give something back. Norwich's fan base have always been amongst the most passionate and loyal in the entire country. They identify with their club in a way that the supporters of many bigger clubs will never be able to do and to see the looks on people's faces when we turned up at their events was an absolute joy.

I'd first heard about it back in October 1990 from Mick McGuire, a former team-mate at Carrow Road who was now working for the Professional Footballers' Association. Mick had outlined how the scheme worked and mentioned he thought I might be an ideal candidate to help develop it at Norwich City. I didn't need asking twice if I would be interested and immediately sent a letter to Roger Read, who was based in Manchester and charged with setting up various schemes across the country. It took a while for Roger to get back to me but when he did, again by letter (no e-mails back then!), he mentioned that he found my CV 'most interesting' (is it a good or bad thing when someone says that about your CV?) and that, as he was currently looking to establish a local project at Norwich, he would keep me in mind. It wasn't quite the response I had hoped for but, then again, at least I'd made my interest known.

As I hadn't heard anything back from Roger or from anyone involved with the FITC scheme, I dropped him another line at the end of March 1991 – nearly five months after Mick had told me all about it. Roger's reply was a little bit more encouraging at least, mentioning that his regional director was in the process of making an approach to Norwich City and that, with that in mind, they'd soon be able to more properly consider my application and interest in the job which was now, at least, at the point of being brought into actual existence! Three months later I heard from him again confirming that the club was about to advertise the job and that he would ensure that my CV was considered '... along with all the other applications'.

Thus, a little under a year after Mick McGuire had first told me about the scheme, I was invited to the club in order to attend an interview for the post, which was then cancelled three days before I was due to attend. By this time, I have to say I was beginning to get a little bit weary about how long the whole application process was taking, but I was also determined to see the whole thing through and, following a second interview late in November 1991 (interest in the post was high and, as I now understand it, the club had a high number of very high calibre applicants), I was, eventually, in July 1992, offered the role of Norwich City Football Club's first ever football and community (as it was now titled) development officer. It had been an extremely long haul but it was a role I had always been interested in, indeed, was very excited about. I was delighted to finally accept especially as, a couple of months earlier, I had again enquired about a role at the club, this time as reserve-team manager. That application didn't go very far at all, however, as I soon heard that I was not going to be considered via a terse letter from Mike Walker, who had just taken over as the club's new manager. Mike clearly, as is any new manager's right, had his own man in mind for the role, that man being, as it turned out, the former Luton Town and Leeds United centre-half John Faulkner who went on to do a very good job.

But no matter. I had a new job back at the club that I loved and was very much looking forward to starting and getting to know Ros Watson, who was the club's schools liaison officer. Happy days.

Norwich's scheme might, first and foremost, have been altruistic in nature but that didn't mean we ended up swanning around Norwich and Norfolk doing good deeds for one and all with little care for the costs involved. We had, of course, a tightly managed budget as the scheme didn't, and couldn't, do whatever it wanted to do. So we accounted, carefully, for every penny that went out, just as we did for every penny that came in. And yes, there were occasions when we made a little bit of money as well, money that would immediately be paid back into the scheme in order for us to arrange more and more schemes in the area and make, in the process, FITC as accessible, hands-on and fan-friendly as possible. But it was never going to be as simple as that. The club's financial policy at the time didn't seem to be one that regarded the FITC scheme as a priority. And maybe that's understandable, given that every penny made really did matter back then. In any case, it did appear that the people and the communities we were out there working for couldn't always benefit as much as I thought they might have and that was disappointing.

I know that football clubs have to be run, first and foremost, as a business. It's especially true today of course, but even back then that was most certainly the case. And, just as the club has had to do in recent years with, for example, the sales of players that are dictated by financial need rather than for purely footballing purposes, we had to cut our cloth according to our coat at the time. I didn't like it but I wasn't going to be able to change the way the club was run. But, rather than carry out and put up with things the way they were, I decided to resign from my role and leave the club altogether. In any case, I'd been in it for around four years and had figured that maybe we both needed a change and, for me, it was time to try something else. I was still only 36 and knew I had a lot to offer someone even if it might not necessarily be in football and would certainly not involve Norwich City in any way.

Yet I hadn't, quite, left football behind. Because while I had been working for the Canaries, I ended up doing a bit of a Micky Channon by, just as he did with us in 1985, playing my part in another Wembley cup final when the combination of age plus the club I was at might have meant such a possibility was impossible. And it's all down to another former Canary, Bill Punton, who'd persuaded me to sign for Diss Town for a second time after I'd finished a brief but enjoyable spell playing with Wroxham.

I was delighted to have the opportunity to go back. Diss Town were (and remain) one of Norfolk's great football clubs, one that was, at the time, run by Richard, or 'Dickie', Upson who was the father of Matthew Upson, a local lad (he was born in Eye) who escaped the clutches of both Norwich and Ipswich and went on to play for, amongst others, Arsenal, Birmingham City and West Ham as well as England. Dickie was a great football man and administrator and set the tone at the club, which was to always try to do things in as proper and professional a manner as they could, which was admirable. This included, as I immediately noticed upon my return, a good group of players, many of whom would have been more than capable of playing at a higher level of the game had they wished to do so.

My move back to Diss Town didn't come without its problems. My position at the time as the football in the community officer at Norwich City meant that I wasn't able to play in every game for Diss as my contract of employment with the Canaries meant that I had to be at Carrow Road for every home game. If that clashed with a home game for Diss then I couldn't play for them, something which caused a few problems in the dressing room at the club.

That situation changed as Diss progressed in the FA Vase that season. I'd missed, for the above reason, some of the club's earlier games in the competition that season, but once the club had reached the quarter-finals of the competition Robert Chase gave me permission to play in all of our remaining games, home or away. Bill Punton certainly wanted me in his team and I suppose he was putting a lot of faith in me as he knew I had the sort of experience and know-how that was needed at that stage of a cup competition when more and more attention is drawn to a club and its players. But I wasn't the only decent player at the club. Paul Gibbs and Paul Warne were both more than good enough to play at Football League level; indeed, as time went on, we knew that clubs higher up the pyramid were keeping a very close eye on them indeed.

Our dreams of going to Wembley looked to have ended at the semi-final stage when, in a replay against Tamworth FC, we were losing 1-0 with hardly any time left. Somehow we managed to get an equaliser before, in the dying seconds of the game, Ian Manning popped up with the winner, breaking Tamworth hearts in the process, but at the same time provoking an outpouring of unfettered joy amongst the Diss players and fans I've rarely experienced in football. What a game, what a night and what a team.

This all meant that, just as Mike Channon had enjoyed his unexpected Wembley swansong with Norwich at the age of 37, I was now, at 34, set to have one more chance to play at the famous old stadium, something I wouldn't have expected in even the wildest and most fantastic of dreams when I'd been forced to leave Norwich. Yet, right at the last minute, it seemed as if that opportunity was going to be taken away from me when, two weeks before the match, I pulled a calf muscle in training and realised, immediately, that my chances of taking part in the club's big day were now extremely unlikely.

Bill wanted me to play and made that very clear. So, in an effort to get fit, I had constant treatment until, just before the club were due to travel down to London for the match, one final and very gruelling late fitness test. Make or break time. Fortunately, I came through it and Bill made the choice of starting me on the day, a tough one for him to make as it meant there was no place for Ian Manning who had, if you remember, scored the goal that had got us to Wembley in the first place. I'm sure Ian was bitterly disappointed to have missed out but he was, as were all the lads, a man who put the team ahead of any personal considerations and worked as hard as anyone as we prepared, as a team, for the game which was to be played against Taunton Town from Somerset.

It's well-known history now that we won 2-1 after, I have to admit, as gruelling a 30 extra time as I'd ever experienced, a combination of my injury and age I suppose! Yet I'd always thought our names was on the cup and still thought that way even as we drifted towards the end of injury time after 90 minutes had been played, six minutes in, seven minutes, eight and now NINE minutes into injury time with the Taunton Town supporters torn between celebrating and hiding their heads in their hands, willing the referee to blow the final whistle. They knew we'd never give up and we didn't as, in that ninth minute of injury time, we were awarded a penalty. The pressure on Paul Gibbs as he stepped up to take it was enormous. I could feel it myself so goodness only knows how Gibbo felt. Yet he stuck it away as if it had been a training ground exercise, drilled into the roof of the net to make it 1-1 with all to play for.

No one wanted that period of extra time but here it now was and it was laden with cases of cramp to say the least. Yet, somehow, the Diss boys prevailed with, in particular, Robert Woodcock in goal standing firm whilst, just ahead of him in our back four, Jason Carter stood resolute, very much a man in 'they shall not pass' mode as he had been all season. I was pretty much keeping to my position on the edge of the 18-yard box yet when we got a couple of corners in quick succession moved a little bit further forward, a good bit of anticipation really (or else Bill would have had a right go at me) as I was now perfectly positioned to meet the corner with a firm header towards the goal. Taunton's keeper made the save but I was able to respond quickest to the loose ball that followed and volleyed it in to put us 2-1 up and, of course, win the game and the FA Vase with it.

It was pandemonium all over again, just as it had been against Sunderland back in 1985. I was ecstatic, of course, to have scored the winning goal but what pleased me more than anything else was that I'd repaid Bill Punton's faith in me. He'd signed me in the first place and then proceeded to start me in matches when, at one point, the feeling in the dressing room might have been I was getting preferential treatment because of who I was. He'd then picked me to start the final, leaving out Ian in the process, a very tough call for him to make and one which could, of course, have so easily gone against him. So, however happy I was feeling as we paraded the trophy at Wembley and, later on, in our open-type bus tour around the town, I knew that no one in Diss was quite as happy as Bill was at that moment and I was more delighted for him and the club than I was for myself.

It certainly seemed as good a time as any for me to finally hang up my boots. I'd been working for Norwich City's FITC scheme for two years by then and felt that I now wanted to focus on that role as well as the coaching I was doing with the club that came with it. I also knew that if I kept playing then I'd be aggravating my pelvic injury, not that I thought the condition was going to get any worse but I was suffering a lot of pain after matches (including Wembley finals!) which necessitated taking a lot of tablets to try and nullify the pain. I also found it was taking me up to three or four days to get anything like normal movement back in my body, which all meant, of course, if I wasn't at my best then it was hardly fair on Norwich City, my employers at the time, or the people who I met, on a daily basis, especially those I was putting on coaching sessions for.

At least I'd gone out on a high. And there can't have been too many players who've gone to two Wembley finals and won them both, once as a professional and once as an amateur. So yes, it was the right time to 'properly' retire from playing and, in doing so, give more of a chance to some of the younger lads at the club back then, good players like Ian Manning, Phil Mortimer and Phil Bugg.

And as a Norfolk lad, I couldn't have been prouder at playing my part in helping bring a prestigious trophy like the FA Vase to Norfolk. It hasn't been back since, but the non-league scene in the county is currently very strong so there's every reason to think that it might happen again one day.

I'll look forward to supporting whoever it is in the final when that happens.

With my playing career well and truly finished and, as I wrote earlier, my time as the FITC officer at Norwich City having come to an end, I found myself, in April 1996, having to re-evaluate my life all over again. It wasn't the first time I'd had to do so and I have had to do so again and again on subsequent occasions but, for all that, it never gets any easier and I've never enjoyed the uncertainty and stress that goes with it. On this occasion and after a brief spell of unemployment, I took on a role at a business in Norwich that specialised in designing and manufacturing labels for an assortment of food-related items. It wasn't, as these things often aren't, anything like the sort of position or work I'd expected to end up in but it was a case of needs must at the time and I learnt, during my time in the job, a lot of things that I might never have expected to. So it served a purpose for the four and a half years or so I was there, but during all of that time I knew that, somewhere, there was a position that I could really make my own, one that could make use of my best qualities which I have always believed involved getting out and about and meeting people, making a difference and being, as the modern-day description goes, an 'influencer'.

Which is exactly what the role I took with the East Anglian Air Ambulance Charity allowed me to do. It was, and remains, an outstanding organisation, both the charity and the people that it supports.

The objectives of the East Anglian Air Ambulance were, and are, straightforward and positive. They exist to save lives by delivering highly skilled doctors and critical-care paramedics by air or car to seriously ill or injured people throughout the region. They are a life-saving charity that is only kept airborne thanks to the time given and the incredible generosity shown by their supporters. It was now my job to be the highly visible 'face' of the charity and to get out and about in East Anglia, working alongside both colleagues and volunteers to raise money and awareness as well as to constantly keep the charity moving forward in order to meet the stream of targets that we were set by our executive director.

I was with the charity for nearly five and a half years and enjoyed every second of my time there. It felt as if it was the sort of role I had been made for, one that gave me a lot of freedom to plan and deliver new fundraising initiatives which included the creation and implementation of a structured fundraising plan;

recruiting volunteers and, as part of that process, supporting them throughout their time with the charity as well as utilising all the numerous contacts I'd made in both my working and social life in order to generate maximum publicity and support for the charity, as well as, of course, income. And we were more than successful on that score, constantly surpassing the targets that we'd been set, which meant the charity was able to meet its commitments to the Air Ambulance team in full.

I had a wonderful team of volunteers working for me, one of whom, Elizabeth Moir, was hugely supportive. No matter where we were or what we were doing, she'd be there, signing people up and raising money for us in innumerable ways, a lovely lady who raised tens of thousands of pounds for us on her own!

Life was therefore good, and looking up. I was working in a role that I thoroughly enjoyed; indeed, it was probably, career wise, the most fulfilling time I'd had since my peak years as a player with Norwich City. We'd been successful in making the East Anglian Air Ambulance one of the most high-profile charities in the region, helped by Roy Waller of BBC Radio Norfolk who gave us so much praise and publicity on his programmes. There was also the very important fact that wherever we went with our fundraising activities we were often able to take along one of the stars of the show to meet everyone – in other words one of our helicopters.

They'd attract a crowd in no time at all and I soon realised that the thrill of being so close to such a fantastic piece of technology made people more than happy to put their hands in their pockets and put something into one of our collecting buckets, that or, if they were a local business, to pledge some more substantial support. We were a 'feel good' charity that was dedicated to saving lives and that sort of thing resonated with people. I was, for the first time in quite a while, extremely happy with my work and the way my 'new' career was progressing.

# CHAPTER NINE

# Beauty on the Inside

*... it was that one small act that tipped me over the edge and I reacted in a split second in the most barbaric and horrible way imaginable.*

I GUESS I am my very own 'elephant in the room'.

You may have heard the phrase. It refers to an obvious risk or problem that people don't want to talk about, regardless of its scale. Hence the use of the word 'elephant'. You couldn't be in the same room as an elephant and not see it. It's big, noisy and has a tendency for aggressive behaviour. In your face in other words. Yet, for all that, social norms dictate that if mentioning the elephant would make the people in the room feel awkward, embarrassed or otherwise uncomfortable, then they'd pretend it wasn't there and carry on as if nothing was happening, even if it was in the process of destroying the room around them.

So I'm a sort of elephant really. I can be in a room with a group of people or at a social event or something similar to that, chatting away to lots of people and enjoying myself, yet, all the time I'm there, I know there will be people looking at me or chatting to me who are constantly thinking, 'He's that bloke who stabbed his girlfriend and nearly killed her.'

They're thinking it and I know they're thinking it. I sometimes wish people would bring it out into the open, say something straight away, rather than hide behind all of the straight talk.

'Hi Peter, pleased to meet you. What the hell were you thinking about when you stabbed your girlfriend with a kitchen knife?'

It'd at least get things out in the open. It never happens, of course. I'm more likely to be greeted with something like, 'I was at Wembley on that day Pete,' or 'Do you remember that goal you scored for Norwich against Aston Villa in the cup replay?'

Even people who aren't into football will remember me for another reason.

'Hello Peter, nice to see you. We met when you came round to collect that money we raised for the helicopter, I don't suppose you remember?'

I love meeting people. I'll always try to find time to talk football if someone stops me in the street or recognises me while I'm at work. It's always a pleasure. I hope that, whenever it happens, some of the people I meet will go home and say to someone, 'I met that Peter Mendham today, he's a really nice bloke.'

But who am I kidding? For every one person who might say that, there'll be another nine who'll catch me out of the corner of their eye and think, 'There's that bastard who stabbed his girlfriend.' And worse. It's something I'll have to live with for the rest of my life. And rightly so. I'd never try to convince anyone otherwise because I am that bastard who stabbed his girlfriend.

There's no use hiding from it. And I can't write a book without talking about it. People will read this book to see what I have to say about that night and my spell in prison that resulted from. I'm not going to ignore it as it's something that's never going to go away.

I began to write about that time in my life in the prologue at the beginning of this book. It sets the scene, outlining how and when Charlotte and I met and how, over time, we started to have a relationship. I had, at the time, a great job, a nice home, money in the bank and how lucky was I topping all of that off by being part of a developing relationship with a beautiful woman?

That prologue ends with these nine words:

*So yes, life was good. Very good in fact.*

Except that was a lie. Who was I kidding? Life was anything but good at the time. In fact it was starting to become a very real struggle. And I was beginning to lose control of it and everything around me.

The one exception was my main job. I'd raised in excess of £5 million for the East Anglian Air Ambulance so was, as a result of that, always out and about. Socialising disguised as networking and all for the good of the charity. I was doing well, the charity was doing well and my bosses were very pleased with me. I was working far longer hours than those set out in my contract of employment but who doesn't these days? It was a demanding role but one I was more than happy to go above and beyond in to make it work.

Yet, over time, I was becoming a bit of a recluse.

Things came to a head after I'd gone out one evening with an old friend. When Charlotte found out about it, she wasn't happy and made that very clear. I couldn't blame her. I'd always been out and about working, then when I did have some free time I chose to spend it with a mate. Anyway, she didn't ring or text me at all for a while, neither did she respond to my messages.

I started to brood about it. Why was she ignoring me? Was it all over before it had even started? Was she seeing someone else? Did she think I was seeing someone else? I constantly played all of these scenarios over and over again in my head trying to work out why she was ignoring me and getting absolutely nowhere. Eventually I became a bit obsessed about it. It must, I reasoned, be me. What have I done wrong, what did I do to upset her? I was able to go to work and do what needed to be done but that was about it as far as things went. From the moment I woke up in the morning my mind was on Charlotte and what I had done wrong, that or what I hadn't done, and it stayed with me all day until I got home again. I didn't go out, didn't go to the gym as I usually did, or arrange to meet up with any friends. I started to ignore messages that had been left for me. All I wanted to do was put right whatever I had done wrong. But if I couldn't even get to talk to Charlotte over the phone, let alone meet up with her on a date, then I wasn't going to get the chance to talk it out, to explain myself to her, my actions or inactions, anything at all. I just wanted an opportunity to press the reset button and get things back to normal.

I was trying too hard. I did everything I possibly could to 'win' Charlotte's approval. If she liked the look of something, I'd go out and buy it for her. She might only have mentioned how she liked something but never came anywhere near to actually asking or expecting to have it. It'd be a throwaway remark. 'I like that car' or 'That's a lovely necklace', that sort of thing, which I'd regard as my cue to go out and buy it. I became obsessed. I got her Christian Dior jewellery, Louis Vuitton bags and even a brand new car. All material things. Was I trying to buy her approval, her love and affection for me? I don't know.

Yet the things I wanted more than anything don't cost a penny. Things like love, loyalty and, most of all, companionship; having someone at your side every day who just wants to be with you. My marriage to Gabrielle had, sadly, ended in divorce in 1999 after 16 years and two wonderful children. They'd been good times. But, much as I enjoyed life, I also wanted to be with someone again, someone special, have someone to come home to after a hard day's work. So many people have that, a lot more want it. And, at that time, I knew I wanted it again. But I wasn't in the right place for it. I was a recluse, someone who was covering up his insecurities and loneliness with money, and money he didn't have, convincing himself, in the process, that he could buy a person's love and approval.

On the rare occasions I did see my friends, they'd make little comments to me. A quiet word or two, that sort of thing. They knew I wasn't right. I was feeling vulnerable, insecure and needy. I wanted to be loved and thought it came at a price. A high one at that. But I was prepared to pay it. I became more and more stressed and fell, steadily, into depression. To most people I might still have looked like the old Peter Mendham, always up for a chat and a bit of a laugh. I used all of that to mask how I was really feeling. Because just underneath that superficial surface, I was a mess.

This wasn't something that had come about all of a sudden. That little fallout between Charlotte and me wasn't the cause of my depression, but it did, ultimately, lead me over the edge of the cliff face I'd been standing on. The signs everything was coming to a traumatic head had been there for a long time. A year before all this happened, I lost my driving licence for 12 months. I'd been out with Charlotte, along with a few friends and had been seen, initially, by a couple of policemen as I walked her home along a road in Norwich. They'd recognised me as an ex-footballer and carried on before, almost straight away, spotting my parked car, which was, as they noted, facing the wrong direction in a road close to Norwich's Roman Catholic Cathedral. I couldn't deny it was mine either as it was a work-sponsored Seat which had 'Peter Mendham' sign-written on it.

They sought me out and, smelling alcohol on my breath, asked me to give a sample. I was happy to do so but, because I had a chest infection at the time, wasn't able to do so sufficiently. However, I wasn't going to mess them about or drag things out. I knew I was in the wrong and admitted that I'd been drink-driving. The case duly went to court and I was convicted and banned.

The obvious fallout from this was that the ban would affect my ability to do my job with the East Anglian Air Ambulance charity. I might even have lost my job over it. Quite apart from the fact that driving around the region played a very big part in my job, my ban was also bad publicity for my employer. So they might have felt justified in calling me in and advising that my services were no longer required. I wouldn't have blamed them. But they didn't, they kept faith in me, with, I hope, that £1 million I'd help raise for them every year carrying a bit of weight in my favour.

Why had I been stopped? Because I thought I was doing the best thing I could for Charlotte, even then. We'd been out and she wanted to go home. But we couldn't get a taxi. Stupidly, I said I'd drive her home myself even though I'd had a few drinks and shouldn't have done. I should have called that taxi for her. But, rather than do that, I took a chance and I paid the price. It was a stupid and dangerous thing to do and evidence that, bit by bit, the control I had over my life was ebbing away and continued to do so over the next 12 months until matters came to a terrible conclusion.

That little fallout I mentioned earlier only lasted for a week or so. The sort of thing that happens in all relationships and all of the time. So we were back on track again. Or so I thought. I'd invited Charlotte over to my cottage one Wednesday evening, just a little supper and catch-up time. She wouldn't be able to stay but that didn't matter, it was enough to share a lovely meal with her with some wine and champagne and to enjoy her company, and a nice chance to see her in the middle of the week as well as we were very much a 'weekend couple' at that time, constantly busy with our own lives during the week but able to spend more time with each other at weekends. So a midweek date was a treat and I wanted to make it a special one.

We chatted and as Charlotte went into my hallway she noticed a letter from Christian Dior on the oak chest near to the staircase and asked what it was for. I replied that they were requesting I paid the deposit on a diamond bow bracelet that I had ordered for her, to which she replied that she'd thought I'd already done so.

I hadn't, simply because I was a regular customer at the Christian Dior desk at Harrods in London and the salesman there had let me take it away as he (and Harrods) knew I was good for the money. But I think that, maybe, at that split second Charlotte wondered if I was having second thoughts about buying her the piece after all, hence my delay in making the payment. That wasn't the case, but even so we fell into an argument about the whole matter, for some reason, the last thing I had wanted on what I had hoped would be a very happy midweek date for us both. Cross words were exchanged, but even then I thought things would calm down and we'd go on to have our meal, but, no, Charlotte was now upset and said that she wanted to go home.

Naturally I didn't want her to leave. My wish now was for us to sit down and resolve the matter before eating together. But Charlotte wanted to go home, and as she brushed past me in the hallway on her way to the front door the small of my back hit the end of the banister rail. It was only a short stab of pain but came as a bit of a shock, as her walking past me had caused me to temporarily lose my balance and take a step or two back into the dining room. I know now what people mean when they say that, for whatever reasons, they 'lost it'. Because in that split second I did. I didn't know who I was anymore, where I was, nothing. It was as if my mind completely shut down, like a big switch on a wall had been pulled from *On* to *Off*. I was in a complete daze. It was instantaneous. And it may seem like a tiny and inconsequential thing but, after a year of getting more and more depressed with life, this was the one small thing that tipped me over the edge, and I reacted in that split second in the most barbaric and inhumane way imaginable.

In the confusion, I'd reached out and grabbed the nearest thing to hand and blindly lashed out at Charlotte with it. It turned out to be a knife and, such was the force that I hit out at her, the blade sank deeply into the side of her body and remained there.

It wasn't intentional. It never was. I'd lost it. Completely out of control, and not the person I had always been for all of my life leading up to that second or, I have to say, in all of the days, weeks, months and years that have passed ever since. For a few terrible seconds, I wasn't Peter Mendham. I was someone, something else. I was that bastard who stabbed his girlfriend. Whoever I was at the time hasn't come back and I know he never will. But, right in the white hot heat of that moment in time, one that will forever be frozen in my mind, who I really was and the type of man I really was, didn't matter one bit. All that mattered was that Charlotte was now lying on my hallway floor, bleeding heavily and, for all I knew, dying.

Life suddenly came back into focus again. Clarity. And, at that precise moment, as I looked on, I was sure she was about to die. I wanted to die as well at that moment but I pushed that thought out of my mind. I now had to use that renewed focus to help her.

I'd done a terrible, evil thing and I knew I would be punished for it, but first of all I had to help her. So I went back into the cottage and, as best as I could, tried to make her comfortable. And yes, I know, I've just stabbed the person I loved more than anyone else in the world and I'm trying to do the 'right thing' by making her comfortable. I did what I could before calling 999 and asking for an ambulance, telling the operator what I'd done. She said an ambulance was on the way. I knew a police car wouldn't be far behind.

As I waited, it suddenly dawned on me that the driver might not be able to find the house. So, after checking on Charlotte again, I ran outside and met the ambulance as it arrived, leading the driver and his mate into the house. Later on in court, the prosecution claimed that I'd 'run away' and left her. I hadn't. I knew, through experience, that people found it very difficult to find my home as it was at the end of a partially hidden and narrow lane. And it was dark. What if the ambulance driver hadn't been able to find it either? Unlikely, maybe, but I wasn't going to take the risk. So I ran to the top of the lane a couple of times until, finally, I saw them coming and waved them towards me. She was now in safe hands which meant I could 'let go'. So I laid, face down, on my lawn whilst the paramedics started tending to Charlotte and waited for the police car that was just behind the ambulance. The policemen quickly handcuffed me and put me into the back of their vehicle. For both of us, our lives were now never going to be the same again. What happened to me from then on, quite honestly, I didn't really care. What mattered, all that mattered, from that moment onwards was Charlotte. Her life was saved by that ambulance crew and the medical staff at the Norfolk & Norwich Hospital and she would, over time, be able to lead a new life. It was, for me, when I heard that news, the very faintest speckle of light on what had been a very dark night indeed.

What's my excuse for what I did? I don't have one. I was completely and utterly responsible for what happened that evening. I admitted it at the time and would do so today. No excuses. Yes, my life had been heading into a downward spiral at the time but, even so, I should have had enough of a sense of self-control to not have reacted as I did. I should have taken a deep breath, taken a step back and let Charlotte leave as she had clearly wanted to. What right did I have to expect her to stay when she was clearly so upset? If she had gone home, as she wanted, we could have both had time to think about what was happening and, perhaps, re-evaluate where we were in our relationship and where we wanted to go. It's so simple on paper. And it should have been as straightforward as that.

So no excuses. Ever. But whatever happened to lead me to that dark place? I couldn't look back at my childhood and find any reasons for how my adult life had developed there. Yes, I'd been mentally scarred when I was a child. But I'd been able, over time, to come to terms with what had happened. It would never be right and would always be something that caused me, on occasion, a lot of pain and emotional upset. But I would never have tried to use it as an excuse or some kind of justification for the person that I briefly became that night.

Like I said, no excuses. I had a great childhood. Mum and Dad were always there for us. Mum, especially, who, like me, hated confrontation so she always steered clear of it. She'd have preferred to let things go if I got up to any mischief rather than run the risk of a row, especially if it meant my dad getting involved. That meant I grew up with no real sense of how to be assertive or to argue my point of view but was, instead, a boy and, eventually, a young man who was naïve and gullible. I know I have friends to this day who would argue that nothing has changed there. When I was playing for Norwich, I found it hard to turn down any of the requests I got for an interview or to go along and present a trophy somewhere, give a talk, maybe do a little coaching for a school team or something. If I was asked, I'd go along, no matter what it was. The rest of the lads found it easy to say no thanks to the myriad invitations and demands that were made on our time but I didn't.

This meant, ultimately, that some people started to take advantage of me. Let's say they wanted a signed football. I'd always be the one going from player to player at Trowse getting all the lads to sign it. I'd probably have to pay for the ball myself as the club wasn't in for giving stuff away back then. I'd then let whoever had asked me for the ball know that it was all sorted and they might ask if I'd drive out to somewhere like Swaffham or Fakenham to deliver it. I'd do so without thinking. All in my time, or, as I got older, time I should have been spending with family and friends.

I was so eager to please and to be liked, I would let people walk all over me. I was a doormat, pure and simple. With all the gifts I was getting for Charlotte, I was doing exactly the same thing, trying too hard to be liked and, with it, thinking that spending money on someone was the best way to show you loved them. It wasn't and isn't. I know that now. There really is so much more to life than that.

But the pressure, the expectation to deliver, the depression, all of it mixed together until, on that fateful October evening, it came to a head and I eventually lost control.

I'd long lost control of my finances. My level of personal spending had been excessive and I was living well beyond my means. I was in debt and had outstanding loans on top of that which I was having more and more trouble paying off. Yet, despite all of that, I was going to spend nearly £18,000 on a bracelet.

That's just one example of how out of control I was. Massively in debt but willing to spend even more in order to win, for me, Charlotte's approval and love.

I hadn't done that. But I had 'won' myself a prisoner number that I'll never forget.

Mendham PX7017.

I was arrested at my home and taken to the police cells at Bethel Street station in Norwich. Sat in my cell, it wasn't hard to imagine that my surroundings were probably pretty much identical to those of someone who'd been arrested and placed there a hundred years or so previously. But that was an aside. My real worry, other than Charlotte and how she was, concerned the very real and inescapable fact that my life had changed, in a fraction of a second, beyond all recognition.

I'd lost my liberty. Lost my job and my home. Lost everything that we take for granted in our lives. Friends would probably disown me as might some family members. What I'd done would probably be in the local papers the next day. As would the case in general. Thinking about all those things, as they raced out of control around my head, was torturous. I wasn't in that cell for long. I was taken from there to Norwich Knox Road Prison. It's still hard for me to find the right words to describe the emotions I was going through as we drove that short distance. I was, by then, in a state of deep shock at what had happened and was, desperately, clinging on to the hope that this was nothing more than a terrible nightmare that I couldn't wake myself from. But I didn't wake up and, as the police van slowed down and pulled up outside the main entrance to the prison itself, I knew that it was all very real.

HMP Norwich is an old Victorian prison which, like the cells at the police station, had certainly seen better days. The cell I was put in was very small with just enough room for two bunk beds, a toilet in the corner of the room and an adjacent hand basin. I spent my first five days in captivity in that cell with three others in a part of the prison that was known as the induction unit. It's something that every new prisoner has to go through before being allocated a cell on one of the larger wings in the prison.

As far as I was concerned, that couldn't come quick enough. The cell was small and fairly airless. Not pleasant at the best of times, but what made matters worse was that all three of my cell mates smoked. Luckily my bunk was next to the one very small window in the cell, so I did have some relief there. But it was minimal as spending 23 hours a day in a room (plus half an hour allocated for exercise and the other 30 minutes to take a shower and make one phone call) that's not much bigger than the average bathroom with three heavy smokers is not the best place to be. I asked for a smoke-free cell while I was waiting to be moved on to the main wing and, luckily, got that particular wish granted, although it was a couple of days after I'd made the request in the first place. But no matter, it meant that my circumstances had improved a little and that was something.

My new cellmate was called Jonathan[7] who was a very nice chap and cellmate. He was so nice and well-spoken that I ended up wondering why on earth such a decent-looking chap was in prison in the first place so I committed what I later learnt is a cardinal sin amongst prisoners by asking him what he was inside for? He was happy to tell me and what a story it was. He'd recently purchased a large collection of bird eggs that were displayed in a beautiful mahogany case. What Jonathan didn't realise was that some of the eggs he now owned were those from birds that were protected species, which meant he ended up being prosecuted. He was sentenced to six weeks in prison and, I have to admit, it was a pleasure to serve 'time' with him. And I was, at least on this occasion, lucky. He was someone I could talk to, something which is by no means guaranteed when you get put into a cell with a complete stranger. We soon agreed that one of the worst things about being locked up in the cell was having to go to the toilet in front of one another (he'd announce his needs by declaring, 'I'm afraid I need to do a number two, Peter,' at which point I'd lie on my bunk and face the wall), something we found both embarrassing and humiliating. But you just have to learn to get on with it and, over time, we did.

---

7   All the names of people that Peter met or knew in prison have been changed to protect the privacy of those individuals.

After a short time, I was moved into the main prison block which is where things started to liven up. It was a very noisy place and even seemed a bit lawless at times as many of the prisoners there were prepared to make as much noise as possible in order to disrupt the rest of the block. Little was ever done about that disruption and I began to wonder how I was going to get through the coming weeks and months if it was always going to be like that. I also found, at that point, that I was being targeted by some of the other prisoners because of my background, especially the fact that I used to be a professional footballer.

Fortunately, the officers in the block soon became aware of this. Both they and I would have wanted to move me on as quickly as possible and I got lucky when I heard that a cleaning orderly was required for the healthcare block at the prison. I made an enquiry and was able to get the position which meant another move into another cell with more people to get to know – and whether you liked it or not.

But at least that cell was bigger. Just as well really, as I was sharing it with five other inmates, two of whom suffered from ill health, notably Phil, who had a heart condition, and Don, who was a schizophrenic. Fortunately, despite our all being very different, we got on well and I was relieved that the move had also come with a job, as it meant I now had to do something which would, at least for a little while, take my mind off the situation I was in. My physical health was good, I'd exercised as much as I could from the moment I arrived in prison but my mind and spirit had been crushed. I was desperately sad and very lonely (loneliness can be particularly pronounced in busy places) and had been running the same questions through my mind again and again and again: what was going to happen to me, what did my future hold, did I even have a future? I had all the questions – the only constant certainty that kept arising whenever I asked them of myself was that I didn't have anything remotely close to an answer.

Cleaning duties in HMP Norwich were varied and included issuing clothing and serving meals as well as cleaning out cells. I shared my cleaning duties with Jacky, who came from Glasgow, and Paul, who was a very passionate Irishman. Paul and I struck up a good friendship from day one as we both had a real love of football. So it was through that and our efforts to keep fit in our cell that helped me become focussed and, over time, start to feel a lot stronger in my mind as well as my body. It almost felt as if God had decided to put Paul and I together as, just when I was at the lowest ebb imaginable, he came along to give me the guidance and support I needed as I began my incarceration.

There was certainly a lot of work to do in the healthcare centre. It had two floors with my duties predominantly being on the first floor where I had responsibility for approximately 20 cells as well as an ablutions room in the centre that included two very large baths. These baths were something of a luxury as showers were the only way you could keep clean in the main wings. I determined that those baths were going to be as clean as possible and even enquired about having some bleach to clean them with. Much to my surprise, my request was granted and, for a time, I was referred to as 'Dr Bleach' by both my fellow inmates and the prison staff. Being given permission to use bleach for cleaning purposes may not, upon first reading, seem that much of a big deal but in prison it most certainly is, as bleach is, if it can be obtained, very much a 'weapon' of choice for some prisoners who might have a grudge against another prisoner. It's therefore a restricted substance and my being allowed to use it shows that I was, already, trusted to do the right thing by the prison wardens.

Some of the occupants on the ground floor of that wing were prisoners who were terminally ill as well as those who needed lots of medication. Jacky did a great job of looking after these prisoners and would often give us updates on their conditions. It was certainly a part of the prison I never wanted to be a long-term resident of and I doubled up my efforts to keep fit by constantly running 'doggies' in the exercise yard during those 30 minutes a day I could go there whilst the prison officers looked on, certain, I felt, that I was possessed as I'd constantly be varying my speed in order to lower and increase my heart rate. I wasn't possessed of course, not then, but I knew that I had been, in some way, when I committed my crime, and was determined to never let my physical or mental fitness nosedive in such a way that I'd ever come close to doing something like that again. Paul and I would also exercise by juggling with a rolled-up sock in the cell before, later on, and I have no idea how he got hold of one, a small ball. We'd spend an age keeping that ball in the air without it ever once hitting the floor.

Things were now, on the outside at least, starting to move with regard to my case. I was still on remand and awaiting discussions with my barrister and solicitor about my court appearance and the plea I would enter. They'd advised me I was looking at a five-year stretch with a charge made against me of 'wounding with intent', so five years was the period I had in mind and I was working with that as regards how I was planning the time I'd be spending in prison. It also helped that I had, by now, started to regularly attend the prison chapel on Sundays. The staff and chaplain there were brilliant with me and I found the (temporary) solace that was on offer in that quieter, more controlled environment a great benefit.

There was always an opportunity for me to have visitors at the prison, even when I was on remand, but the two people I really didn't want to see were Mum and Dad as I felt so totally ashamed about what I had done and the sort of place they were now seeing me in. I was, after all, a disgrace to the family name, a name that had always been a respected and steadfast one in the local community. But they insisted on coming to see me not long after I'd been sent to Norwich Prison and I was so very glad that they did. It was a special visit and, far from them condemning me for what I had done, they were very positive and did a lot to help me keep my spirits up as they were at rock bottom. Two weeks after my incarceration, however, and not that long after they'd been to see me, I was called away by the prison chaplain into the chapel where he gently broke the news to me that my mother had suffered a massive heart attack, one that had been so severe it was unlikely she would recover.

I was devastated. My first reaction was to blame myself and, at that point, I wanted nothing more than to die myself. I could not, initially, be consoled, but eventually my thoughts were with my dear father and how he would be coping. It seemed unreal. Mum was a fighter, we knew that, even if the medical profession didn't, and I hoped and prayed that she would pull through. The prison service were, at this point, extremely helpful as they allowed me to go and visit her at the Queen Elizabeth Hospital where she remained unconscious. I was led to her bedside, double cuffed between two prison officers where, along with my family, I was able to spend some last, precious time with my mother. Her eyes were closed but I talked to her and hoped that she was able to hear my words. It was a hugely emotional time for us all and one that, given my circumstances, I was finding almost impossible to deal with. Fortunately, the prison officers who escorted me to King's Lynn on the day did so with compassion and respect, which meant I could, at least, be given time and some space to grieve for what had happened to my mother, even if I had no privacy to do so.

Mum, as we all knew, fought a brave fight but eventually she passed away on 13 November 2006. It was a day where I think I must have felt as low as I have ever done in my entire life. I was alone and almost numb with grief. Much of that was because I was blaming myself for what had happened to Mum. In fact, I was full of guilt but was unable, because of where I was, to unburden myself, to be able to share that grief with anyone. It became so bad that I realised, through my tears, that I just didn't want to live any more. Those feelings didn't quite translate into self-harm or contemplating suicide, but at the time I understood exactly why some people do think that way and go on to do just that.

A fellow inmate, Big Tom, said a prayer one evening and after hearing him say that I shared with him how I was feeling the following night. It helped because from that moment I was able to focus on what I had achieved in my life and what I was going to do with it, not just when I got out of prison but for however long I was in prison. I vowed that whatever happened I was not going to be beaten and I was not going to give up on hope. Quite where I found all that new strength, coming so soon after I was at absolute rock bottom, I'll never know but I now had it in abundance and, so much so, that I was not only helping myself but found myself in a position to help others as well. People talk about miracles occurring from the most improbable of situations and that early stage of my incarceration and leading up to Christmas 2006 was mine, one that helped me get through the most desperate and wretched few weeks I'd ever had in my life.

Christmas on the inside is what the prisoner makes of it. I did my best to get through it by remembering all the wonderful times I'd had at that time of the year on the 'outside'. But it wasn't as bleak a time as I might have first expected. I got a lot of cards from family and friends as well as many from people who I'd never met before. Those cards and the letters some of them contained meant the world to me, a lifeline, for, if at any time I found myself slipping into a depressed state, I'd get them out and read through a few. Most of them contained very encouraging messages while some people mentioned how much they'd enjoyed watching me play football. They couldn't, of course, make up for the situation I was in, but receiving so many kind words from so many people meant a great deal to me.

My case eventually got to court in February 2007 with the conclusion reached that I should serve seven and a half years in prison. It also meant that I would be moved from the prison in Norwich to a different place in order to start serving out my sentence. I was hoping that it would be at Her Majesty's Prison (HMP) at Wayland, which is situated approximately halfway between King's Lynn and Norwich and would, as a result, mean it would be fairly easy for both my father and my sons to visit me. But you don't get the luxury of choosing which prison you go to.

As it turned out, I was still quite fortunate as I ended up being transferred to HMP Highpoint which is in Suffolk. I was later told that they had sent me there rather than Wayland as there was concern about how much media attention I would generate if I was at Wayland, which seemed rather strange reasoning to me as once I'd been sentenced I knew that interest in me and the case would die down and be largely forgotten, which turned out to be pretty much what happened.

Just as I had done at Norwich, the first thing I had to do at Highpoint was go through another induction course. That sounds all very proper and professional but let me assure you it is most certainly not that at all. In fact, it's little more than a quick and harsh lesson in learning to survive in prison. There were no social niceties at that time. It was tough and you either made it or … well, you just had to make it, it wasn't as if you could quit and go somewhere else. It was a case of fighting for everything, sometimes literally. For example, take meal times when I might find myself eating the scraps of whatever was left after the 'top men' had taken what they wanted.

You couldn't complain about this of course, you just had to put up with it and fight for what you wanted just as everyone else was. It's a harsh but very effective way of finding out every little detail about how the prison is run at this time, and not just from the prison staff but your fellow, more 'established', inmates. While I was on the induction wing at Highpoint, I met up with a friendly guy called Robert as I waited to make a phone call one evening. Robert had got involved in a racket he maybe should have walked away from while on the outside, something that might have made him a few quid and, while I could understand his reasons for doing so, was sure that, like me, he knew he'd made the wrong decision in life. We clicked almost straight away and resolved to do everything that we could to not only make our own lives in prison more bearable, but also, if we could, to help others who, like us, might have been finding it a bit of a struggle. One of the courses I enrolled on was related to victim awareness, which had a waiting list of around a year for interested prisoners so I was going to have to be patient as far as that was concerned, not that I was going anywhere in the meantime. Robert and I also found time to play a lot of table tennis, something which rapidly became one of my favourite pastimes while I was inside, and something that was not only great fun but helped to keep me fit and, of course, pass the time.

And, like it or not, there is a lot of time to 'pass away' when you are in prison, with one of the biggest concerns, I am sure, for any first-time prisoner being how they are going to fill that time productively, but not only that, how they are going to do so productively and not crack under the pressure. I was at Highpoint for one and a half years and made a very great effort to better myself during that time, making the most of every opportunity I could in order to find employment when I was eventually released. My first job at Highpoint was assisting the librarian in the prison library. It proved to be a very useful role to have as it gave me access to the sort of information I needed to help me apply for grants that paid for some distance learning courses. So, for example, the Professional Footballers' Association (PFA) provided funding for my diploma in sports psychology while some local charities supported me with my application to take a diploma in counselling.

Not the typical pursuits you'd associate with a former professional footballer, but I wanted to find out why I had reacted as I did, what had made me lash out so violently against a person I loved and cared for more than anyone on earth. I needed to know who I was and the courses helped me get some sort of understanding there. I also kept myself busy by writing letters, hundreds and hundreds of letters to family and friends, all written in the evenings after 'bang up', which is the worst time of all in prison. If I wasn't writing those, then I was busy doing some in-cell workouts to help keep my fitness up as well as, in the daily 30 minutes or so we'd get out there, running around the prison's very large exercise yard.

I also wanted to get some fitness-related qualifications to help me with the work I was doing in both the gym and sports field, so I applied to become a gym orderly, something I had first enquired about when I had my gym induction early on. During that time, one of the gym officers had approached me and said, 'Do you remember me?', to which I could only reply, 'No, I'm afraid I don't. Should I?' He smiled in response before saying, 'You should do as you presented me with a football trophy when I was 12.'

I still couldn't remember him but the next day he brought in a photograph to show me, and there I was, presenting him with that trophy at North Walsham Community Centre. He'd since grown into a 6ft 4in giant of a man! I got the job in the gym and have to admit it probably helped that he was a big Norwich City fan! So was I, of course, and one lucky enough to be able to do his workouts in some spare kit that Terry Postle, who was then the kit manager at Carrow Road, was kind enough to send me. I remain, to this day, grateful to Terry for his thoughtfulness and generosity – cheers pal!

I loved my time in the gym and sports hall. It was a real buzz on a daily basis for me as I knew that all of the inmates who were attending wanted to be there. But not only that as, because working out was an opportunity for them to 'escape' the tedium of prison life, my fellow inmates would usually have a big smile on their faces all the time they were there. It was a very positive atmosphere to work in and, after a while, I decided that I wanted to give society a little something back, so I organised a charity day in the sports hall with the objective of raising some money for Victim Support. Among the items we received that were auctioned off were two signed footballs that were sent by Chris Hughton, who was then at Tottenham, as well as a signed copy of his book by Bryan Robson and an Everton shirt and autograph sent to me by my former team-mate Chris Woods, who was then coaching at the club. Fantastic gestures that were hugely appreciated by all of us involved at Highpoint, just as we were for all the smaller ones that were made as well, including those made by a lot of inmates who dug deep into their limited resources to donate whatever they could. My time in the gym was certainly productive. I passed my levels I and II in gym instruction as well as level II in circuit training. It all helped to make me feel as useful a member of the prison community as I could be and the days, weeks and months started to come and go more and more quickly.

I was forever looking to improve both my life and my inner self while I was inside. One of the things I did with regard to the former was ask where the best units were in the prison. I soon found out that this was where the 'lifers' were serving their time – and for good reason. As they are, by definition, going to be in prison for a very long time, allowances are made for that. And I was lucky enough to be allocated one. These cells do not only have a separate WC and hand basin but also a shower, something that was a blessing for me after a hard day's work at the gym.

I'd become a prison 'listener' by now; that is someone fellow prisoners can approach and ask to spend some time with in order to share any fears or worries they might have, or, quite simply, for a bit of company and conversation if they're feeling down. One of the things my fellow inmates worried about the most was their families and loved ones on the outside. People tend to forget that it is tough for them as well, especially if their loved one who is now inside was the breadwinner. I was one of eight listeners at Highpoint and can truthfully say that the time I spent doing that was by far the most fulfilling and valuable of my whole sentence. It was hard work at times. The training was tough and some of the role-play scenarios I found myself in were extremely thought-provoking. But it was all a big learning curve. One thing I was already aware of before I started the 'listener' course was that self-harm and suicide were very common in a lot of prisons so our work was vital as we would, potentially, be the person who might be in a position to stop that from happening.

Sadly, though, there were still two suicides at Highpoint during my time there, with one of them taking place on my watch. I had been made aware of, and seen, letters from this man's partner saying she was moving away, along with their children, and that he was not, upon his release, to come looking for them. Stan was naturally devastated at receiving this news and I believe started to plan his suicide from that moment onwards. I shared the news and my fears with some of my colleagues and we vowed to do all that we possibly could to support Stan but it was to no avail as a day later he was found dead in his cell. He'd left a note for me that I still have telling me that he saw no way out other than this and thanked me for my friendship and support during the brief time we'd known each other.

There is, as you are learning, a lot of support and advice at hand for any prisoner who might need it, regardless of whether they are inside for just a few months or are serving a life sentence. This is in direct contrast to the lack of support that is provided for them once they have left prison; it felt, to me, as if once a man walked out of the doors at Highpoint then it was a case of 'out of sight, out of mind'. If the support that is so desperately needed is not there then many find it increasingly difficult to cope once they are on the outside, a belief of mine which is strongly supported, then as now, by the amount of cases that come to court that involve someone reoffending. It makes complete sense to me why this happens. In prison there is discipline, yes, and, of course, you have lost your liberty. But there is also order, a structure to the day, shelter, food and medical care when needed, plus a certain degree of companionship. Once you are out then most of that is gone and people have found it very difficult to pick up their lives again, so no wonder a return to prison is sometimes the inevitable option.

What is the answer? I wish I knew. The cause of imprisonment is, of course, the crime. So why are crimes committed? Whatever the motivation behind the crime – money, mental breakdown, drugs, sex, alcohol, the list is nearly endless – certain individuals are prepared to take the very real chance of ending up in prison by committing a crime. So one answer is, naturally, how can we lessen the chance of someone committing a crime in the first place? Should this start at school with more time and energy spent on preparing people for life rather than swamping them with largely useless information that they'll likely never need?

Let's start to give young people lessons in life at an early age as maybe, just maybe, that will help make them better prepared for it and therefore lessen their chances of ever offending or even wanting to offend. It sounds so simplistic I know, but I am convinced that the answer is not in catchphrases like 'tough on crime, tough on the causes of crime' but in an education that looks to lessen the chances of crime happening in the first place. I know it's something I could have done with having. I left school with a knowledge of poetry, for example, as well as the capital cities of our world. I knew all about the history of the country that we all live in and the wars we have fought. I learnt about the arts and sciences, I could pretty much recite my times tables backwards by the time I was seven.

But did I leave school with any life skills? How much did I know about relationships? Or opening a bank account? Purchasing a house or car? How to be a good father?

How to be aware of a deteriorating state of mental health?

No.

When I was nearing the end of my time at Highpoint, I attained Category D prisoner status, which meant I was eligible for release from prison on a temporary licence. This didn't 'kick in' immediately and I remained at Highpoint for a few more months, working in the gardens and the officers4' canteen until I was moved again, this time to HMP Hollesley Bay near Woodbridge in Suffolk. This was where prisoners could go out into the community and work on a voluntary basis until, as you reached the last few months of your sentence, you were eligible to commence paid employment. I started off by working in a special needs school in Ipswich before working for a packing company near Needham Market. That was dull and very monotonous work but my thoughts during my time there were brightened by the prospect of having a little money put by which would be useful when I was released – or so I thought.

Two days before my release date of 20 April 2009, I was called to the governor's office to be advised that I would not be released to my father's home in King's Lynn but was, instead, being 'ghosted' (in other words, smuggled!) out on that afternoon in an unmarked police car to a hostel that was situated on the Old Norwich Road in Ipswich as the prison service were, again, concerned about the possible press and media attention that would surround my release. It was a knock to my morale I have to admit as I had worked hard to earn my release and had been advised that I would be with my father, only to have that positive thought taken away from me at the last second.

This frustration wasn't a one-off either, as for the next two and a half years, while I was on licence, it became the norm. Obstacle after obstacle was placed in my way. Now I accept, fully, that I was still serving my sentence, albeit doing so out in the community, but the restrictions that were now being placed on me during this time made it almost impossible to integrate into society in the way the licensing scheme was meant to work. Eventually a friend of mine called Phil offered me a job working at his home and on his estate in Cumbria, something which was a great opportunity for me as it was not only a great job to have but, being situated way up in the north-west of England meant I was also well out of the way of any of this perceived media interest I was supposed to be attracting, as no one in Cumbria would have heard of me or known who I was!

Things didn't always go to plan. At one point whilst I was in Carlisle, Charlotte rang me on my mobile as she wanted to talk to me about something she was going through back in Norwich. We chatted and that was that. Except, of course, part of the conditions of my parole were that I was to have absolutely no contact with her. I should, of course, have informed my probation officer that she had rung me and we'd had a conversation as a result of that. But I didn't, which meant I was recalled to prison and had to go through the process of applying for parole again. I was able to do so successfully and ended up back in Cumbria, determined to do my very best for Phil and, at the same time, ensuring I followed the conditions of my parole to the letter.

Phil's offer meant I was transferred to a hostel run by Cumbria probation, which I stayed in for several months until I was eventually given clearance to move into Phil's property. He certainly had plenty of space for me there as it was at Edmond Castle, which is part of the enormous Hayton Hall estate. It was a fantastic opportunity and I will always be grateful to Phil and his wife Deb for not only giving me the opportunity to live and work there but also to renew our friendship. I ended up helping Phil to manage the estate as well as being 'quartered' in a corner of the castle that I pretty much had to myself, so, all in all, it was an absolutely fantastic way for me to make my return to society and in a community that was a very close-knit and friendly one. It couldn't, I don't think, have worked out any better for me.

Being so far away from Norwich and Norfolk did, of course, have its advantages to begin with. No media intrusion for a start, not that I think there would have been much in the first place, but at least being in Cumbria kept the probation service happy. It was hard to be so far away from my father though, the 500-mile round trip if I ever wanted to get back to see him was not at all practical, so popping back for a night wasn't possible. He was living on his own now of course and his health was failing, which meant I knew I had to be with him, no matter how good my new life in Cumbria was. He'd been so supportive to me as I had been progressing in my football career, so now it was time to pay him back a little and be there for him. Once I'd made up my mind to leave, I told Phil and Debs of my plans. They were, as I'd expected, more than a little surprised, mentioning, in the course of the conversation that followed, that I was now living in a place I loved with people who supported me and doing a job that I really enjoyed. I couldn't argue with them. That was definitely the case and, had the circumstances been different, I could have seen myself living and working up there for a long time. Phil was like a brother to me, so it was a hard choice for me to make but I knew that it was also the right one.

It was tough to start with. I'd applied to Norwich City Council for a one-bedroom flat to live in but hadn't been at the top of their list. It seemed wrong having to ask them for help not all that long after I'd been celebrating the success of the East Anglian Air Ambulance Charity with them, or, years previously, standing in City Hall with all my Norwich City team-mates as part of the civic reception put on after we'd won the Milk Cup – but life can be like that. I ended up living in the back of my van on the outskirts of Norwich and, despite what people said, it wasn't that bad. I had a bed and other bits and pieces with me while I was able to wash and change at the gym I was a member of. Then there's the fact I'd been used to being banged up in a prison cell for 23 hours out of every 24. Living in a van might sound rough but at least you can walk in and out of that tiny space whenever you want to.

I also launched a charity called the Yellow Brick Road Foundation. Its objective was to raise funds to offer cash grants to worthy causes in the area, whether that was other charities or individuals. It was named after the famous road in the *Wizard Of Oz* as I'd been inspired by the thought that the Tin Man, the Lion and the Scarecrow were all walking along the road together to get to the place where they wanted to be, making that journey to not only better their own lives but also those of the people around them. I was in my element when I'd worked for the East Anglian Air Ambulance and just wanted to do something like that again with my own charity, to help out the people who really needed it the most.

So there was lots going on. And now I was back with Dad. That was important. As his health deteriorated, he needed more constant care so I was able to move, van and all, back home where I became his full-time carer. It meant giving up the job I had in Norwich but it was a decision I never regretted making. Not once. I loved being with Dad and living at home again, we had a great time together enjoying, as was always the case with us both, the simple things in life. Like, for example, having lunch in the Silver Spoon restaurant in King's Lynn or seeing him terrorise the people of the town as he sped along the pavement in his mobility scooter. We made each other happy and that is, I believe, the most important thing, as was the fact that Dad was no longer alone and lived out the rest of his days with a smile on his face and a little piece of that Bill Mendham taste for adventure forever in his heart.

RIP Dad. I bet you and Mum are having a great time in Heaven together!

# CHAPTER TEN

# Life on the Outside

*I later received a letter from Mr Hughes who stated that, 'Judging from your letter, you do seem to have a problem understanding what direct play is and, therefore, I am not surprised that you do have difficulties with coaching certain aspects of the game.'*

WHEN MY case had eventually come to trial at Norwich Crown Court in February 2007, I was sentenced to seven and a half years in prison for wounding with intent.

As the verdict was read out, I felt numb. But also very calm as I wanted to go to prison. I had no excuses, I deserved to be punished and was ashamed and shocked by what I had done. Neither my solicitor nor barrister had attempted, in any way, to mitigate what I had done and fully expected, as did I, that a custodial sentence would be imposed upon me.

What they hadn't expected was the length of that sentence. So, and immediately afterwards, they lodged an appeal against that.

The appeal was heard four months later and in order for me to be able to attend I was transferred, for one night, to HMP Brixton.

Three High Court Judges were involved in my case and as part of it they discussed a previous one that had been very similar to mine where an estranged husband had, after looking after their children for an evening, stabbed his wife 14 times when she'd returned home. His sentence for stabbing his wife 14 times was five years in prison, whereas mine for stabbing my girlfriend once (and that's once too many, I fully accept that) was seven and a half years.

So there was an inconsistency. And that was the core of their argument.

It was soon decided that my original sentence had been excessive and its length was duly reduced by two and a half years, which meant that I now had a new release date (on licence) of 24 April 2009 which, at the time, would have seen me return to live with my father in Gaywood until, as things turned out, I ended up in Cumbria.

When my time on licence came to an end and I was finally regarded as a 'free man', the temptation to get back into football was very strong. My time in prison hadn't dulled my desire to coach, but, for all that, I knew it would be difficult to find a club, certainly initially, that would employ me as the newspaper headlines would, inevitably, be about how the club's new coach had served a prison sentence then, before you knew it, all the headlines would reappear and that would be that. This is pretty much exactly what happened when, shortly after my release, I was appointed as assistant manager of non-league Newmarket Town. They're hardly one of the best-known names in the game within East Anglia, even at non-league level, but they were a well-run club that wanted to progress so it was an obvious appeal to me, the opportunity to restart my life and career in football at a good club.

Kevin Grainger was the manager of the team at the time and he made me feel as welcome as possible, stating, publicly, that in his opinion what had happened in my past had happened and that it was now nobody else's business. He went on to say that the experience in and knowledge of the game that I had would be invaluable and that he was very much looking forward to working with me. I'd gone along to see them play in their Ridgeons League Premier Division match against Yarmouth Town the previous weekend and had been impressed with how they had played in their 6-1 win.

It seemed a perfect opportunity for me, whilst the backing I'd got from Kevin was hugely appreciated. I hoped, as we all did, that he'd nipped any stories or gossip firmly in the bud and I'd be able to get on with the job and my life. But that was never going to happen. The press interest was immediate and intrusive, so much so that after just two days in the job I had no option but to quit, much to the disappointment of everyone concerned. This was, it seemed, how my life was going to be from now on.

It wasn't as if I hadn't prepared myself for a career in the game once my playing days were over. In June 1994 I'd attended the FA's advanced coaching licence course at Lilleshall, joining, amongst others, the likes of Paul Barron (ex-Arsenal and Crystal Palace), Terry Connor (Leeds and Brighton), Kerry Dixon (Chelsea) and Peter Fox (Stoke City), all of whom took the course at the same time as me and who were, at its conclusion, awarded their advanced licence, as was Alan Pardew, who has since, of course, had a good career in coaching and management. They were all good lads, as were nearly all of the others who I shared the course with, having, in the process, an enjoyable but very productive time.

I did well and got some good feedback while I was on the course. I certainly had no reason to expect that I might not have passed it which is why the subsequent letter I got from the FA came as such a shock.

There were aspects of the management and administration of that course which didn't seem right at the time. Part of that seemed, to me, to be a willingness on the part of the FA to not award the advanced licence on merit, but to seemingly do so judged on who the student was and his status in the game, rather than their performance on the course. One student, an extremely well-known player in the game, was able to take the whole course, even though he'd only turned up on the fifth day.

How can you be accepted on to a course of any kind if you miss about a third of the syllabus covered?

I wasn't happy and I made my grievance very clear in my reply to the FA on 3 August 1994. But it wasn't all negative, as in addition to my offering a little of what I believed was constructive criticism about the course to Mr Kelly, I also talked about my work with Norwich City as their community officer as well as congratulating them on the appointment of Terry Venables as England coach, together with Don Howe who'd impressed me while I was on the course.

So I wasn't, contrary to what the FA might have believed, having a go at anyone and may well have accepted the fact that I hadn't passed the advanced course if certain other individuals hadn't still fared a lot better than me with their results despite missing much of its commencement or even, as I found out, passed the course despite securing lower marks in their assessments than me.

One issue that I felt particularly passionate about was that the FA still seemed to favour the coaching techniques and philosophies that were championed by Charles Hughes, who worked as their director of coaching. Mr Hughes was a great student of the game and had concluded, through watching and coaching games and basing his analysis on over 100 matches played at all levels (including Brazil), that most goals were scored from three passes or fewer, meaning that it was important for attacking teams to get the ball forward as swiftly as possible.

This led him to come up with the now famous acronym POMO, meaning Position Of Maximum Opportunity. In other words, getting the ball forward and into the opposition's penalty area (the POMO) with as little fuss as possible, which placed an importance on set pieces, long balls and crosses into the box.

It is an aspect of the game that has its merits, of course. Furthermore, it has been one that has proved to be successful for a number of teams in the past such as the Wimbledon team of the

1980s. I played against them for Norwich home and away during the 1985/86 season and they battered us on both occasions, with their 2-1 win at Carrow Road on 5 October being our only home defeat that season. They knew how we liked to play the game and just got in our faces, long balls, plenty of set pieces and no holding back in the tackle. It worked as they came up with us at the end of that season, and, two years later, they famously beat Liverpool in the FA Cup Final and would, had it not been for the ban on English clubs that came in following the Heysel tragedy in 1985, have taken their rumbustious style into the following season's European Cup Winners' Cup competition which would, had they drawn one of the top-rated Spanish, German or French clubs, have made for some very entertaining viewing.

Charles Hughes had more than an adequate case in favour of his coaching philosophy, therefore. But it was one that didn't go down well with many coaches and managers in the English game who thought it old-fashioned and one that discouraged players from learning new technical skills or understanding different playing strategies. Nevertheless, it had its advocates and although I would never be one I had to admit that it was effective.

But I also thought the FA believed in it and its methods a little too closely, which is why, in my letter to the FA, I praised the appointment of Terry Venables, a man and coach who, like John Bond and Ken Brown, the two managers I'd had at Norwich, was as far removed from the dreaded POMO as you could possibly get.

The problem was, as I saw it, that those players and ex-players who were attending the FA course I was on who favoured or were more enthusiastic about that coaching method seemed to do better than some of us who had dared, and I use the word advisedly, question it. I later received another letter from someone at the FA that defended its stance, adding, 'Judging from your letter, you do seem to have a problem understanding what direct play is and, therefore, I am not surprised that you do have difficulties with coaching certain aspects of the game.'

It was, it seemed, a very clear case of '… it's my way or the highway'!

Other matters that had greatly concerned me included one candidate whom I noted was referring to a textbook as he took his exam, whilst another, who was leading a group that was working on beating the goalkeeper when clear of the defence, had one of his players make a very obvious mistake during the routine. Yet, rather than stopping the exercise and talking his player through what he had done and taking steps in order to prevent it happening again, he let the exercise continue, and when asked if he'd seen the mistake that had happened he admitted, and I quote, 'No, I wasn't looking.' Yet he still received high marks for that exercise, seemingly, to me, because he was, and remained, a passionate advocate of Charles Hughes's ideals.

I'd discussed all of these issues at some length with the Professional Footballers' Association (PFA) so it didn't really come as too much of a surprise to me when, towards the end of August 1994, I received a fax from the journalist Brian Glanville, who was then working for the *Sunday People*. It was straightforward and to the point, no niceties or introductions included or required:

> PFA sent me your alarming letter about the coaching course. Please could you ring me about it on 071 *** *** any time today til midnight. Otherwise mornings or evenings.

I wanted what I had seen and experienced out in the open and gave Brian a call. He took up my cause and wrote some superb articles about it for his newspaper, including one piece when he claimed that 'the hinterland of Hughes's narrow theories is one of sheer chaos', adding, in conclusion, that, 'as things stand, the Lilleshall courses are exposed as a fiasco'. (*Sunday People*)

Naturally, it didn't take long for matters to reach the ear of my employer who was, at the time, Norwich City Football Club. I had, as far as they were concerned now that the matter had gone very public, dragged the club and its good name into a personal spat with the FA and they weren't happy. I consequently received a written warning as to my future conduct from the club secretary, which was swiftly followed by one from Mr Chase which was, to all intents and purposes, a very strongly worded written bollocking! He had, at the time he'd written the letter, thought that I had not only gone to Brian Glanville directly (it was the other way around) but had sent him copies of my correspondence to the PFA, which was not the case. Brian reassured Mr Chase that I hadn't named any of the players involved who he mentioned in his feature but that he had obtained the names himself, as all good journalists do, from another source.

I kept my job which came as a great relief to me as I had never wanted to involve Norwich City in the matter in any way. I was also grateful that Brian had exposed some of the FA's shortcomings and hoped that, in time, the whole coaching system would be overhauled so that incidents like those I had witnessed were never allowed to happen again. Fortunately, Terry Venables's appointment as England coach did coincide with a greater awareness of coaching and tactical methodologies other than those advocated by Charles Hughes, with the proof of the pudding being the ongoing rise at that time of such coaches as Arsene Wenger, Ruud Gullit, David Pleat and Gerry Francis, all of whom believed in the sort of pass and move, pass and move football that was also encouraged at Norwich under John Bond, Ken Brown, Dave Stringer and, of course, Mike Walker.

Looking back now it seems something of a pyrrhic victory. I'd had my say and the matters I'd raised had been publicly aired, for which I was grateful. It did, however, make me wonder if I had, at least under the regime at the time, burnt all of my bridges with regard to ever getting a coaching job at Norwich City whilst, undoubtedly, the gossip on the football underground would cite me as a whinger or troublemaker, someone who was not to be considered even if he did make an application to a club.

Now, some 15 years later on, I'd found, after just two days, a position that I had been given in the game was indeed untenable, albeit for completely different reasons. It did make me realise, however, that, as much as I wanted it, it was looking increasingly unlikely that I would ever work in football again, a prediction which, to this day, has proved to be absolutely correct.

Life had to go on then as it does today. But my involvement with football is now and will always be as a fan. At least that is something that can never be taken away from me.

It means, of course, that since my release from prison I've had to adapt myself to working in a non-football or sporting field. But it's not as if I am afraid of hard work. I'm not, indeed, unlike my dear father in that respect in that I will always roll my sleeves up, get my hands dirty and put in a good shift. I was, for several years, an employee of my ex-wife Gabrielle at a company called Ecoglass as a driver. It wasn't a fancy job or title. I loaded the glass on to a van, drove to where it was required and unloaded it for the client. Hard work, dirty work, long hours.

But I always put my shift in. Never hid, never shirked, not for one second. That's not my way and it never will be. All of my life experiences have helped mould me into the person I am today – a very fortunate one who possesses good health in both body and mind with enough tools in my bag to help me manage most situations. I love and embrace life to the full and enjoy sharing my time with people who like me. I am particularly proud of my two sons and the achievements that they have made in their lives and am happy for them both. As for me, well, I'm currently self-employed and enjoying a variety of projects that include landscaping, removals and deliveries and general house maintenance.

I'll be 60 next April (2020) and although that's a time that most people seem to start to slow down I really do aim to prove, even if it's just to myself, that life really can begin at that age, refreshed, new and exciting. And doing so while knowing who the most important person in my life is – that's ME. Something which should apply to everyone.

One of the hardest lessons I have ever learnt made me realise that. For much of my life, I was trying to be all things to all people.

Whatever it was I was doing, I wanted to please everyone. Even when I was playing, I'd go the extra mile if I felt it would make someone happy. If there was an event on at some club or a social occasion where a Norwich City player's attendance was needed, I'd be the one to go along, I'd be the smiling face and willing helper. If it meant putting my hand in my pocket and spending some money, I'd do it. I had it, I could afford it, no problem. But there is, as I know and appreciate now, far more to life than trying to be larger than it. I was focussing too much on being someone I wasn't rather than taking time to step back and look at the bigger picture, the more rounded and realistic one. But, over time, it became very draining and my mental and emotional health suffered as I tried to be all things to all people, suffering to such an extent that we all know now where that fragility of mind eventually led me.

So if you're a busy person, don't forget to take time out on occasion for yourself. Make sure you are well in both body and mind. Enjoy what you are doing, and remember laughter really is the best medicine. And appreciate the simple things in life. I try to do all of those things now. I take time out for me as much as I possibly can, time to escape with my myriad thoughts and with my well-being in mind. I love walking along the beautiful North Norfolk coast, I love fishing at some of my favourite stretches of water, including, of course, chasing those beautiful carp at Barford Lakes. I took my co-author Ed there for his first-ever fishing trip as we were starting out with the book and he is now, excuse the pun, totally hooked!

Maybe you'll bump into me at the side of a lake or on one of Norfolk's magnificent beaches one day. If you do, come along and say hello. I love a chat, especially if it's about fishing or sharing a footballing story or two with a fellow Norwich City fan.

But, most of all, if you enjoyed this book then, even if you don't say anything else, at least tell me that. It'll make my day.

Thank you.

*Stop being a prisoner of your past.*
*Become the architect of your future.*

Robin Sharma

# Afterword

*I'm sure that one of the first questions people will now ask me is why did I feel the need to write a book?*

IT'S BECAUSE I wanted to share all of the things that have happened to me, to 'have my say' as I said right at the start. Yet, having now completed it, I'm now convinced that writing our life stories is something that we can all do and benefit from as we can, as I have, not only learn so much about ourselves by looking back, but continue to do so as we look forward and share our own life experiences with others.

If anyone was to ask me for a bit of advice with regard to their life, football, anything at all in fact, I know exactly what I'd say. Make your own life work for YOU because you are worth it. If we all do that and make the right decisions for ourselves then we can come as close as possible to 'having it all'. I don't think money is the key to life, but I do think attaining personal contentment is. I do believe that is something that I have now come close to achieving and have never felt so at peace with life and myself.

There has been a lot of trauma in my life which I allowed to happen and, ultimately, I only have myself to blame for what happened.

Yet, ultimately, and I hate to say this but it's true, the time I spent in prison ended up saving me from myself.

**Peter Mendham**

# Afterword

LIKE SO many Norwich City fans, I first knew about Peter when he made his first appearance for the club, going on to play 267 first team matches for the Canaries between 1976 and 1987, including the victorious League Cup Final at Wembley in 1985. Peter was a talented player and a fans' favourite about whom his manager Ken Brown once said: 'If you cut him open, his blood would flow yellow and green.' Indeed, Peter would always display total commitment and give every last ounce of his energy and effort to the team. It is no wonder that Ken Brown thought so highly of him.

It was after what Peter has called his 'moment of madness', back in 2006, that I really came to know him well. In those early days after his arrest, through contacts in the chaplaincy service at Norwich Prison, I was able to see Peter there, whilst he was on remand. He was a broken man, but very soon set about taking positive steps forward, quickly earning the respect of prisoners and prison staff. For a time, he remained on the Young Offenders' Wing in Norwich, largely because his positive influence on some of his fellow inmates there was recognised and utilised for the good.

As a priest, I was able to make pastoral visits to Peter without taking up any of the valuable visitors' passes, which could be prioritised for family use. It was a privilege to spend time with Peter at prisons around the country, as he moved from Norwich to Highpoint in Suffolk, and later to Wetherby near York and Hollesley Bay near Ipswich. Everywhere, it was clear that Peter was bringing a tremendous influence to bear on those around him, and not least in his role as a listener, rather like the work of the Samaritans, out in the community.

Peter Mendham is the classic case of a good man who has done a bad thing. His story is about his journey through life, and about how he has responded to the challenges of imprisonment and of rebuilding his life. I have been privileged to play a part in his journey, and as we travelled together, we formed a bond of friendship that will never be broken.

Thank you, dear friend for giving me the opportunity to be part of your story and for inviting me to contribute to *Life on the Inside*, but most of all, thank you for your sincere and precious friendship.

**Bert Cadmore**
Former Chaplain to Norwich City FC (2001–17)
Sports Chaplaincy UK Trustee

# Acknowledgements

MY THANKS commence right at the very beginning with my beautiful parents Bill and Molly Mendham. A dad and mum in a million who were devoted to us all and played such a big part in the lives of me, my brothers and my sister.

It gets a bit more difficult now as if I was to name every single person who has played a significant or supportive role in my life, then this book would need to have a few hundred extra pages!

Much love and kindness has been shown to me by so many over the decades, I thank you all.

Gabrielle has been a wonderful mother to our sons, Ross and Jamie. I would also like to thank her husband Roger for the kindness, support and patience he has shown.

Then there are the wonderful supporters of all the football clubs I have played for. My thanks to each and every one of you.

The teachers at the schools I went to, the managers and coaches I have played under and the tutors who have helped get me through all of the courses I have taken in the past few years. Thank you.

Thanks to Gordon Taylor and all at the PFA for their help and support, there for me right from when I started my career at the age of 16 to the present day. You have always been there and that is priceless.

There is always a good woman or man behind any man, and in this case the woman in question is Sarah. Thank you so much for supporting me throughout this project.

Finally, last but by no means least, my ghostwriter and close friend Ed. This has been an incredible experience for me and I cannot thank you enough for all the time and effort you have put into producing this book.

**Peter Mendham**
August 2019

# Acknowledgments

FIRST AND foremost, I'd like to thank Pete for trusting me to write his story. It's been a pleasure and an enormous privilege mate. Never let the sun go down on that big smile of yours. It's infectious.

Grateful thanks are also due to the following:

Paul and Jane at Pitch Publishing. We all met up to discuss this project on a cold and very icy morning in Arundel. They backed me straight away and their faith in this title from that moment onwards has been total. This is the third book I have written for Pitch, I hope there are more to come.

Paul Hazlewood for the cover photograph of Pete – plus his excellent company on the day of the shoot!

Michelle Grainger for editing the manuscript.

Ian Clarke and Siofra Connor at Archant.

To Lord Russell Baker for his support and encouragement throughout this project.

Daniel Brigham at Norwich City FC; Holly Ainslie and Carole Slaughter at Jarrold in Norwich and all at the Maids Head Hotel in Norwich.

To Ken Brown for writing the foreword. A Norwich City legend.

Numerous fellow Norwich City fans who have either helped with the book or been very supportive of me in my work overall deserve a nod here as well, including Michael Bailey, Rob Butler,

Phil Daley, Chris Goreham, Jeremy Goss, Gary Gowers, Stuart Hodge, Paul King, Ronnie Moulton, Chris Reeve, Jack Reeve, David 'Spud' Thornhill and Connor Southwell.

To Hans Zimmer and Pink Floyd for providing an ideal musical background whenever I am writing.

And finally to my mum, who is always telling me to 'have a rest'. Once I write a best-seller Mum, I promise.

**Edward Couzens-Lake**
August 2019

# Index